TRILLIONS

THRIVING IN THE EMERGING INFORMATION ECOLOGY

PETER LUCAS
JOE BALLAY
MICKEY McMANUS

WILEY

JOHN WILEY & SONS, INC.

Published by John Wiley & Sons, Inc., Hoboken, New Jersey.
Published simultaneously in Canada.

For general information on our other products and services or for technical support, please contact our Customer Care Department within the United States at (800) 762-2974, outside the United States at (317) 572-3993 or fax (317) 572-4002.

Wiley publishes in a variety of print and electronic formats and by print-on-demand. Some material included with standard print versions of this book may not be included in e-books or in print-on-demand. If this book refers to media such as a CD or DVD that is not included in the version you purchased, you may download this material at http://booksupport.wiley.com. For more information about Wiley products, visit www.wiley.com.

Library of Congress Cataloging-in-Publication Data:

Lucas, Peter,
  Trillions : thriving in the emerging information ecology / Peter Lucas, Joe Ballay, Michael McManus. — 1st ed.
       p. cm.
  Includes index.
     ISBN 978-1-118-17607-8 (hardback); 978-1-118-22715-2 (ebk.);
     978-1-118-24006-9 (ebk.); 978-1-118-26478-2 (ebk.)
  1. Information technology. 2. Information society. I. Ballay, Joe, II. McManus, Michael, III. Title.
  T58.5.L835 2012
  303.48'33—dc23
                                                          2012012395

Printed in the United States of America.

10 9 8 7 6 5 4 3 2 1

To Diana, Sue, and Lynn

Contents

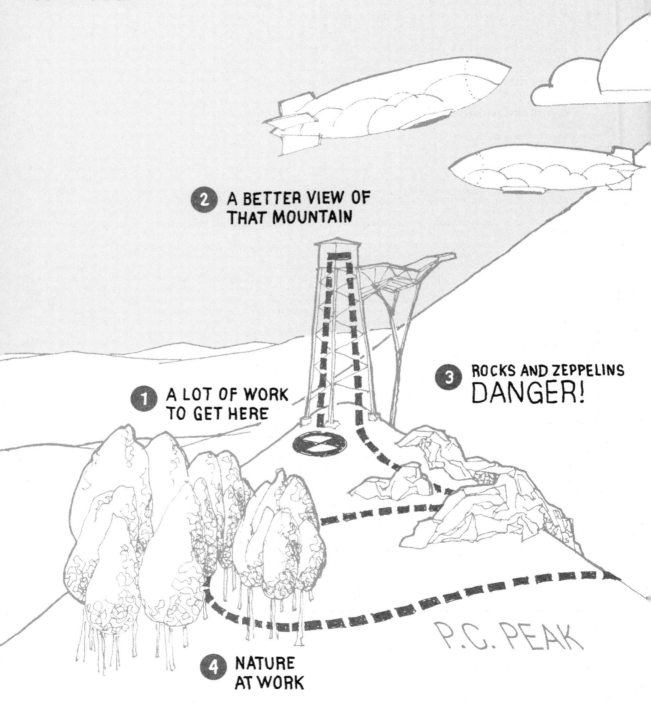

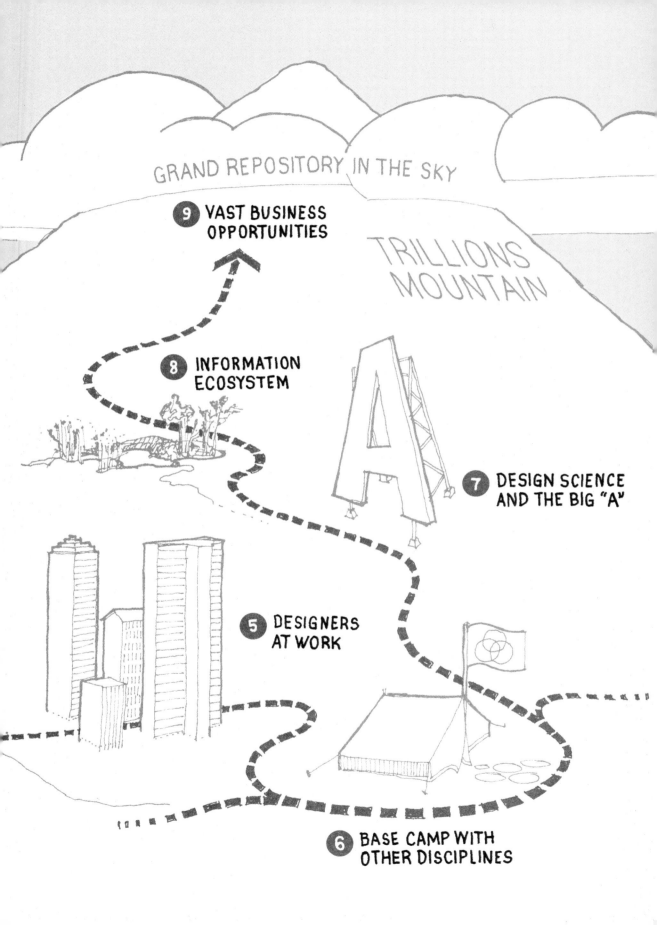

Preface

TWO MOUNTAINS

The ruling metaphor for technological change is that of successive waves of innovation. We envision each paradigm shift and its corresponding rearrangement of the way we live as a wave that comes crashing down on our beach just as the tumult of the previous one begins to recede. This book is about two such waves—the rise of mass-market computing and the age of pervasive computing that is about to supplant it. For reasons that will become clear, we have chosen a slightly different metaphor to describe this particular sequence: that of climbing two adjacent mountains.[1]

Anyone who has climbed a real mountain (at least if they did so in the days before GPS) knows the experience of a long slog through the forest, during which one's exact position (and thus the status of the climb) can be known only vaguely. But then suddenly the timberline is reached and the accompanying long, clear sight lines produce an abrupt sense of orientation and perspective, after which one's relationship to the summit is correspondingly clear. When we started MAYA Design in 1989, we, and the industry we proposed to serve, had not yet reached the timberline of PC Peak. (This was an era in which the most complex technology to be found in the average home was a VCR, with its flashing "12:00" serving as a taunting harbinger of usability nightmares to come.) Our plan was to offer our services as a kind of mountain guide for the many industries that suddenly found themselves in the complexity business. Nobody quite knew what we were climbing toward or how long it would take to get there. But everybody knew that climb we must. It did not take long for the view to clarify. By the mid-1990s the Internet had gone mainstream, more or less everybody had a PC, and the agenda for the next decade or so was pretty much set. The path to the summit was suddenly obvious.

But, there was more to this newly clear view than most people noticed. While most eyes were (and remain today) firmly fixed on the summit, those who cast their gaze more widely discerned a surprise. PC Peak, which we have been climbing since the 1970s does not stand alone in the technological landscape. It has an adjacent companion—one with a much higher summit. This second peak is called Trillions Mountain, and it towers far over our current perch.

---

[1]The metaphor isn't actually all that different, mountains merely being waves in an unusually viscous medium.

For many years, the only important computing device in a typical home or business was the personal computer (PC), first on the desktop and then on the laptop. In only the past few years, this has suddenly changed, with smartphones and tablet computers well on the way toward eclipsing the PC for most purposes. The term *pervasive computing*[2] refers to the assumption—now widely held by people who pay attention to such trends—that this transition, dramatic though it is, is just the first step in a far more fundamental change. Rather than moving computation out of one kind of box into other—smaller and more portable—boxes, by the end of this transition computing will for all practical purposes be confined to no box at all. Computation (and thus data) will all but literally have escaped into the ambient environment. We already put microprocessors into nearly every significant thing that we manufacture, and we are quickly figuring out how to make those processors usefully communicate with each other, and with us. Moreover, the cost of routine computing and storage is rapidly becoming negligible. We are, as we shall see, well on our way to a world with trillions of computers. Once these trends get past their initial chaotic stage, they will quickly coalesce into something new and disruptive: an *environment* of computation. Not computation that we *use*, but computation that we *live in*.

We are by no means the first to make this observation. As we have said, these trends are widely recognized. But most of what has been written on the topic comes in one of two forms. The first of these comprise world of tomorrow gee-whiz stories about the wonders to come—how houses will cater to our whims; power grids will become intelligent; and tractors will drive themselves through fields sown not just with seeds, but also with millions of "smart dust" moisture and nutrient sensors. The second form is written by and for computer scientists, dealing with tricky nuts-and-bolts issues such as distributed databases, self-configuring mesh networks, and "device discovery" protocols.

This book is neither of these. Although we do present examples, and at places verge on the technical, neither represents our main point. The book is really about *people*—how we might arrange for them to live well in this new kind of built environment, and how we might botch the job. In other words, it is about *design*. Exactly what that means, and what it takes to be an effective designer is a topic that needs a fresh look in each technological epoch. What it takes in the present era and the profound impact of this new mode of design on the business world are the major themes of this work.

The occasion for the book is the upcoming twenty-fifth anniversary of our company, MAYA Design. However, it is not intended as a self-congratulatory

---

[2] Academics love to fight about names. The term *pervasive computing* has a major competitor in the literature: *ubiquitous computing*. As far as we can tell, the terms are synonymous. However, there seem to be sensitivities attached to the use of one or the other term, apparently having to do with concerns over whom history will recognize as the founders of the discipline. We have no dog in that fight. We use *pervasive computing* because we think it sounds better than the awkward *ubiquitous computing* and especially its common but hideous contraction *ubicomp*. Such things matter.

festschrift. We will keep our personal war stories to a minimum, and those we do tell are offered more in the spirit of a foot soldier's diary than a general's memoir. But they are, we think, worth the telling. For, they were culled from almost a quarter-century of intimate collaboration with engineers and marketing professionals from many of the world's most successful and advanced organizations.

As a business, MAYA is uniquely structured. In many ways, we reflect the tradition of the great industrial design consultancies of the 1940s and 1950s.[3] The majority of our work involves long-term consulting relationships with firms that develop and market technological products and services. But we also have many of the attributes of an industrial R&D lab, performing applied research in areas of relevance to our commercial work. In any given week, a designer at MAYA might spend time helping a new tech startup launch a tablet-based pervasive computing service; working on a project with one of our Fortune 500 clients developing a long-term product architecture; and exploring a DARPA-funded technology that will not be commercially viable for a decade. The hybrid nature of this project mix is virtuous in both directions: It lets us help our commercial clients see past the pressures of the next quarter and thus avoid the often-fatal pitfalls of local hill climbing, and it encourages us to focus our research efforts toward practical issues that are likely to really matter to the humans that are always at the center of our attention.

This is a book with three authors, a fact that would be blatantly obvious even absent the names on the cover. We have tried to even out the voices, at least in the main body of the text. But truth be known, we have not tried all that hard. The presence of three very different voices, and several others that show up from time to time, is an essential part of our story. They reflect a belief—at the very heart of MAYA's approach to design—that the problems we and our clients now face are beyond the ken of any one disciplinary tradition. From the day we opened our doors, we have brought together engineers, human scientists, and visual designers in the conviction that triangulating from all three of these disciplinary perspectives represents our best hope for getting the future right. We have never looked back.

We created MAYA at a time when the practice of interdisciplinary design was rare and the idea of human-centered design in computing and information systems was nascent. We maintain a belief that the hard problems that people, organizations, communities, and cultures will face in the coming years can only be solved at the intersection of how people think, how technology works, and what form and function the desired solution takes.

---

[3] Our name, "MAYA"—an acronym standing for "Most Advanced Yet Acceptable"—is an homage to Raymond Loewy, one of several role models from among this group, who often spoke of his goal for a design to reach "the MAYA stage."

A FIELD GUIDE TO TRILLIONS MOUNTAIN

And so, we find ourselves at the very apex of PC Peak. It was a long, tough climb, but we made it. We desperately want to go even higher, so we have taken to building fire towers, and extensions upon those. But the skills that got us to this eminence don't help much here at the top, so the towers are rickety and dangerous. Everybody sees Trillions Mountain out there across the valley, rising far above us into the clouds. But most people avert their eyes. We climb up, not down; and down appears to be the only way to get over there. Plus, we don't even know how to climb that kind of a mountain. So, it's back to the fire towers. Others busy themselves trying to cantilever a bridge out in the new mountain's direction. That isn't going too well, either.

But a few of us are ready to bite the bullet and start the trip, even if it means reversing some hard-won progress and then mapping a whole new territory. If you're up for the journey, we hope that this book will be of some assistance.

We begin with an overview of what we can see of Trillions Mountain from our present viewpoint. Most of the prerequisites to the emergence of pervasive computing are already in place, and many of the remaining developments are well underway. Although these claims are not really controversial, their implications are not well-known to many people, even within the industry, so Chapter 1 is intended as a kind of executive summary of progress to date. Chapter 2, while a bit more speculative, explores a set of possibilities that are certainly possible and in our judgment both likely and desirable.

Chapter 3 concerns itself with those rickety fire towers. As the industry climbed upward from the spacious foothills of the current mountain to the crowded heights, increased competition for a dwindling set of opportunities has led to some pretty risky behaviors. Here we will explore some of the less-than-healthy aspects of today's computing scene, with special emphasis on those that represent significant threats to the unfolding of a safe and sane technological future.

We then begin to plan our climb up Trillions Mountain. There are many novel challenges ahead, but most of them share a common basis. That basis is *complexity*. More than anything else, what will distinguish computing in the future from computing in the past are sheer scale and the complexity that comes with it. Devices will exist in unprecedented numbers, as will occasions for human–machine interactions. The design techniques that have served us well on PC Peak will be wholly inadequate for the problems of scale that we will soon face.

These are unfamiliar issues to the computing world, but they are not without precedent. The next section of the book examines some of these precedents and what we might learn from them. Chapter 4 examines the ultimate master of distributed complexity: Nature herself. We explore the basic self-organizational patterns of natural systems and how they inform steps toward the creation of an ecology of information devices. Chapter 5 looks at the design process itself, both from an historical and contemporary perspective. Finally, Chapters 6 and 7 bring science into the story, examining the thesis that the notions of *design* and *science* are not, as is often assumed, disjoint activities. We pay special attention to the generalization of the concept of architecture as the basis for a scientific approach to the design process.

The last two chapters, Chapters 8 and 9, attempt to pull this material together into a coherent, if fuzzy, image of life in the foothills of Trillions Mountain. We know better than to be too specific here, but it is possible to discern the broad strokes of how the story of pervasive computing is likely to unfold, and in these chapters we lay them out in as much specificity as we dare.

Finally, scattered throughout is a fair amount of supplementary material, which we hope will support and reinforce the main thread of the text. Each of us indulges in a bit of first-person storytelling, as do a few of our MAYA colleagues. Included here are a number of case studies describing both examples of our research activities and commercial work done in collaboration with our clients. You will also encounter references to various audio, video, and interactive material, which can be found at the book's website: TRILLIONS.MAYA.COM.

There are also two "interludes" — minichapters whose purpose is to place examples of these trends into their historical context. We end the book with an epilogue containing material specifically aimed toward members of the business community as they face the challenges raised by the advent of pervasive technologies.

Some topics that are discussed in *Trillions* really deserve dedicated books in their own right. Much of the research work that has been done by our small band and by others is still very much in progress as this book goes to print. However, where possible, we have included pointers in the end pages to where you can drill deeper into the topics we have touched.

Acknowledgments

It is customary for authors of works of nonfiction to whine to their readers about the impossibility of thanking everyone that they should. We certainly have no cause to break with this tradition. Indeed, our situation is worse than most. The contents of this book are not the results of a bounded research project. Rather, they are the collective product of a quarter-century collaboration, not only among the authors, or even among the hundreds of design professionals who have worked at MAYA over the years. Rather, the circle of credit extends in a most fundamental way to include the many extraordinary clients with whom we have been privileged to work. The countless intimate collaborations with our clients' engineers, designers, marketers, and managers are the wellspring of whatever insights we may have to offer. To mention even a few would be a disservice to many others of equal importance, so we can only acknowledge the depth and breadth of our debt here. And, of course, the collective contribution of everyone in the MAYA family—past and present—is vast beyond calculation.

In thanking those with a direct hand in the creation of the book itself, we must begin with Ralph Lombreglia. Whatever success we have had in making unfamiliar and complex topics accessible to the general reader has benefitted greatly from his fine rhetorical sensibilities and his unfailing good advice throughout the project. A number of longtime MAYAns have also been direct contributors to the text: Jeff Senn—a genuine polymath who has been a core member of the MAYA family since the day we opened our doors—has made countless contributions both to the ideas and to the words themselves. Bill Lucas (no relation to Pete) and David Bishop have each taken the time to write essays that we have gratefully included in the text.

Nearly everyone in the MAYA companies has read early drafts of the manuscript, and many have provided valuable feedback. Special recognition must go to Dutch MacDonald, who has regularly provided detailed feedback on all aspects of the project while also managing to keep the business on an even keel during our frequent bouts of book-driven inattention. Lori Paul, our treasured executive assistant (a title that vastly understates her value), has been characteristically masterful at keeping the process moving forward amidst the background chaos of a busy consultancy. Thanks are also due to Chris DeMarco for technical support and Christen Adels for attending to legal matters.

This is a book of significant breadth and deceptive complexity, and the brunt of our compulsion for fact-checking and general rigor has fallen on Susan Salis and Susan Zelicoff (collectively referred to as "the Susi"). Their diligence and care in managing the minutiae of the project were frequently the only things standing between us and chaos.

Nearly all the members of MAYA's visual design group have contributed their fine talents to the project. Special recognition is due to Greg Gibilisco, who is responsible for the bulk of the graphics, and also So-Eun Ahn and Daniel Szecket for valuable contributions. Matt Ross, our amazing filmmaker, is largely responsible for the films and animations found in the supplementary material.

We offer our grateful thanks to the entire editorial team at John Wiley & Sons. In particular, we will always be indebted to acquisitions editor Tim Burgard for getting excited about our idea at a time when everybody else was giving us blank stares. We also thank our development editor Stacy Rivera and our production editor Todd Tedesco for their skill in balancing our sometimes-wacky vision against the realities of getting a real book onto the shelves and into the current chaos of the eBook realm.

Finally, we are profoundly grateful for the patience, support, and love of our spouses Diana Dee-Lucas, Sue Ballay, and Lynn Lofton.

TRILLIONS

CHAPTER 1

The Future, So Far

Behind all the great material inventions of the last century and a half was not merely a long internal development of technics: There was also a change of mind.

—LEWIS MUMFORD

There is a point of view—generally called "technological determinism"—that essentially says that each technological breakthrough inexorably leads to the next. Once we have light bulbs, we will inevitably stumble upon vacuum tubes. When we see what they can do, we will rapidly be led to transistors, and integrated circuits and microprocessors will not be far behind. This process—goes the argument—is essentially automatic, with each domino inevitably knocking down the next, as we career toward some unknown but predetermined future.

We are not sure we would go that far, but it is certainly the case that each technological era sets the stage for the next. The future may or may not be determined, but a discerning observer can do a credible job of paring down the alternatives. All but the shallowest of technological decisions are necessarily made far in advance of their appearance in the market, and by the time we read about an advance on the cover of *Time* magazine, the die has long since been cast. Indeed, although designers of all stripes take justifiable pride in their role of "inventing the future," a large part of their day-to-day jobs involves reading the currents and eddies of the flowing river of science and technology in order to help their clients navigate.

Although we are prepared to go out on a limb or two, it won't be in this chapter. Many foundational aspects of the pervasive-computing future have already been determined, and many others will follow all but inevitably from well-understood technical, economic, and social processes. In this chapter, we will make predictions about the future, some of which may not be immediately obvious. But we will try to limit these predictions to those that most well-informed professionals would agree with. If you are one of these professionals (that is to say, if you find the term *pervasive computing* and its many synonyms commonplace), you may find this chapter tedious, and you should feel free to skip ahead. But if the sudden appearance of the iPad took you by surprise, or if you have difficulty imagining a future without laptops or web browsers, then please read on.

TRILLIONS IS A DONE DEAL

To begin with, there is this: There are now more computers in the world than there are people. Lots more. In fact, there are now more computers, in the form of microprocessors, manufactured *each year* than there are living people. If you step down a level and count the building blocks of computing– transistors–you find an even more startling statistic. As early as 2002 the semiconductor industry touted that the world produces more transistors than grains of rice, and cheaper. But counting microprocessors is eye-opening enough. Accurate production numbers are hard to come by, but a reasonable estimate is ten billion processors per year. And the number is growing rapidly.

Many people find this number implausible. Where could all these computers be going? Many American families have a few PCs or laptops—you probably know some geeks that have maybe eight or ten. But many households still have none. Cell phones and iPads count, too. But *ten billion a year?* Where could they all possibly be going?

The answer is *everywhere*. Only a tiny percentage of processors find their way into anything that we would recognize as a computer. Every modern microwave oven has at least one; as do washing machines, stoves, vacuum cleaners, wrist watches, and so on. Indeed, it is becoming increasingly difficult to find a recently designed electrical device of any kind that does not employ microprocessor technology.

Why would one put a computer in a washing machine? There are some quite interesting answers to this question that we will get to later. But for present purposes, let's just stick to the least interesting answer: It saves money. If you own a washer more than ten years old, it most likely has one of those big, clunky knobs that you pull and turn in order to set the cycle. A physical pointer turns with it, showing at a glance which cycle you have chosen and how far into that cycle the machine has progressed. This is actually a pretty good bit of human-centered design. The pointer is clear and intuitive, and the act of physically moving the pointer to where you want it to be is satisfyingly literal. However, if you have a recently designed washer, this knob has probably been replaced with a bunch of buttons and a digital display, which, quite possibly, is not as easy to use.

So why the step backward? Well, let's think for a second about that knob and pointer. They are the tip of an engineering iceberg. Behind them is a complex and expensive series of cams, clockwork, and switch contacts whose purpose is to turn on and off all the different valves, lights, buzzers, and motors throughout the machine. It even has a motor of its own, needed to keep things moving forward. That knob is the most complex single part in the appliance. A major theme of twentieth-century industrialization involved learning how to build such mechanically complex devices cheaply and reliably. The analogous theme of the early twenty-first century is the replacement of such components with mechanically trivial microprocessor-based controllers. This process is now ubiquitous in the manufacturing world.

In essence, the complexity that formerly resided in intricate electromechanical systems has almost completely migrated to the ethereal realm of software. Now, you might think that complexity is complexity and we will pay for it one way or another. There is truth in this statement, as we will see. However, there is a fundamental economic difference between complexity-as-mechanism and complexity-as-software. The former represents a unit cost, and the latter is what is known as a nonrecurring engineering expense (NRE). That is to say, the manufacturing costs of mechanical complexity recur for every unit made, whereas the replication cost of a piece of software—no matter how complex—approaches zero.

This process of substituting "free" software for expensive mechanism repeats itself in product after product, and industry after industry. It is in itself a powerful driver in our climb towards Trillions. As manufacturing costs increase and computing costs decrease, the process works its way down the scale of complexity. It is long-since complete in critical and subtle applications such as automotive engine control and industrial automation. It is nearly done in middling applications such as washing machines and blenders, and has made significant inroads in low-end devices such as light switches and air-freshener dispensers.

Money-saving is a powerful engine for change. As the generalization from these few examples makes clear, even if computerized products had no functional advantage whatsoever over their mechanical forebears, the rapid computerization of the built world would be assured. But this is just the beginning of the story. So far, we have been considering only the use of new technology to do old things. The range of products and services that were not practical before computerization is far larger. For every opportunity to replace some existing mechanism with a processor, there are hundreds of new products that were either impossible or prohibitively expensive in the precomputer era. Some of these are obvious: smartphones, GPS devices, DVD players, and all the other signature products of our age. But many others go essentially unnoticed, often written off as trivialities or gimmicks. Audio birthday cards are old news, even cards that can record the voice of the sender. Sneakers that send runners' stride data to mobile devices are now commonplace. Electronic tags sewn into hotel towels that guard against pilferage, and capture new forms of revenue from souvenirs, are becoming common. The list is nearly endless.

Automotive applications deserve a category of their own. Every modern automobile contains many dozens of processors. High-end cars contain hundreds. Obvious examples include engine-control computers and GPS screens. Less visible are the controllers inside each door that implement a local network for controlling and monitoring the various motors, actuators, and sensors inside the door—thus saving the expense and weight of running bulky cables throughout the vehicle. Similar networks direct data from accelerometers and speed sensors, not only to the vehicle's GPS system, but also to advanced braking and stability control units, each with its own suite of processors. Drilling further down into the minutiae of modern vehicle design, one finds intelligent airbag systems that deploy with a force determined by the weight of the occupant of each seat. How do they know that weight? Because the bolts holding the seats in place each contain a strain sensor and a microprocessor. The eight front-seat bolts plus the airbag controller form yet another local area network dedicated to the unlikely event of an airbag deployment.

We will not belabor the point, but such lists of examples could go on indefinitely. Computerization of almost literally everything is a simple economic imperative. Clearly, ten billion processors per year is not the least bit implausible. And that means that a near-future world containing trillions of computers is simply a done-deal. Again, we wish to emphasize that the argument so far in no way depends upon a shift to an information economy or a desire for a smarter planet. It depends only on simple economics and basic market forces. We are building the trillion-node network, not because we can but because it makes economic sense. In this light, a world containing a trillion processors is no more surprising than a world containing a trillion nuts and bolts. But, of course, the implications are very different.

CONNECTIVITY WILL BE THE SEED OF CHANGE

In his 1989 book *Disappearing through the Skylight*, O. B. Hardison draws a distinction between two modes in the introduction of new technologies—what he calls "classic" versus "expressive":

> To review types of computer music is to be reminded of an important fact about the way technology enters culture and influences it. Some computer composers write music that uses synthesized organ pipe sounds, the wave forms of Stradivarius violins, and onstage Bösendorf grands in order to sound like traditional music. In this case the technology is being used to do more easily or efficiently or better what is already being done without it. This can be called "classic" use of the technology. The alternative is to use the capacities of the new technology to do previously impossible things, and this second use can be called "expressive." . . .
>
> It should be added that the distinction between classic and expressive is provisional because whenever a truly new technology appears, it subverts all efforts to use it in a classic way. . . . For example, although Gutenberg tried to make his famous Bible look as much like a manuscript as possible and even provided for hand-illuminated capitals, it was a printed book. What it demonstrated in spite of Gutenberg—and what alert observers throughout Europe immediately understood—was that the age of manuscripts was over. Within fifty years after Gutenberg's Bible, printing had spread everywhere in Europe and the making of fancy manuscripts was an anachronism. In twenty more years, the Reformation had brought into existence a new phenomenon—the cheap, mass-produced pamphlet-book.

Adopting Hardison's terminology, we may state that the substitution of software for physical mechanism, no matter how many billions of times we do it, is an essentially classic use of computer technology. That is to say, it is not particularly disruptive. The new washing machines may be cheaper, quieter, more reliable, and conceivably even easier to use than the old ones, but they are still just washing machines and hold essentially the same position in our homes and lives as their more mechanical predecessors. Cars with computers instead of carburetors are still just cars. At the end of the day, a world in which every piece of clockwork has experienced a one-to-one replacement by an embedded processor is a world that has not undergone fundamental change.

But, this is not the important part of the story. Saving money is the proximal cause of the microprocessor revolution, but its ultimate significance lies elsewhere. A world with billions of isolated processors is a world in a kind of supersaturation—a vapor of potential waiting only for an appropriate seed to suddenly trigger a condensation into something very new. The nature of this seed is clear, and as we write it is in the process of being introduced. That seed is *connectivity*. All computing is about data-in and data-out. So, in some sense, all computing is connected computing—we shovel raw information in and shovel processed information out. One of the most important things that differentiates classic from expressive uses of computers is who or what is doing the shoveling. In the case of isolated processors such as our washing-machine controller, the shoveler is the *human being turning that pointer*. Much of the story of early twenty-first century computing is a story of human beings spending their time acquiring information from one electronic venue and re-entering it into another. We read credit card numbers from our cell phone screens, only to immediately speak or type them back into some other computer. So we already have a network. But as long as the dominant transport mechanism of that network involves human attention and effort, the revolution will be deferred.

Things are changing fast, however. Just as the advent of cheap, fast modems very rapidly transformed the PC from a fancy typewriter/calculator into the end nodes of the modern Internet, so too are a new generation of data-transport technologies rapidly transforming a trillion fancy clockwork-equivalents into the trillion-node network.

An early essay in such expressive networking can be found in a once wildly popular but now largely forgotten product from the 1990s. It was called the Palm Pilot. This device was revolutionary not because it was the first personal digital assistant (PDA)—it was not. It was revolutionary because it was designed from the bottom up with the free flow of information across devices in mind. The very first Palm Pilot came with "HotSync" capabilities. Unlike previous PDAs, the Pilot was designed to seamlessly share data with a PC. It came with a docking station having a single, inviting button. One push, and your contact and calendar data flowed effortlessly to your desktop—no stupid questions or inscrutable fiddling involved. Later versions of the Palm also included infrared beaming capabilities—allowing two Palm owners to exchange contact information almost as easily as they could exchange physical business cards.

In this day—only a decade later—of always-connected smartphones, these capabilities seem modest—even quaint. But they deserve our attention. It is one thing to shrink a full-blown PC with all its complexity down to the size of a bar of soap and then put it onto the Internet. It is quite another to do the same for a device no more complex than a fancy pocket calculator. The former is an impressive achievement indeed. But, it is an essentially classic application of traditional client-server networking technology. The iPhone truly is magical, but in most ways, it stands in the same relation to the Internet as the PC, which it is rapidly supplanting—namely it is a terminal for e-mail and web access and a platform for the execution of discrete apps. It is true that some of those apps give the appearance of direct phone-phone communications. (Indeed, a few really do work that way, and Apple has begun to introduce new technologies to facilitate such communication). But it is fair to say that the iPhone as it was originally introduced—the one that swept the world—was essentially a client-server device. Its utility was almost completely dependent upon frequent (and for many purposes, constant) connections to fixed network infrastructure.

The Palm Pilot, in its modest way, was different. It communicated with its associated PC or another Palm Pilot in a true peer-to-peer way, with no centralized "service" intervening. Its significance is that it hinted at a swarm of relatively simple devices directly intercommunicating where no single point of failure can bring down the whole system. It pointed the way toward a new, radically decentralized ecology of computational devices.

The Pilot turned out to be a false start, rapidly overtaken by the vastly greater, but essentially classic capabilities of the PC-in-a-pocket. But the true seeds of expressive connectivity are being sown. A design engineer would be hard-pressed to select a current-production microprocessor that did not have some kind of communications capability built-in, being thus essentially free. Simple serial ports are trivial, and adequate for many purposes. USB, Ethernet, and even the higher-level protocols for connecting to the Internet are not uncommon. Wireless ports such as Bluetooth, ZigBee, and WiFi currently require extra chips, but they are increasingly trivial to add. Although these capabilities often go unused, they are there, beckoning to be employed. And the demand is growing. It is the rare manufacturer who does not have a connectivity task force. What CEOs are not asking their CTOs when their products will be controllable via a mobile "app?" Much of MAYA's business in the last decade has involved helping our clients understand their place in this future information ecology. Whether they are manufacturers of kitchen appliances or medical devices or garage-door openers, or whether they are providers of financial services or medical insurance, the assumption of universal connectivity is implicit in their medium-term business planning. We won't just have trillions of computers; we will have a trillion-node network. Done deal. The unanswered question is how, and how well, we will make it work.

COMPUTING TURNED INSIDE OUT

As consumer products go, the personal computer has had quite a run. From its origins in the 1970s as a slightly silly geek toy with sales in the thousands, PC sales figures sustained a classic exponential growth curve for more than

35 years. Cumulative sales exceeded one billion units quite some time ago. In 2008 it was reported that there were in excess of one billion computers in use worldwide. In comparison, after 100 years of production, there are an estimated 600 million automobiles in use worldwide. For the postindustrial world, the PC is the gift that keeps on giving.

After all these years of consistent growth, it is difficult to imagine a world without PCs. But the phrase *post-PC era* has entered the lexicon. The precipitous collapse of an entire industry is the kind of thing—like a serious economic recession—that happens only a few times per career. As a result, many mid-career professionals have never actually witnessed one and therefore lack a visceral understanding of what such an event is like.

Fall of the Minicomputer
By Pete

In 1987, I received an invitation to attend something called "DECWorld '87." This was a one-company event sponsored by a computer manufacturer called Digital Equipment Corporation (DEC). It was part trade show, part technical conference, and all party. It was by far the most opulent business event of any kind that I have attended, before or since. DEC was a company that was making more money than it knew what to do with, and they were determined to entertain their friends in style. As part of the celebration, they chartered the *Queen Elizabeth II* and brought it to Boston Harbor. A decade later, DEC was out of business.

Sandwiched between the IBM-dominated mainframe era of the 1950s and 1960s and the PC age of the past three decades was a nearly forgotten period during which most of the underlying technologies of modern computing were introduced and perfected. This was the era of the minicomputer, and it was when I came of age as a technologist. The first computer I ever touched was an exotic machine called an Adage Graphics Terminal. Despite its name, it wasn't just a terminal. It was a full-fledged computer. Being only the size of a few refrigerators, it was marvelously compact for a 1970 computer. And, most amazingly, it was a single-user device. When you signed up for an hour on this machine in a windowless upstairs room at the Penn State Computation Center, you were signing up for an up-close-and-personal experience in which it was just you and the computer. It is difficult to capture just how unique an experience this was in an age in which the closest typical users ever came to a computer was when they passed a deck of punched cards over a counter to be submitted, along with many other such decks, into the input queue of some back-room mainframe. Just to put things into perspective: The Penn State Science Fiction Club once attempted to commission the Adage for an evening in order to hold a *SpaceWar* tournament. (*SpaceWar* was the first real graphical computer game, and the Adage was the only machine on campus capable of running it.) Although the sci-fi fans were willing to pay the relevant fee (which, if I recall, was something like $100 1970 dollars per hour), their request was denied by University officials as an "inappropriate use of University facilities."

Within a few years, machines faster, cheaper, and smaller than the Adage had become the mainstay of industrial and scientific computing. The trajectory of the minicomputer industry represents a microcosm of the coming PC revolution. Smaller in scale and a bit shorter in duration, to those who lived through it the era nonetheless had all the same feeling of inevitably and seeming permanence as our current turn of the screw—right up to the time when it suddenly collapsed.

That collapse was truly stunning. In a 1986 article, *Fortune* magazine called DEC's founder Ken Olsen "America's most successful entrepreneur," saying:

> In 29 years he has taken Digital Equipment Corp. from nothing to $7.6 billion in annual revenues. DEC today is bigger, even adjusting for inflation, than Ford Motor Co. when death claimed Henry Ford, than U.S. Steel when Andrew Carnegie sold out, than Standard Oil when John D. Rockefeller stepped aside.

DEC's revenues peaked the very next year, and then it promptly entered its death spiral. As things turned out, when we founded MAYA in 1990, Digital was our first client. More on this in Chapter 6. My point here is that we had an insider's view of how a truly great company could have been so utterly insensitive to the implications of the PC revolution, a revolution that by that time nobody—certainly not DEC—doubted was coming. As the screw prepares to turn again, I can think of no story more relevant.

But, as a consumer product, the PC is dead—as dead as the eight-track tape cartridge. In another decade, a desktop PC will look as anachronistic in a home office as a CRT terminal looks today. Your parent's Dell tower over in the corner will remind you of your grandparent's doily-covered console record player. The laptop form-factor will survive longer—maybe even indefinitely. But such machines will increasingly be seen as outliers—ultra–high power, ultra-flexible machines tuned to the needs of an ever-dwindling number of professionals who think of themselves as computer workers, as opposed to information workers.

We are not saying that keyboards, mice, or large-format displays are going away. This may well be the case, but this chapter is about sure things, not speculations, and our guess is that more or less conventional input/output devices will linger for quite some time. But the Windows-based PC has seen its day.

There are many ways to measure such things, and the details vary by methodology, but, generally speaking, PC revenues peaked almost a decade ago. Unit sales in the developed world have recently peaked as well.

The nearly complete transition from desktop to laptop PCs represents a mere evolution of form-factor. The modes of usage remain fundamentally unchanged. The same cannot be said about the transition to the post-PC era. The functions that were once centralized in a single device are increasingly being dispersed into a much broader digital environment. People who write a lot and people who spend their days crunching numbers still reach for their laptops, and they probably will for a while. But surfing the web is no longer a PC thing. People may still like the experience of viewing web pages on a spacious screen using a tangible mouse, but they like getting information when and where it is needed even more, even if it involves poking fat fingers at a pocket-sized screen. E-mail is no longer something kept in a PC—it is something floating around in the sky, to be plucked down using any convenient device. And, of course, in many circles e-mail itself is something of a quaint formalism—rather like a handwritten letter—appropriate for thank-you notes to grandma and mass-mailing party invitations, but a poor, slow-speed substitute for phone-to-phone texting or tweeting for everyday communication.

The important point in all of this is not the specific patterns of what has been substituted for what, but rather the larger point that, for the first time, all of these patterns are in play. During the hegemony of the PC, it was difficult for most people to see the distinction between medium and message. If cyberspace was a place, it was a place that was found inside a computer. But, the proliferation of devices has had the effect of bringing about a gradual but pervasive change of perspective: The data are no longer in the computers. We have come

"I don't know. I press F10 and suddenly I'm watching CNN."

Figure 1.1 Datamation Magazine, *March 15, 1991. Just 20 years ago, the very idea of television playing on a computer was fodder for absurdist humor. Today, no one would get the joke.*

Source: Courtesy of the artist.

to see that *the computers are in the data*. In essence, the idea of computing is being turned inside out. This is a new game. It is not a game that we are yet playing particularly well, but the game is afoot.

THE POWER OF DIGITAL LITERACY

There is one more topic that belongs in this chapter—one that is rarely discussed. It does not directly relate to evolving technologies per se, but rather about the evolving relationship between those technologies and nonprofessional users. Put simply, people aren't afraid of computers anymore. Computers today are part of the air we breathe. It is thus difficult to recapture the emotional baggage associated with the word *computer* during the 1960s and 1970s. This was a generation whose parents watched Walter Cronkite standing in front of a room-sized UNIVAC computer as it "predicted" Eisenhower's 1952 presidential election victory (Figure 1.2). Phone bills arrived on punched cards, whose printed admonitions not to "spindle, fold, or mutilate" became a metaphor for the mutilation of humanity by these mindless, omnipotent machines. The trend toward uniformity of language and thought that began with the printing press would surely be forced to closure by these power tools of conformity.

In his dark 1976 critique of computer technology and culture, Joseph Weizenbaum reflects this bleak assessment of the effects of technology on the humane:

> "The scientific man has above all things to strive at self-elimination in his judgments," wrote Karl Pearson in 1892. Of the many scientists I know, only a very few would disagree with that statement. Yet it must be acknowledged that it urges man to strive to become a disembodied intelligence, to himself become an instrument, a machine. So far has man's initially so innocent liaison with prostheses and pointer readings brought him. And upon a culture so fashioned burst the computer.

Moreover, computers were quite correctly seen as huge, expensive, vastly complex devices. They were in the same category as nuclear power plants and spaceships: futuristic and maybe useful, but practical only in the hands of highly skilled professionals under the employ of large corporations or the government. And as with all members of this category, they were frightening and perhaps dangerous.

These were the market conditions faced by the first-generation of PC manufacturers as they geared up to put a computer in every home. The 20-year journey from there to the iPhone represents one of history's greatest market transformations. It was a triumph, and it was no accident. But it was not fundamentally a triumph of marketing. Rather, it was a triumph of human-centered design.

Figure 1.2 *1952: Walter Cronkite watches UNIVAC predict the electoral victory of Dwight Eisenhower.*

Source: U.S. Census Bureau.

The story might have been very different had it not been for an extraordinarily devised but unfortunately named innovation known as the WIMP paradigm. WIMP, which stands for "Windows, Icons, Menus, and Pointers," was a highly stylized, carefully crafted architecture for human-computer interaction via graphical media. Jim Morris, one of the founders of MAYA, worked on the team that invented the first computing system that used the WIMP paradigm and watched the story unfold firsthand. Its development at the famed Xerox Palo Alto Research Center (Xerox PARC) and its subsequent appropriation by Steve Jobs during his famous and fateful visit is well-documented and oft-told. Less often discussed is the pivotal role of this story in paving the way for mass-market computing.

The details aren't important to our story. What is important to point out is that the WIMP paradigm presented the first generation of nonprofessional users with a single, relatively simple, standardized mode of interaction. Equally important was the fact that this style was essentially identical for all applications. Whether the user was playing a game, sending e-mail, using a spreadsheet, or editing a manuscript, it was always windows and icons. Why is this important? The obvious answer is that simple, logical rules are easier to learn than complex, idiosyncratic ones. Moreover, the transfer of learning that results from a high level of consistency more than makes up for the disadvantages associated with a one-size-fits-all approach to design. And, of course, limiting the "creative" freedom granted to workaday designers was not necessarily a bad thing back in a day when experienced user interface (UI) designers were few and far between.

But the biggest advantage accruing from such a rigorous framework (or from any other widely-accepted architectural framework) is that it forms the basis of a *community of practice*. That is, such frameworks encourage a virtuous cycle in which early adopters (who, generally speaking, can take care of themselves) take on the role of first-tier consulting resources for those who come later. As a whole society struggled together to figure out these strange new machines, having everybody trying to sing the same song was of inestimable value.

But along with this value, there were significant costs. Most notably, rigid UI standards brought with themselves a deep conservatism. In 1987 when Apple's Bill Atkinson released the HyperCard multimedia development environment (in our opinion one of the most important innovations of the pre-web era), it was widely criticized for a few small and well-motivated deviations from the Apple WIMP style-guide. As the years went by and a new generation of digital-from-birth users entered the marketplace, the costs of this conservatism eventually came to exceed the benefits. A long string of innovations, including interactive multimedia, hypertext systems, touchscreens, multitouch displays, and above all immersive video games, gradually forced developers and platform providers to mellow out and relax the doctrinal grip of WIMP. This has led to a far less consistent but much richer and more generative computing environment. The interfaces aren't always good, but new ideas are now fair game.

Concomitant with this evolution has emerged a market populated by users who are pretty much up for anything, in a way that just wasn't the case even a few years ago. Having learned to use keyboards and mice before pencils and pens, they are not fazed by such mysteries as dragging a scrollbar down in order to make text move up. And, if Apple decides to reverse this convention (as it recently did, presumably in order to improve consistency with touch-oriented devices), that's fine with them. The minor mental rewiring involved is taken in stride. This underappreciated trend is a significant market enabler, which sets the stage for bigger changes to come.

CHAPTER 2

The Next Mountain

In design . . . the vision precedes the proof. A fine steel building is never designed by starting to figure the stresses and strains of the steel. We must get off the ground with an impulse strong enough to make our building stand up, high and shining and definite, in our mind's eye, before we ever put pencil to paper in the matter. When we see it standing whole, it will be time enough to put its form on paper and begin to think about the steel that will hold it up.

—WALTER DORWIN TEAGUE

Chapter 1 was about some changes in the technology landscape that very likely *will* happen, and happen soon. We now turn to some potential consequences of those changes. These are things that certainly *can* happen, and in our judgment they *should* happen. In the long run, we are inclined to believe that they are inevitable (but then, we are optimists). There is, however, reason to fear that the long run may be unnecessarily slow in coming. In Chapter 3, we'll address some of the things standing in the way of progress toward Trillions Mountain. It would be disingenuous to claim that the industry is obviously on a trajectory toward the trends we are about to describe. But this is merely to say that these changes are *disruptive*. It is part of the definition of disruptive technologies that they seem to the inattentive to come suddenly out of nowhere. But just because the trajectory isn't obvious doesn't mean that it isn't discernible. There are long-term trends and fundamental processes at work, although the details are still very much in play. The prize to those who correctly discern the large-scale trends is the opportunity to influence and profit from those details.

In this chapter, we will sketch out a future computing landscape based upon the trillion-node network. This picture has three basic facets: (1) fungible devices, (2) liquid information, and (3) a genuine cyberspace. We will explore each in turn. All three of these facets are architectural in nature. They are dependent on the development and wide adoption of broad organizational principles and well-articulated standards and practices, developed and maintained by a community of designers.[1] We will speak more about the "how" of this essential process in later chapters. This chapter focuses on the "what."

FUNGIBLE DEVICES

The titles of both this section and the next involve terms borrowed from economics. This is no coincidence. There has only ever been one human-devised system with a level of complexity comparable to that of the coming trillion-node network, and that is the worldwide economy. In a real sense, the discipline of economics amounts to the study of unbounded complexity and how to manage it. It is thus no surprise that some of its basic concepts will show up in our study. Two such concepts are those of *fungibility* and *liquidity*. We will argue that *device fungibility* and *information liquidity* represent the holy grail of our search for a manageable future.

For the benefit of readers who may have slept through Econ 101, the term *fungibility* refers to the ability to freely interchange equivalent goods. An item is fungible to the extent that one instance is as good as another. If I lend you

---

[1] The word *designer* is used to label practitioners of activities that range from the ridiculous to the sublime. Later on we will give significant attention to the concept of "design." For now, suffice it to say that our use of the term is broad. Engineers, for example, are certainly designers in our book.

$1,000 (or, less plausibly, an ounce of gold), you do not expect to be paid back with the same actual dollars or gold. One dollar is as good as another. It is often assumed that fungibility depends on physical similarity. This may be true of gold, but it is certainly not true of dollars, even if we limit the discussion to U.S. dollars. No two dollar bills are physically identical, and many transactions don't involve physical bills at all. It is not the physical similarity that is important; it is the functional equivalence that matters. Fungibility is a desirable trait for the obvious reason that it greases the skids of commerce. If you compare a market based upon fungible currency to a barter economy the difference is stark. You may trade a goat for two rolls of fabric today and trade one of those rolls for 100 pounds of flour tomorrow. While this works tolerably well in local enclaves, it doesn't scale or interoperate very well. It's very hard to separate the value of the good from the good itself. It is the fungibility of currency that makes it superior to barter as a medium of exchange.

Looking Back at a Look Forward

In 1998, at the threshold of the new millennium, The Defense Advanced Research Projects Agency (DARPA) put out a rather unusual request for proposal. It was a challenge to researchers to mount an "Expedition to the 21st Century" with the goal of exploring and reporting back on the information technologies of the future. MAYA was encouraged to propose, and we did so. Below is the preface to our successful proposal, transcribed verbatim:

The Post-Computer Era
Components and Information Architecture in the 21st Century
BAA: #99–07 (Information Technology Expeditions)
Dec 07, 1998

We have received a preliminary report from our advanced reconnaissance mission to the 21st Century and it contains surprising and sometimes puzzling data. As expected, this culture is awash with information devices of all description. Indeed, it is rare to encounter a manufactured item of any type whatsoever that does not possess at least some capability to process information. A great many of these devices are based on a technology known as JAVA++, but early predictions that this language would become the universal development environment proved to be overly optimistic, especially on the numerous low-end devices. For example, most magazine ads contain animations printed in semiconductor inks comprising polymer integrated circuits powered by amorphous solar cell paper. Although the resulting processors are impressive, heroic efforts to port the J++ virtual machine to this

(Continued)

platform have not gone well, so producing apps for them remains a craft industry involving low-level programming.

Despite such limitations, it is a striking fact that virtually all such devices appear to have at least some ability to interoperate. (Even the magazine ads can—if the reader touches a designated spot—dispense short messages to a wristwatch/PDA.) Short-range RF, bodylan techniques, and other technologies not fully understood act as the threads that stitch together literally trillions of separate devices into a seamless worldwide dataflow of computation. Information flows freely through this landscape of devices like water in a brook—effortlessly finding the shortest available route to its destination, flowing around obstacles along the way.

Although the Internet has continued in its role as the "spinal cord" of society, 20th Century assumptions that all devices will essentially become Internet terminals have proven wrong. A great deal of information flows through ad hoc, spontaneously self-organizing networks that function as "tributaries" to the Internet. (Contemporary researchers were amused to discover that a tiny but measurable percentage of the transcontinental data traffic flowed by hopping from vehicle to vehicle along Interstate 80.) The component architectures, data models, security and routing algorithms necessary to support this vast, ever-shifting, heterogeneous sea of packet-switched computation remain a complete mystery to our investigators.

But, the most astonishing finding about 21st Century society is that it is practically devoid of "computers"! The term rarely appears in print; the PC as an artifact can be found only in museums; and the employment advertisements contain no category for "computer programmer." Although a huge amount of computation obviously takes place in service of this society, it appears to occur primarily as an emergent property of the milieu of special-purpose information devices. Evidently, the status of "computer" in society went the way of the electric motor—evolving over time from being a centerpiece of technology to a mere component that disappears entirely into the inner workings of countless appliances.

There are many things that we don't understand about the functioning of this technology. Everyone—and no one—seems to be a programmer. Device interoperability seems to be complete. It is quite common to see random collections of stuff being composed—even by children—into sometimes strange but always functional ensembles of information devices. Military units in the field have been known to improvise computational resources out of spare vehicle parts. It is clear from these examples that the component revolution has succeeded far beyond anything contemplated today. Moreover, component interoperability on such a grand scale must be mediated by some universal information architecture that greatly surpasses current art (this is especially astonishing given the aforementioned fact that these devices are not based on any single implementation technology or object model). Finally, since the sheer numbers of devices involved preclude any kind of centrally orchestrated component integration, how global system coherence and integrity are maintained is a complete mystery.

The goal of our proposed expedition is to discover and prototype architectural principles that will support radically complete interoperability among huge numbers of wildly diverse information devices. We will create generic, field-composable components—both hardware and software—that can be quickly assembled to duplicate the functions of contemporary personal computers, while also supporting ad-hoc assembly into unique, special purpose devices of great diversity. The design of such devices will follow architectural principles geared toward unprecedented scalability. Some of the prototyped devices—such as network interfaces and data display software components—will be of broad applicability, while others—such as sensors and domain-specific simulators—will be quite specific. But, no matter how diverse, or how randomly matched any set of devices may be, each will be able to meaningfully exchange data with the others. Storage devices, displays, and general computational resources will all be orthogonally composable. For example, one will be able to plug in a keyboard and monitor to a cell phone in order to edit its configuration. This will be accomplished not by providing VGA and keyboard ports on the phone. Rather, "semantic interconnects" mediated by simple universal "information objects" will permit such operations to be mediated at the message-passing level.

Our application of this concept to computing devices is slightly metaphorical and not quite precise. But the basic idea is the same. To the extent that building blocks of a system are fungible, that system is easier to build, easier to maintain over time, and more likely to benefit from the positive forces of free market processes. This is the point of modular architectures of all kinds. A toy structure built out of Lego bricks is vastly easier to build than a similar structure made out of hand-carved wood. Even better (at least from the consumer's perspective), once any relevant patents have expired, a successful line of modular products invites competitors. There now exists a thriving market of Lego-compatible toys. Although it is true that some of these products directly compete with the real thing, many others represent extensions to new (often niche) markets—expanding the customer base into areas where the original innovator cannot or chooses not to go. There are businesses specializing in Lego-compatible ninja dolls; medieval weapons; custom colors; and on-demand customized graphics. It is unlikely that the existence of this market represents a net loss to The Lego Group. Fungibility builds markets and empowers users.

Where We Stand Today

How does the computer world score in terms of fungibility? At first glance, that answer appears to be "very well." What is more interchangeable than the PC? If you can perform a task on one modern Window's box, you can pretty much assume that you could do it on another one as well. And even the dreaded PC vs. Macintosh divide is not what it used to be. Modern development environments have vastly simplified the process of creating cross-platform applications, and robust "virtual PC" environments are available to fill in the gaps. However, this interchangeability was largely achieved at the expense of diversity. General-purpose computers are mostly interchangeable because they mostly all run the same software.

This lack of diversity has two very serious negative consequences: First, this kind of interchangeability implies generality, and generality implies complexity. Second, whenever we put all of our eggs in one basket, we are asking for trouble. A lack of diversity inevitably leads to fragile and vulnerable systems. In the case of the PC, this fragility is manifest in many ways, but most prominently in the utter absurdity of the current Internet virus situation. Books have been written on this topic, so we will restrain ourselves here. The following statistic seems sufficient: A PC plugged into the Internet without a firewall will almost certainly become infected with a virus (and thus become co-opted as a source of spam or worse) within a few minutes. The modern PC, it seems, is not a very wise choice as our only egg basket. This path to device fungibility is not going to get us much farther.

But what of less general devices? As we work our way down the computing food chain, does fungibility increase? In fact, the opposite is the case. The current crop of high-end mobile devices generally avoids the virus plague via a set of techniques known collectively as the *walled garden* approach. This means that the devices are "tethered" to their manufacturer so that even after the device is in its owner's hands, the mother ship retains ultimate control over what software may or may not be run on the device. If, for example, Apple decides that a piece of software is insecure, of poor quality, or otherwise inappropriate, then that software cannot be run on a stock iPhone. Apple even retains the ability to delete software from all iPhones after the fact. Such arrangements are the rule and not the exception with contemporary smartphones, as well as DVRs, cable and satellite boxes, and most other subscription-based devices. This approach for the most part does an excellent job at keeping these devices safe in a way that PC users can only dream about. But it reduces the fungibility of these devices to almost zero. Your TiVo contains all of the hardware and most of the software to serve as a general-purpose computing device. Moreover, one can imagine many compelling uses of a computer constantly connected to your TV. But, unless you happen to be a very well informed tinkerer with a lot of time on your hands, you are out of luck. That powerful, video-enabled PC in your living room will only do what the TiVo people permit. Smartphones have apps and so are much more flexible, but they are not much more fungible. If you wish to switch from an iPhone to an Android device, you will pretty much be starting over. And, using that lovely touch screen for some ad hoc spur-of-the-moment purpose is simply out of the question.

So, how about really low-level products? Again, from a fungibility perspective, things only get worse. Your clock radio and your cordless phones and the half-dozen remote controls that have no doubt accumulated on your coffee table all contain reasonably powerful computers, and as we have seen, newer models may well have some kind of communications capability. And, just as with a TiVo, it is not difficult to imagine useful, convenient, and creative ways to customize or repurpose these devices to better fit the particulars of your life. But if you are tempted to try, be prepared to learn to use a soldering iron.[2] Every device is an island, locked in to a very specific use that is almost impossible to change. This is particularly galling in the case of all those remote controls. Yes, most new remotes have "features" that purport to make them "universal," yet somehow some necessary function always seems to fall between the cracks, and the collection on the coffee table continues to grow. In more than a quarter-century of trying, the technology industries have proven incapable of even making the half-dozen devices found in a typical entertainment center work together well enough to be tolerated by any sane consumer.

Where We Can Be Tomorrow

There is an exception to that last statement. A home theater can often be made to work seamlessly if you follow one simple rule: Just buy all your stuff from one manufacturer. This is essentially the moral equivalent of the walled-garden approach. Simply by ceding all decision-making power to a single corporation, most of our problems are solved. Another example of the viability of this approach can be found in a different industry: Imagine a world in which all of your doors and windows were automated; in which the security system was automatically and unobtrusively activated at all the right times; and in which you were instantly reminded if you leave your keys in the lock. This description is either futuristic science fiction or it is utterly mundane, depending upon whether it is describing your home or your car. What's the difference? Simply that cars are designed and built as a unit and houses are not.

Unfortunately, a walled-garden home would leave something to be desired. It is one thing to be forced to choose between Apple and Android when buying a smartphone, it is quite another having to make a similar choice when buying a home. A consumer would be a fool to agree to a single-vendor commitment when investing in something as complex and long-lived as a home or an apartment. Imagine deciding five years into owning a home that you'd like to change something. Maybe you'd like to update the lighting, or the furniture, or the refrigerator, or the doors. Sorry, if the manufacturer doesn't make those things or have a deal with someone who does, you are just out of luck. And don't even think about trying to install that heirloom furniture from your childhood home. This, in a nutshell, is the challenge of pervasive computing: How do we build a world

---

[2]This is no exaggeration. It is common, for example, for professional home-theater installers to physically modify consumer devices in a heroic effort to lash together disparate products into a system with a modicum of usability.

that hangs together well enough to be worth living in without giving up the ability to pick and choose among competing offerings? If the industry is going to find
an answer to this question, it is going to involve a change of perspective, and the
giving up of some very ingrained habits. Instead of using deliberately incompatible designs and protocols, manufacturers must begin to see themselves and their
products as participating in an *ecology*—an ecology of information devices.

This will involve a change in mind-set. In today's market it is extremely
common for the manufacturers of consumer electronics to go out of their way
to make it difficult for third-party devices to interoperate with their products.
But in an information ecosystem, interoperability must become a sacrament. The
sheer scale and diversity of the world that we are in the midst of building implies
that going it alone is a fool's errand. Attempting to do so once this trend gains
steam will represent a choice analogous to that made by the early online service
providers such as Prodigy and CompuServe as the open Internet slowly but inexorably overtook their proprietary models—and the results will be the same.

How will this kind of universal interoperability be accomplished? Is it even
feasible? This is a fair question. A straightforward extrapolation from today's
networking practice might lead to a certain pessimism. Will a trillion devices all
be nodes on the Internet? Are we going to burden every light switch with the
complexity required to speak the complex suite of Internet protocols plus some
standardized home control protocol? And do we expect existing standards bodies to produce such a protocol and negotiate its universal adoption? Does our
goal of device fungibility in an open market imply detailed published specifications and standards for every possible feature of every possible product?

The answer to all of these questions, fortunately, is "no." First of all, a
trillion-node network does not imply a trillion-node Internet. The vast majority
of pervasive computing devices will only ever communicate with their immediate neighbors in a preconfigured peer-to-peer arrangement. This is not to say that
there will not be data paths to and from the Internet to such devices. But in a great
many cases those paths will be indirect, often involving numerous hops over much
more primitive data paths. On the matter of protocols and standardization, the
first thing to recognize is that very many devices have very little to say for themselves. Imagine putting all the complexity of a PC into a doorbell to get it "on"
the Internet. Today, due to our lack of modularity, the most practical path often
involves something nearly this complicated. A doorbell need communicate only
one message, and that message is only a single bit long. This may be an extreme
and atypical example, but if we go just one more step, to a protocol containing
exactly two messages (which still requires a payload of only one bit), we will have
captured the needs of a great many devices, including simple light switches, desk
lamps, motion detectors, door locks, and many, many other devices. If we allow
ourselves four bits (16 unique messages), we will have subsumed the needs of
numeric keypads, simple telephone dialers, many security panels, and so on.

The previous paragraph may seem trivial and simplistic, but it is the key to
the path forward. The trick is to recognize that the set of all devices requiring

only, say, two messages forms a class. At MAYA we call such a class a *realm*. Once we have conceptualized the notion of realm, several key pieces of the puzzle quickly fall into place. First of all, although some realms—such as the Internet—have a great many different messages and so are quite complex, many others, including the ones just described, have very few different messages and so are extremely simple. The value of this observation lies in the fact that simple realms require only simple protocols, and simple protocols are easy to get people to agree to. If we can only manage to resist feature creep, there just isn't very much to fight about.

The next realization is that if we avoid making unnecessary assumptions about how a realm will be used, we can get a great deal of interoperability for free. So, for example, if we are careful to define the two messages for our light switch not as "on" and "off," but as "true" and "false" (or, equivalently, as "1" and "0"), then the same protocol can be used for all other two-valued devices, which means that any two such devices can speak directly to each other.[3] This means that in one fell swoop, we have achieved universal interoperability among the vast number of devices—existing and potential—in the "True/False, On/Off, 1/0" realm. This in turn implies that, for example, all motion sensors will have achieved near-complete fungibility, and also that some blue-collar installer out in the field can be sure that any one of them can be used to control, say, any light fixture.

This is still pretty trivial. But we next observe that realms can be *nested* in the following sense: We can easily arrange for the 2-message realm to be represented as a proper subset of the 16-message realm (e.g., by agreeing that "1" means "True" and "0" means "False"). If we then add the simple requirement that all devices ignore any message they don't understand, we now have a situation in which the simple 2-state devices can be directly mixed with members of the more capable 16-state realm. So, our simple light switch could serve as a source of messages for a controller that understands numeric commands, and vice versa. Moreover, even if we fail at coming to universal agreement on realm definitions, this will create a market for simple devices to bridge incompatible realms (we call such devices transducers).

The plausibility of this story clearly depends upon keeping things simple. It is one thing to talk to a light switch. But the list of messages we would need to control, say, a satellite TV set top box would be another matter. And what about device fungibility in the case of such a box? The features of such a device are so numerous and idiosyncratic that it would seem that we have made very little progress toward our goal. The answer to both problems involves one of the most basic patterns of nature: recursive decomposition. This is just a fancy way of saying that complex things should be built out of simple things. We can think of our satellite box as a wrapper around several simpler devices: a tuner box, a box that sends pictures to your TV, a user-interface box, a diagnostic

---

[3] We are simplifying here just a bit. In addition to agreeing on the messages, we also have to agree to how those messages are actually transported, but this is only a little harder.

box, a movie-ordering box, a video decryption box, and so on. Some of these boxes may be made up of even simpler boxes, perhaps down several levels. Thought of this way, no single part of the system needs to be all that complex—at least in terms of the messages we might want to exchange with it. If we can then figure out a way to expose the internal interconnections among these simple components to the outside world, we will be off and running. Figure 2.1 sketches this concept as applied to the components of a clock radio.

Please note that we are not necessarily suggesting that satellite boxes or clock radios should be *physically* modular—cost, space, and aesthetic considerations often preclude this. What is absolutely essential, though, is that we as the architects of Trillions start to think recursively and resolve to keep any given module simple enough and open enough that it could in principle serve as a fungible building block of new and unanticipated assemblies. Today, computing is largely thought of in terms of hardware versus software. The concept of fungible information devices drives a refactoring of this approach. Instead of thinking of hardware and software, we suggest that a more fruitful way of thinking about information systems would be to start with the distinction between *devices* and *information*. In essence the

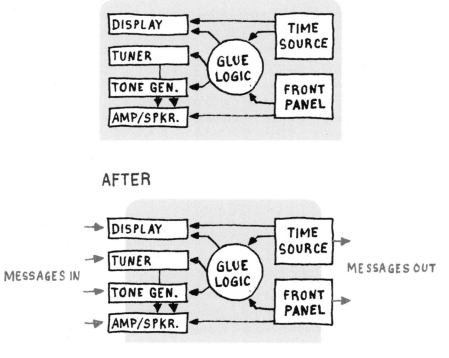

Figure 2.1 *Componentized clock radio: a common appliance re-imagined as a modular device*

divide is between physical and metaphysical. Devices can then be further divided between hardware devices and software devices. These are built in very different ways, but they do exactly the same thing: They process information. In practice a particular building block may start out as a software module and, later, it may be replaced by hardware—or vice versa.[4] This may happen because someone else in the market produced a version of the building block that was faster or more energy efficient or more robust along some other dimension. In a world of fungible components, such substitutions will become routine—they can be done without disrupting the basic architectural integrity of a design.

If we can make the transition to interchangeable information devices that are fungible between software and hardware, we will quickly see an explosion of innovation. We will discover that our customers will amaze us. Far from costing sales, interoperability will cause our products to be used in ways we could never have imagined, and in numbers we could only have dreamed of.

These ideas are simple, but they are not simplistic. This kind of thinking lights the way toward an open, competitive marketplace of incrementally evolving device families that collectively will deserve the label *ecosystem*.

LIQUID INFORMATION

Liquidity is the other side of the fungibility coin. In economics the term is used in various ways, all generally relating to the free flow of value in an economy. Similarly, our metaphorical usage refers to the ability of information to flow freely where and when it is needed. At one level of analysis, the Internet itself is a triumph of information liquidity. There are perhaps five billion or more devices connected to the Internet, and any one of them is capable of sending packets of data to any other one almost instantly. But users don't care about packets; they care about meaningful units of information, and at that level, the liquidity scores are much more mixed.

Where We Stand Today

There is so much information available on the Internet, and there are so many different ways to measure quantities of information, that any statistic about how many petabytes, or exabytes, or whatever, of information on the Net is essentially meaningless. But there is a lot—eclipsing anything the world has seen by orders of magnitude. And a significant percentage of it can be summoned to a screen near you with a few clicks of a mouse. Doesn't this count

---

[4] It is important to note that, although software is often thought of as data rather than as mechanism, this is incorrect. Computer *code* indeed comprises data, but a piece of code is in fact merely a plan (a blueprint, if you will) for the creation of a *running computer program*. The latter, although existing inside the memory of a computer, is an operational mechanism—taking up space in memory and consuming energy. It is in every essential respect a *machine*.

as liquidity? Not really. The term *liquidity* evokes images of a bubbling brook, with water finding its own course around boulders and down waterfalls; merging with other streams; being scooped up into buckets and poured into bottles and glasses. The flow of information from a web server to your screen is nothing like that. It is a highly regimented, rigidly engineered process by which largely predetermined chunks of data are dispensed in predetermined formats. Every website is like a discrete vending machine where we go to procure a certain particular kind of information. When we need a different kind, we move on to another machine. In this sense, it is less a matter of the data flowing to the user than the user traveling to the data.

There are modest exceptions to this pattern. The most obvious example involves what is known in web jargon as *mashups*. The term refers to the practice of gathering information from multiple sources around the Net and displaying them together on a single web page. The most common example involves using Google maps as "wallpaper" in front of which various geocoded data points may be displayed. This is indeed a big step forward, but in most cases the effect is more like the layering of one or more transparent acetates over a map than a true intermingling of independent data objects. A more aggressive plan for promoting information liquidity involves a family of protocols and interfaces that have been developed by the web technical community with the explicit goal of getting the data to flow. These include mechanisms with names like RSS (real simple syndication) and SOAP (simple object access protocol). These are parts of a broader framework going under the name of *web services*, and comprise techniques for sharing small amounts of information from one machine with another on demand. Again, such techniques represent real progress, but for the most part their designs assume a conventional client/server pattern of data flow, in which all aggregations of data ultimately reside in large servers controlled by single corporate entities. The data flow, but only begrudgingly.

As we have already seen, the low-level Internet is a marvel of liquidity. If you can represent something digitally, you can transport it using the Internet. Word processing files, photos, web pages, spreadsheets, music, movies, computer programs, encrypted files whose contents are a total mystery—it makes no difference. If your target device is on the Net and it has enough room, the Internet can get it there for you. We've come to take this fact for granted, but if you think about it, it is quite a trick. How is the trick done? How did a small group of designers working in a day when CNN on a computer was an ironic joke manage to anticipate all this diversity? The answer is very simple: The Internet slices everything up into a bunch of little data containers called *packets*. The problem thus reduces to a relatively simple one of creating mechanisms for moving around packets. The strategy is the same as that seen in the use of standardized shipping containers for the transport of physical goods. Instead of having one system for moving machinery and another one for moving dry goods and so on, we simply put everything into standard containers, and then design all our cranes and trucks and ships and railcars to efficiently move those containers.

The Box That Flattened the World

On a spring day in 1956, an alert ship spotter in Newark, New Jersey, might have caught a glimpse of something odd. Steaming out of port was a converted oil tanker with 58 trailer trucks lashed to its deck, bound for Houston, Texas. The ship's name was *Ideal-X*, and her voyage was something of a rapid prototype of an idea that changed the world: the intermodal shipping container. In the decades following this experiment, those hacked-together trailers evolved into a worldwide fleet of 100 million highly engineered standardized containers in which the vast majority of the planet's goods are transported. These containers are the common currency of a global ecology involving ships, trains, trucks, forklifts, cranes, and a hundred other specialized devices and facilities (Figure 2.2).

Standardized containers are so familiar and so seemingly obvious an idea that it is difficult to remember that half a century ago virtually all freight was shipped *break bulk*—loose bundles of product loaded onto ships using big nets and arranged carefully (or not) into the holds of ships, one item at a time by muscular longshoremen. When the ships reached their destinations, the process was repeated in reverse, as the items were transferred into boxcars or delivery vans for the next step of their journey. Nor is it easy to imagine the years of struggle—technical, economic, and political—by a few industry visionaries that were required to pull off this apparently simple innovation. And yet today's global economy would have

been impossible had those visionaries not prevailed.

The analogy between physical shipping containers and information objects such as Internet packets is striking. In both cases, simple technologies serve to catalyze the development of highly integrated, standardized systems for the liquid flow of value. In both cases, containerization supports a clean separation of payload from transport—making a true integrated system possible without requiring an unrealistic degree of standardization of payload. Today, 50 years after the *Ideal-X*'s voyage, the technique she prototyped has become nearly universal. The world's semantic data, however, are still shipped break bulk. We will not make it very far up Trillions Mountain until this changes.

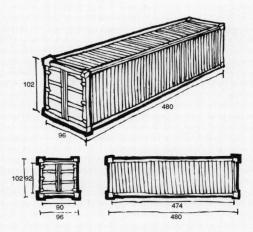

Figure 2.2 *The intermodal shipping container: a standardized interface between shippers and carriers*
The concept of containerization is further explored online at http://trillions.maya.com/ Containerization.

Packets are small, they are simple, and most importantly they are (at least so far) non-negotiable. If you want to be part of the Internet, you need to deal with packets, and if you want to use the Internet, you need to turn your payload into packets. This is not to say that packets are always the best way to represent data. For any given task, a clever engineer can usually conceive of a bespoke representation that would be more efficient and/or convenient. But almost never is this worth the trade-off.

Regrettably, nothing like the packet exists at higher levels of our information infrastructure. Our *semantic stack* progresses nicely from the bit to the byte to the packet. After that, however, standard practice degenerates to a chaos of "just so" protocols that bear a closer resemblance to longshoremen with nets than to the structured simplicity of shipping containers. The emergence of a uniform data container is in the critical path to the world of Trillions.

Where We Can Be Tomorrow

Suppose we *did* have a "container" for data. Nothing fancy like XML or its ilk. Just one small step up from the packet. Think of it as a little box into which you could fit an e-mail message, or a single image, or a chapter of a book, or a single scene from a movie. Let's add just one more feature: On the outside of each "box" we could put a unique number. Not a name or a date code or an owner or anything like that (those things will be inside the box), just a number that is different on every box.[5] Think of this number as being like the barcodes that we routinely put on the outsides of virtually all shipping containers. Such numbers aren't *names* because they don't identify the contents of the box, only the box itself. (This is important: It encourages all boxes to be treated on an equal basis. Plus, in most cases, it is none of the transporter's business what is in the box, anyway.) We could then use these numbers as *pointers* that allow the contents of one box to refer to other boxes. In this way, for example, there could be a box that in effect refers to an entire book or movie, simply by containing a list of other boxes' numbers.

Such a concept (except for the unique identifier) was proposed in 1997 by Michael Dertouzos, then head of the MIT Laboratory for Computer Science. He prefaced the proposal with the following quotation:

> Achieving some basic degree of understanding among different computers to make automatization possible is not as technically difficult as it sounds. However, it does require one very difficult commodity: human consensus.

---

[5] If you are worried that there aren't enough numbers to go around, just do the math: 34 bytes would be enough to label each atom in the known universe.

As Dertouzos suggests, this idea is, from a technical perspective, really quite trivial. Making it happen in practice is quite another matter. The problem is that the way of thinking implied by this simple little idea is completely at odds with the way the web deals with content. For this reason (and this reason alone), the challenges are significant. But let's fantasize for a moment and assume that in the future all content is shipped around the Net in our little boxes. What would such a world be like?

For starters, it would be a much simpler world. Even though the Net is based only on packets, if we go up a level we discover that it is replete with special-purpose protocols and standards, all of which do pretty much the same thing. There is a protocol called SMTP that is only used for sending e-mail. There is a different protocol for fetching e-mail (actually, there are two: POP and IMAP). There is HTTP for web pages, NTP for the time of day, the aforementioned SOAP and RSS (among others) for "web services." We will not belabor the point, except to note that as of this writing, the Wikipedia list of such so-called application layer protocols contains 51 items. There is no doubt that every one of these protocols has some handy features and optimizations that were important back when computers were orders of magnitude slower and when the Internet was accessed via dial-up lines, but we can assure you that with today's technology there is no data payload being transported by any of them that couldn't be successfully put into our little boxes.

Thus, all 51 protocols could be replaced by a single protocol. (Let's call it LBTP—Little Box Transport Protocol). Such a change would be guaranteed to vastly increase information liquidity. This is true for several reasons. For starters, both data transport and data storage would become much more standardized and general. Instead of requiring devices to have the complexity of a relational database or some one-off remote access protocol to fetch and store information, we just ask for a trivial ability to get little boxes and give little boxes. This becomes increasingly important in the age of Trillions, since it permits relatively simple devices to retain generality. If a device can transport and store one little box, it can do so with another. The computers in your car might or might not be able to display pictures from your camera or save the state of a video game, but in our hypothetical world they will surely be able to back them up in a network dead zone and pass them on whenever service is restored.

Additionally, since the boxes are assumed to be relatively small, designers will be forced to break up large blocks of data (such as web pages and large databases) into smaller units. Although it is true that this could be done stupidly (e.g., by breaking the data up into semantically meaningless blocks at arbitrary cut-points) this is not what competent engineers will do. Rather, they will tend to make their slices at semantic boundaries. So, for example, if a web page comprises a list of travel information about 50 cities, each city will tend to be given its own box. This, in turn, will tend to support the evolution of user interfaces that make it possible to tear off parts of visualizations that are of interest to the user. Such fragments of data could be mixed and matched and caused to flow into tight spaces of the pervasive computing world, performing functions that today would require the cost and complexity of a PC or an iPhone.

The liquidity resulting from this kind of containerization of data is an essential step in the emergence of the trillion-node network. The traditional Internet serves as the arteries and veins of the worldwide information circulatory system, and it will continue to do so. The advent of a network of many billions of cheaper, less-capable, but far more ubiquitous devices represents the emergence of a system of capillaries, reaching all the cells of our technology and of our society. This is only going to work if the viscosity of our information lifeblood is reduced to a minimum.

CYBERSPACE FOR REAL

The word *cyberspace* has not fared well in recent years. Its common usage has devolved into a geeky synonym for "Internet." This is a shame, because it originally referred to a distinct idea that is both nonobvious and important. It was coined by science-fiction writer William Gibson in 1982—a time in which the idea of a public information network was not even on most people's radar. Gibson's cyberspace was in effect a parallel reality, a "place" filled with "things" made of bits rather than atoms. Most importantly, it was a place where people "went" to interact. The idea was captured evocatively by author and sometime Gibson collaborator Bruce Sterling in the following:

> Cyberspace is the "place" where a telephone conversation appears to occur. Not inside your actual phone, the plastic device on your desk. Not inside the other person's phone, in some other city. *The place between* the phones. The indefinite place *out there*, where the two of you, two human beings, actually meet and communicate.

In Gibson's stories, cyberspace is accessed via a "consensual hallucination" produced by a machine involving the attachment of electrodes to one's head. Although the real Internet may or may not someday come to that, the mode of access is beside the point. For present purposes, the inconvenient presence of a plastic screen between user and cyberspace is incidental. What is not incidental is that cyberspace is a (almost) literal *place* where people can "go" to find and interact with digital "things" and also with other people.

In writing these words, we are painfully aware of the triteness that many readers will perceive upon first reading. *Everybody* talks about the Net this way. What we are trying to say, though, is that *these ideas are not metaphors*. The places between our telephones where we have our conversations are not *physical* but they are quite *real*. They exist, and they have done so for the century and a half since the invention of the telephone. Also real is the one-dimensional "path" defined by the radio dial, along which one can travel and occasionally bump into "objects" in the form of radio channels. The computer and the Internet have expanded the scope of these places almost beyond imagination. So, a little imagination is called for.

Where We Stand Today

What exactly do we mean by *place*? The idea is related to what mathematicians call *manifolds*. This notion generalizes the idea of *coordinate system* and lets us talk about "where" things are and "how far apart" they may be. The surface of the Earth is a manifold, and so the world has "places" where we can go and where we can put things. If you use a modern personal computer, its so-called desktop is a manifold. It is a place where you can put icons representing your digital stuff. You can drag them around and group them in ways that you find meaningful or pleasing—just as on your physical desktop. This desktop metaphor has been with us since the early 1980s, when it was introduced at the Xerox Palo Alto Research Center and popularized by Apple with the original Macintosh computer. It was a toe in the water of a true cyberspace.

At the time, there was a great deal of research in a field called Information Visualization[6] on how this metaphor could be extended from the desktop out into the Internet so as to form the basis of a single, worldwide collaborative information space—a true cyberspace. But there was a competing vision. Its name was "hypertext." This term was coined in the 1960s by an eccentric visionary named Ted Nelson in the context of an extremely ambitious plan for a distributed, text-based information system known as Xanadu. Nelson's vision was sweeping and largely beyond our scope, but the core idea was that of the hypertext link—a technique by which disparate units of text could be associated such that a single click of a mouse can take the reader instantly from one place to another. In cyberspace terms, hypertext links can be thought of as "magic wormholes" from one point in space directly to any other.

Thanks to Nelson and a small community of researchers exploring the technical and human factors of hypertexts, the idea was in the air as the World Wide Web emerged in the early 1990s, and it was a very appealing one. If it lacked the new frontier romance of the cyberspace vision, it made up for it with relatively straightforward answers to pressing questions concerning how users were going to find their way around the vast new world of data that was rapidly forming itself. Moreover, being essentially text based, hypertext techniques were better suited to the graphically primitive personal computers that were commercially viable for consumer purchase at the time.

As a result, the vision (if not the term) of cyberspace basically disappeared from the industry's road map. The first web browsers presented the Internet

---

[6] Our late colleague and fellow MAYAn Steve Roth was one of the founders of this field.

primarily as columns of clickable lists leading to other such lists. Soon, those columns were to give way to billboards of clickable images, but the basic model remains the same. The World Wide Web is literally a tangle of arbitrary links. There is no sense of "distance" in the web model. One can ask how many clicks it takes to get from one web page to another, but beyond that, it makes little sense to ask how "far apart" they are.[7] It is analogous to living in a town arranged randomly, completely without neighborhoods. We have made up for this randomness with the miracle of Google. This approach has gotten us a long way. But it is not the end of the story.

In the mid-1970s, an interesting piece of software was making the rounds in the computer community. Its name was ADVENT, which was short for *Adventure* (file names were limited to six characters back then). If you happened to stumble upon this program without knowing anything about it, it was a fascinating and disorienting experience. After the briefest of introductions, your terminal (most likely a teletype machine) would type the following:

```
You are standing at the end of a road before a small brick
building. Around you is a forest. A small stream flows out of
the building and down a gully.
>
```

A user at that time would recognize the ">" character as a prompt that it was his or her turn to type. After some fumbling, it became clear that you could type things like "GO SOUTH" or "ENTER." Typing the latter would result in the following:

```
You are inside a building, a well house for a large spring.
There are some keys on the ground here.
There is a shiny brass lamp nearby.
There is food here.
There is a bottle of water here.
```

It turned out that the well house stood near the entrance to "Colossal Cave," a huge underground labyrinth filled with treasures to be found and puzzles to be solved. Not only could you move around in and near the cave, you could pick up, carry, use, and drop objects like the keys, lamp, food, and bottle. And, if you dropped something at a particular location and then came back later, the object would *still be there!*

Users of *Second Life* will be unimpressed, but in 1975 this was a revelation. Perceptive observers (whether or not they had any interest in the novel idea of playing games on computers) were quick to extrapolate this relatively simple stunt to something very new. This was the computer, not as the realization of Charles Babbage's vision of "calculating by steam," but computer as

---

[7] For math geeks: Distances on the web are "topological" in nature. A true cyberspace can support "topographic" distances.

medium—a medium sufficiently expressive for the creation of what amounted to real places[8]—places where you could put what amounted to real *things*. It didn't take a lot of imagination to picture multiuser versions of the game in which people could "go" to meet and collaborate (this was not long in coming). Those familiar with the nascent Internet could extrapolate from a virtual model of a Kentucky cave to a virtual model of an office building or hospital; or of a city; or . . . of the world.

As we have seen, this represents a path not (yet) taken. We have been distracted by the low-hanging fruit of the hypertext-based World Wide Web. But it is too compelling a path to believe that we will not get back to it soon. It is as if every piece of real estate in the world somehow had an undiscovered companion lot right next to it, waiting for development. How valuable would some of those lots be?

Is Cyberspace "Real" or "Fictitious?"

You may be bothered by the claim that the "places" and "things" in *Adventure* (or more generally, cyberspace) are "real." But consider: Uncounted thousands of players have stood in front of that well house, each having essentially the same experience. Strangers can have conversations about their experiences in the virtual Colossal Cave, just as they can about those in the physical one. This is, of course, the same as asking whether places that occur only in literature are "real." Is there, for example, a Middle Earth? Tolkien (who wrote extensively on similar topics) called himself a "subcreator"—the builder of a reality embedded in the larger one provided by nature. Our use of the word *fiction* as a literary category notwithstanding, it is a little hard to call such subcreations fictitious. The word means *not real*. Middle Earth is *artificial*, but once created can we really say that it is not real? We think not. In this regard, it seems to us that what is true of literature is true of cyberspace: It is synthetic, but it is quite real.

And, then there are those keys, the lamp, the food, and the bottle. The really important difference between the hypertext and the cyberspace models lies here: Virtual places imply virtual *things*, that is to say, *digital objects*. What do we mean by this term? What counts as a *thing*? Philosophers have earned good livings attempting to answer this question ever since Plato, and anything we say on the topic will annoy somebody. So, let's keep it simple: *Things* have identities

---

[8] Significantly, Colossal Cave *is* a real place. The author of *Adventure*, a computer scientist named Will Crowther, was also a caver, and he based the game's topology on a particular cave in Mammoth Cave National Park in Kentucky. It has been claimed that cavers who knew the cave could find their way around the game, and vice versa.

that persist over space and time. If this is what we mean by *digital objects*, then it is fair to say that not a lot of the stuff out there on the Net qualifies. Is a web page a digital object? Well, a page is defined by a URL (the thing that starts with "HTTP:"). But, a URL does not actually point to the contents of a page. Rather, it points to the place in some server (or server farm) where the page can be found. This is more than a semantic distinction. It means that the content itself has no real identity. There is no precise way to point to the content without also pointing to the location. And if the content is moved (if, say, it is taken over by another custodian), its identity changes. These are not characteristics of *objects*. Anyone who has clicked on a dead link immediately wonders what that *thing* was and if she can find it somewhere else. We, and our ancestors, all grew up in a world of objects, so we try to treat web pages as digital objects; we fool ourselves into thinking they are. Until they disappear with a click.

Where We Can Be Tomorrow

Think back to those little boxes of data that we discussed earlier. Each box has a unique number on its outside. The numbers are called universally unique identifiers (UUIDs). The number identifies the container, regardless of where it is located, and regardless of whether the contents of the box change. Such containers thus meet our minimal definition of digital object. We now have everything we need to start to build a truly public information space. We say *public* because the little boxes are capable of maintaining their identity independently of where they are stored or of who owns them.

This may sound like a minor point, but it is not. Let's fantasize a little more: Suppose we assigned a UUID to everything in the world that we wanted to talk about: every place, every organization, every product, every document, every dubious claim, every abstract concept—everything (there are plenty of numbers to go around, trust us). We don't have to assign the numbers all at once, and we don't have to be completely consistent—we can fix up the problems as we go along. Nor do we need some central authority to assign these numbers. If you need a number for some entity, you would simply check something like Google to see if somebody else already gave it one, and if not, you just make one up. (It is not quite as simple as that, but pretty close.) There is no need to fight over who gets to decide—they are just numbers—one is as good as another.

152D48A50E5F411D68DFC10D4364407

Once we have these numbers, we can start to have fun. Let's say you have a nice experience at a restaurant and you want to write a review. First, you create a note on your phone, describing the experience. The phone will automatically generate a new little box with a unique identifier for the note. You publish the note wherever you like—your favorite blogging site, some Yahoo! Group, Facebook . . . whatever. In fact, you can send it to all of those places. They will all remember the UUID, so there will be no confusion. In fact, if you prefer, you could publish the note yourself, cutting out the middleman, if you are willing to run a simple server on your PC—peer-to-peer style. Next, you send a little message to a Google-like indexing service, which associates the number of your review with the unique number of the restaurant (compared to what Google can already do, this is duck soup). If you wish to identify yourself, you can also include a third UUID identifying you as the author (after all, you are certainly unique). That way your friends can find your reviews in particular.

And that, except for some not-very-hard details, is pretty much it. Of course, this is just one example. Obviously, the Google-like service will associate the UUID of the restaurant with the identity of its location (all the search engines do this kind of thing already). All the publishers will have UUIDs, too, so it will be easy to find the note, or to update it if the publisher allows it. There will be UUIDs identifying the intellectual property status of your note, so people and machines can tell whether and how they may use your review. You can give your UUID to friends, so they can search for all of your reviews, and so on and so forth.

A Pioneer in the Reputation Business

Back in 1841 a company was started to provide reliable information about the credit worthiness of businesses. It was built on a web of credit reporters who roamed the business landscape investigating companies. Abraham Lincoln and three other future U.S. presidents were respected credit reporters of this firm. The company, originally called simply the Mercantile Agency, is now worth billions of dollars and is known as Dun & Bradstreet (D&B).

Stripped to its essence, D&B's business is reputation. They are one of the world's great connectors. In this role, their prime imperative is to make sure that when they are reporting risk they don't confuse one company for another. As the economy grew, so did the scale of this challenge. By the 1960s, they had embarked upon a systematic effort to computerize their information. They invented a unique numbering scheme for companies and began assigning identifiers to each and every company that they knew to exist. When a new company came into existence, a new number was assigned.

Today those identifiers—called DUNS numbers—are used around the world to identify businesses. The United States government requires all companies that do business with it to have one. By assigning unique identities to businesses,

(Continued)

D&B was able to revolutionize the process of making decisions about an organization's riskworthiness.

A few years ago, D&B asked MAYA to explore the idea of broadening its unique identity system to include not only businesses but also locations, offices, and business leaders. The idea was to assign an identifier to represent everything reportable about a business.

As an experiment we were given 10,000 random records from the D&B database. After breaking up these records into uniquely identified information objects, we began to experiment with new modes of pattern discovery. Within the first day of playing in our new information sandbox, we discovered a way to uncover hidden cases of business fraud that, if expanded to D&B's entire database, would lead to unprecedented new forms of value for the firm's customers.

The first pattern we found involved a custom vehicle builder who was ranked as moderately safe by a number of credit firms. However, by assigning him and his facilities unique identities to go along with the DUNS numbers for his businesses we were able to discover a disturbing pattern that had previously gone unnoticed.

We created a visualization of his business relationships mapped to his credit scores and found a series of waterfall-shaped curves. He seemed to have a tendency to start a company, establish a good credit score, and when it started to drop, fire all his employees, move next door, and open up a slightly different business. While this may have been something Honest Abe would have discovered, there aren't quite enough credit reporters to go around now that we have hundreds of millions of businesses in the world. Fortunately, information architecture combined with new techniques for information visualization and pattern analysis are laying the foundation for networks of trust that scale.

What we have essentially done in this story is to turn the web inside out. Today, everything on the web is organized by publisher—if you want to read something, you need to go to a (usually single) website that contains it. In cyberspace, things can be organized by topic. Information objects make this possible by separating the identity of the object from its location (and, thus, its effective owner). The search engines try to do this with today's web, but it is a losing battle, since the hints they have to work with are obtuse and unreliable. In cyberspace, things are much easier, since the creator of a piece of information gets to decide where to put it. And by *where* we don't mean places like Yahoo! or Facebook. Rather, we mean places like "at the restaurant to which the review pertains," or "the appliance that this user manual describes." This will not put Yahoo! or Facebook out of business—quite the opposite. But it will cause their business models to evolve—no doubt in interesting ways.

As evidence that this capability has vast business potential consider the explosion in the number of location-based services of late. They allow you to do something that may appear on the surface to be similar to our story. However, they are regrettably tied to each company's own servers and systems and in many cases custom-designed database schemes. When (not if) those companies change business models, fall prey to malicious attacks, or go out of business, all your carefully curated information will disappear, and you will find that those web things you considered information objects didn't in reality pass the test for true objectness.

Taken together, device fungibility, information liquidity, and a true cyberspace suggest a new and radical path forward in the evolution of computing. Once we have liberated the world's data from their proprietary silos, they will be free to flow downward into the rapidly emerging capillary web of devices, where they can start to interact via a trillion sensors and transducers with the ground-truth of the real world. The promise of such interactions is not just about computing as such, but about the blending of the digital and physical world into one seamless whole. Cyberspace becomes much more compelling when it reflects, informs, and is informed by the real world.

The rest of this book is in essence an exploration of the prospect and problems of this process.

Yesterday, Today, Tomorrow: Platforms and User Interfaces

This first interlude deals with the intertwined history of platforms and user interfaces (UIs). It's not a matter of forcing two issues into one discussion. Standardized user interface paradigms are in fact a kind of platform—platforms used by developers to deliver standardized user experiences to end users.

The computer represents a profound discontinuity in the history of technology, and though the term *platform* is relatively new to the scene, the idea that it describes goes to the heart of that discontinuity. Computers as such don't actually do anything useful. Their utility lies in their ability to serve as a medium (read platform) for software. Much of the action in the evolution, business, and politics of computing is intimately related to the evolution of various hardware and software platforms.

YESTERDAY

For a long time, the only platforms were large boxes of hardware. In the 1950s and 1960s, if you were a business with a need for computing,[1] you bought or leased a mainframe from IBM, Burroughs, UNIVAC, or RCA, or later, a minicomputer from DEC, Data General, or Prime. Difficult as it is to imagine today, nobody to speak of had yet conceived of the possibility of making money on software. What little software came with these machines from the manufacturer had to do with low-level hardware bookkeeping and was considered a necessary evil. The manufacturers would no more consider charging for it than they would for the pallets and crates in which the machines were shipped. Beyond these most basic programs, you were on your own. If you needed a piece of software, you wrote it yourself or you swapped for it with your colleagues at the annual users group meeting of your particular hardware tribe.

In those days, each brand of computer—indeed, each particular machine—was an almost completely isolated island. There was, of course, no Internet. But nor was there any other practical way to connect even pairs of machines together. If you needed to move information (code or data) from one machine to another, your choices were (a) to retype it; (b) to carry around a stack of punched cards; or (c) if you were at a high-end shop, move it via magnetic tape. Not that any of these were very useful—there was little chance that the information from one machine would be of use on any other. There existed languages like FORTRAN and COBOL that were, in theory, cross-platform, but in practice all but the most trivial programs were tied to the idiosyncrasies of particular machine architectures. If you owned a Lionel train set, there wasn't much point in borrowing your friend's American Flyer engine.

Then, at roughly the same time, two watershed developments occurred. First, transistors evolved into integrated circuits (ICs), setting the stage for the microprocessor. In addition to reducing size and cost, this development had crucial effects on the nature of computing platforms. Before the microprocessor, each computer architecture was more or less the result of handicraft—different machines influenced one another, but each was ultimately unique. The emergence of a small number of industry-standard microprocessor families changed that. Machines built around the Intel 8086 CPU chip, for example, were all pretty much the same, no matter whether the logo on the box said IBM, Digital,

---

[1] At this stage of the game, the idea of an individual owning a computer was about as practical as an individual owning a bulldozer—and about as useful.

or Dell. It was this fact that opened the door for Bill Gates & Co. to redefine the notion of platform for a generation.

Concurrent with the birth of the microprocessor emerged the notion of the graphical user interface (GUI), with the introduction of the experimental Xerox Alto, and its commercial successor the Star office workstation. A little-noted characteristic of these platforms was that they were not organized around applications. In the Xerox Star, if you wanted to compose an e-mail message or a business letter, you did not "run" an e-mail application or a word processor app. Rather, you simply "tore off" a new document of the appropriate type from a "stationery pad" and began typing.

This "document-centric" approach to interface design represented a compelling and important simplification of the computing landscape—one that, regrettably, did not survive the GUI revolution. When Steve Jobs appropriated the GUI concept after his famous visit to Xerox PARC, the notion of document-centricity did not survive the transplant from Alto to Macintosh. The reasons for this were fundamentally economic and organizational. Seamless document-centricity requires a high level of architectural integration that is much easier to achieve by a single development team than in the context of an open, multivendor platform. The required architectural techniques were simply not widely available at the time. In addition, exposing the application as the currency of software provided a convenient unit of commerce—something for third-party developers to put in a box and sell without the necessity to directly interact with the authors of the operating system. As a result, the Macintosh and its more successful imitator Windows evolved not as platforms for *information* (even though this is what users actually care about), but as a platform for *applications*, which are at best viewed by users as a necessary evil.

The consequences of this rarely discussed choice are hard to overstate. Viewed from an information-centric perspective, each application for all practical purposes acts as a data silo: Data created by and for one application are commonly unavailable to other applications. If a document happens to be born as an e-mail message, it is doomed to that fate forever. It cannot, for example, be placed onto a calendar, or entered into a cell of a spreadsheet, or added to a list of personal contacts. It is what it is, and what it is was determined by the application used to create it. Things don't have to be this way. They weren't that way for users of the Star in the 1980s, and they will not be that way for users of the successors of the World Wide Web.

TODAY

The Internet, as originally conceptualized, represents possibly the most well conceived piece of de novo engineering design in the history of technology. Starting essentially from scratch, the designers of the Net managed to imbue it with such an ability to scale, such a bias toward liquid data flow, such a propensity toward neutrality, that it has so far withstood every insult to which the vicissitudes of the marketplace have subjected it. The subtlety of this design has been exhaustively examined, and we will not repeat it here, except to say this: Implicit in the ideal of the Internet is the existence of a free, open, distributed, seamless public information space. This ideal is directly at odds with the idea of "applications" as the fundamental building block of the "platform" for worldwide computing. This is not news—the tension has been felt for a long time. This tension has led to several attempts at reform (e.g., CORBA and Java "applets"). The only one that can claim large-scale success is the web browser. The browser is in fact a meta-application, aspiring to be the "last application." That is to say, it aspires to be The Platform of the Future. This is all well and good.

The problem is, the web browser is not a very good platform.

For starters, it is incredibly impoverished as a UI environment. One of the most important innovations of the GUI revolution was the idea of direct manipulation: that we represent data objects as almost-physical "things" in almost-real "places." Yes, the "places" are unfortunately behind an inconvenient piece of glass, but we can equip users with various prosthetic devices— mouse, trackpad, touchscreen—that empower them to reach through the glass and directly manipulate these new kinds of things in their new kinds of places. In this way, all the skills that the human species has acquired in a million years of coping with the physical world would be more or less directly applicable to the brave new world of data. It was a compelling, even thrilling, vision, and the so-called desktop metaphor of the 1980s barely scratched the surface of its potential. By the early 1990s, we were on the verge of dramatic breakthroughs in this realm.[2]

But then came the web browser. This innovation was focused exclusively on another Big Idea, that of the Hypertext Link: a magic wormhole that permitted users to "travel" instantly from one part of the Information Space to any other part with a single click of the mouse button. Here, as we have seen, was a quick-and-dirty answer to some very sticky questions about how to empower users to navigate the huge new "space" of the burgeoning Internet. The 4,800-baud modems of the early 1990s were far too slow for a proper GUI experience, but they supported the click-and-wait pattern of hypertexts quite well. Well enough, in fact, to take the wind out of the sails of direct manipulation. Progress in the realm of designing and interacting with data objects virtually ceased, its potential all but forgotten.

As always, the good became the enemy of the great. Moore's Law and the advent of ubiquitous broadband have long since removed the technical impediments to direct-manipulation Internet navigation. But the train had left the station. The browser is the End of History. For better or worse, we are stuck with it.

---

[2] Our own "Workscape" effort, done in collaboration with Digital Equipment Corporation, is but one example.

This, of course, is nonsense. We are already moving on. Even within the current paradigm, there are those who won't take no for an answer. For example, through some truly heroic engineering, Google and the developers of a technique known as Ajax have managed to reintroduce a remarkably refined set of direct-manipulation operations to Google Maps. But one can't shake the feeling that this (and the rest of the suite of techniques that are often lumped under the label of "HTML-5") is a stunt—remarkable in the same sense as Dr. Johnson's dog walking on its hind legs. Direct manipulation bends a web browser in a direction for which it was not designed, and no long-term good can come from this. We know how to do much better, and it is time to do so.

A second problem with the browser paradigm is that it is intrinsically asymmetrical. The line between suppliers of web content and its consumers could hardly be brighter. Most of us get to "browse" web pages. Only the elite (mostly large corporations) get to "serve" those pages. Yes, it is possible for sufficiently determined individuals to own and run their own web servers, but it is an uphill battle. Your Internet Service Provider quite possibly blocks outgoing web traffic through your home Internet connection; they very likely change the address of that connection at unpredictable times; and they most certainly provide a much slower connection for traffic leaving your house than for your inbound connection. It is also true that some websites let users "contribute" information for others to see, but it is *per force* under terms and conditions dictated by the owner of the website. End users can take it or leave it. If the power of the press is limited to those who own the presses, the web has not fundamentally improved the situation.

Yet, here again, things don't have to be this way, and they did not start out that way. The World Wide Web was created at a Swiss physics lab, and its ostensive original purpose was to permit scientists to more easily share drafts of scientific papers without the need for mediation by a central "publisher." The vision of everyone's computer communicating directly with everyone else's presents technical challenges, but these challenges are not obviously more difficult than the ones involved in creating immense central server farms to permit millions of users to browse the same pages at the same time. The difference is less technical than economic. Of the many ways that one could imagine making money via a mass-market Internet, hoarding data is merely the most obvious. But it has proven to be an extremely effective way, so there has—so far—been little incentive to explore farther. Thus, the client/server interests are deeply vested, and users remain emasculated.

Thirdly, information on the web is extremely *illiquid*. Data flow almost exclusively from server to client. Lateral data paths, either client-to-client or server-to-server are practically nonexistent. For all practical purposes, most data are trapped within a given server's data silo. This fact has two primary negative consequences: (1) When data flow together and intermingle, their quality and value multiply. Anyone who has ever successfully merged two ostensibly redundant databases knows that all large datasets contain many errors, and that the merged dataset is always of greatly higher quality (since each serves as a check on the other). This is just one example of the many synergies that occur when data intermingle. (2) Data illiquidity tends to prevent reuse and repurposing of existing data. On the web, the person who decides what data are available is the same person who decides how they are displayed. The architects of the web gave lip service to the separation of data from formatting, but never really delivered on this promise. The many half-hearted attempts to address this glaring deficiency—things like RSS, SOAP, and especially the so-called Semantic Web—have made some progress, but it is far too little and far too late.

Finally, and perhaps most basically, the web is *poorly engineered*— embarrassingly so. This is something of a taboo topic. The relatively few people who are entitled to an informed opinion on this subject almost all have a vested interest in the status quo. Moreover, most of them are too young ever to have experienced a genuinely well-engineered computing system of any kind. They quite literally don't know what one looks like. Well, there is the Internet itself. But the Internet is so well engineered, so simple, so properly layered, and so stable that it tends to recede from consciousness. It is like the air we breathe— rarely thought of, much less studied, but a thing of beauty, economical and elegant. In stark contrast, the web and its machinery is a huge, unprincipled mishmash of needlessly complex, poorly layered protocols, *ad hoc* mechanisms driven by the needs of shallow UI features, held together with Band-Aids pasted upon Band-Aids, and devised for the most part by volunteer amateurs.

How could this be? Judged by the bottom line, the web is miraculous. Everyone uses it, and it very obviously changed the world. If the engineering is so bad, how could we have accomplished so much? The answer is simple and can be stated in two words: "Moore's Law." As everyone knows, Intel founder Gordon Moore proclaimed in 1965 that the number of transistors on a commercially viable integrated circuit would double every two years. The fact that this is more or less a self-fulfilling prophecy does not lessen the mind-numbing implications of what has proven to be an astoundingly precise prognostication. Exponential growth can balance out many deficiencies, even those as egregious as the way we run the web. The fact is that the amount of raw computing power now at our disposal is such that almost *anything* can be made to work, after a fashion. The question, then, becomes not one of how we manage to make the web creak along, but what we are missing by squandering our wealth on the support of amateurism.

TOMORROW

We find ourselves at a peculiar juncture in the evolution of computing platforms. Some aspects of the status quo are good, and others not so good. This is, of course, always the case. What is unusual about the current juncture is that the parts that are good are extraordinarily good, while the parts that are bad are bad almost beyond belief. Moreover, the bad parts—at least so far—tend to manifest themselves as lost opportunities and retarded progress, rather than as crash-and-burn disasters. As we argue elsewhere in this book, this will soon change. In the meantime, however, the net effect is that everyone—sellers and buyers alike—are having such an overwhelmingly good time with the good parts, that it is difficult to even begin a conversation about the merits of roads not followed. As has often been observed, not even the denizens of *Star Trek* have devices with the capabilities of the iPhone. As Pangloss would say, "This is the best of all possible worlds and couldn't possibly be any better."

But history is not over, and we can already glimpse the future. As has already been noted, direct manipulation of data objects is struggling back onto the user interface scene. Spearheaded by the heroic engineers of Google Maps, even web browsers have been coaxed into supporting a quality of interaction design that threatens to approach that of the early 1990s. More ambitious efforts, most notably Google Earth, have demonstrated that life outside of the browser is still viable when the payoff to the user is sufficient. Apple's Applescript scripting language and its Quartz Composer visual programming environment, although platform-specific and limited largely to technically savvy developers, provide a glimpse of the future of software development. Enthusiasm among the digerati for the Semantic Web, although naive in the extreme, is illustrative of a widespread understanding that the future lies in the separation of data from presentation.

These trends, among others, provide a reasonably clear suggestion of the future. None of them, however, represents a viable path forward. The situation is analogous to aviation technology in the 1940s: Propeller-driven airplanes were advancing steadily toward the speed of sound. None, however, ever reached it. Achieving that goal took new thinking and new architectures. The transition to the next stable plateau of computer platform design will be marked by a similar discontinuity.

What will a "platform" look like in such a world? Attempting a detailed answer to such a question is, of course, doomed to failure. But, there is much we can say with reasonable certainty about the characteristics of the next platform.

The first and most important such characteristic is, it seems to us, an inevitable consequence of the emergence of a global public information space. As the data are liberated from their long entrapment within our machines, and assuming that we dodge the current efforts to re-entrap them within large, corporate pseudo-cloud silos, the notion of "application" will invert: Rather than being vessels for containing and manipulating specific kinds of information, apps will be *applied to* a vast sea of diverse information. That is to say, they will become tools for navigating, visualizing, accumulating, publishing, and sharing disembodied information objects (Figure I1.1). They will become *information centric*.

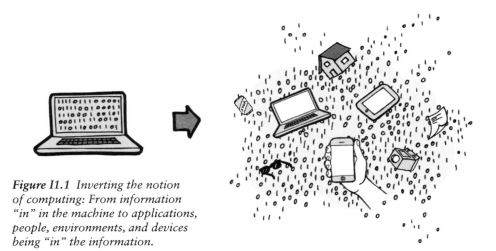

Figure I1.1 *Inverting the notion of computing: From information "in" in the machine to applications, people, environments, and devices being "in" the information.*

Articulating exactly what this means is something of a challenge. However, we can get some purchase on the topic by extrapolating from the status quo:

Let's start by pointing a web browser to a familiar web page: say, today's CNN.com homepage (Figure I1.2).

Figure I1.2 *CNN.com homepage interpreted as a collection of information objects*

This is a good choice in that it benefits from a carefully thought out internal structure—one inspired by traditional newspaper layouts. More so than in many less-well-designed websites, this structure is clear at a glance: The "currency" of this page is the "story"—made up of headlines, text, pictures and video. There are dozens of them—their headlines immediately available for human browsing, their contents available at a click. Across the top, there are numerous "tabs"—stylized buttons that allow one to change focus to other sets of stories, topically grouped. Each "story box" is carefully rendered to look like a "thing"—separate from all the other things on the page. It is almost as if users could "clip" the stories that interest them and "paste" them into a scrapbook of accumulated knowledge for later reference. Almost.

Actually, in some cases, exactly that can be done. Assuming you are using a modern browser, you can drag any photograph that may catch your fancy and drop it onto your computer's "desktop." This will immediately and invisibly copy the picture file onto your local disk drive, where it will stay until you discard it.[3]

This is rather nice. It works in part because in the web, images (for reasons lost in history) have a weak kind of identity in the form of a URL. They are well-defined, so the drag-an-image feature was an obvious one to implement. Unfortunately, this is not true of most of the other things on the page. If you try the same trick on a video clip, for example, it will look like it worked. But, the thing you will get on your desktop will not be a video, it will just be the image used as a thumbnail to represent the video. If you try to drag an entire "story" you will discover that their nice thingness is only skin-deep. They can't be dragged at all.

And then there are the little "tabs" along the top of the page. The "tab" metaphor suggests that they represent a collection of today's stories about a given topic ("sports," "politics," etc.). Dragging one of *them* would be very nice: I could, for example, save all of today's political stories in a single gesture. Does it work? Of course not. You can drag the tab all right. But you don't get a collection of stories at all. Instead, you get a URL that points to whatever collection of stories happens to be available on CNN at the moment. This is just a shortcut to a "place" on the web. It doesn't refer to a collection of specific stories at all.

This little thought experiment illustrates that the web is a long way from information centricity. But that is not the point. The point is that all of this is easily fixed. Let's imagine a slightly different CNN.com home page. It looks and works exactly like the current one, except that there is a little "locked" icon in the upper right corner of the page. Clicking on that icon "unglues" all of the "stories"—allowing them to be dragged around (much like holding your

---

[3] Actually, and somewhat ironically, the image was very likely *already* on your disk drive, stored in a mysterious and invisible place called your cache. Further, the same images have been copied to millions of other users' caches. But this is for the benefit of your browser, not for you. The pieces of the global information space are already there—they are just not doing anyone much good.

finger over the icons on an iPhone for a second permits you to rearrange them). Now you can easily redo the whole page to your needs: moving interesting articles to the top; grouping similar articles according to your taste; deleting silly sports stuff entirely.

Even better, you could create new empty pages to be used as containers for your stuff—dragging things that interest you and making new pages that you can save and share with your friends. And, of course, just as with pictures, you can drag articles, videos, and even entire tabs onto your desktop, into e-mail messages, or anywhere else that strikes your fancy. Suddenly, all of your data have ceased being mere pixels on a screen, and have turned into well-defined, concrete *things*, and things can be moved, arranged, counted, sorted, shared and subject to human creativity. The data have been liberated. They have become liquid. It is hard to overstate the significance of this seemingly small step.

It will come as no surprise that this future scenario plays out using the little boxes of data we discussed in Chapter 2. These boxes have the potential to become the currency of an entire information economy. More than an economy: an *ecology*. Remember these same containers can hold more than text and pictures: They can contain numbers. With just a tiny bit of standardization (far, far simpler than currently proposed schemes for standardizing web pages), these numbers (as well as the text and pictures) can become the fodder for apps. For, you see, the very act of making the little boxes easily manipulable by people also makes them easily manipulable by code. These apps—since they will also be stored and delivered in the same little boxes—will themselves be manipulable, sharable (not necessarily for free), and composable.

That last point—composability of apps—is worth some elaboration. The act of moving from a world in which the data are in the apps to one in which the apps are applied to the data has profound effects on the potential for interoperability across apps. When all apps are essentially operating on the same pool of data objects, it becomes far easier for the user to creatively assemble composites of independently developed apps to solve complex problems. This, in turn, will promote the emergence of simple component architectures designed to facilitate the construction of complex, purpose-built "virtual appliances" out of collections of simple, general-purpose tools. This is the essence of what it means to be a "platform." When a public information space blossoms, it will be the Mother of All Datasets. It will give rise to the Mother of All Platforms.

CHAPTER 3

The Tyranny of the Orthodoxy

At any given moment there is an orthodoxy, a body of ideas which it is assumed that all right-thinking people will accept without question. It is not exactly forbidden to say this, that or the other, but it is "not done" to say it. . . . Anyone who challenges the prevailing orthodoxy finds himself silenced with surprising effectiveness. A genuinely unfashionable opinion is almost never given a fair hearing, either in the popular press or in the highbrow periodicals.

—GEORGE ORWELL

INFORMATION INTERRUPTUS

On November 6, 2008, an AOL staffer named Kelly posted a message on the America Online (AOL) customer-relations blog called "People Connection."

Hometown Has Been Shutdown

Posted on **Nov 6th 2008 1:30PM** by Kelly ███████

Dear AOL Hometown user,

We're sorry to inform you that as of Oct. 31, 2008, AOL® Hometown was shut down permanently. We sincerely apologize for any inconvenience this may cause.

Sincerely,

The AOL Hometown Team

permalink | email this | im this | comments [28] | share |

AOL Hometown was an online tool that let AOL members build and maintain their own web sites hosted on AOL's system. Many of AOL's customers had embraced Hometown as a repository for priceless personal information. The service was once wildly popular. As early as 2001, it is reported to have hosted more than 11 million web pages.

The first official notice of the impending demise of the service appears to have been posted on September 30, 2008, along with a procedure for retrieving user data (during the 30-day period before the plug was pulled). This procedure involved the use of a low-level file transfer protocol called "FTP," which a typical AOL Hometown user had probably never heard of.[1] In any event, many of the users apparently didn't get the memo. User comments on Kelly's post expressed disbelief, grief, and finally outrage. AOL member "Rick" was brief and to the point:

> Things like this is why I left AOL, they think they own your internet expereince!

---

[1] After all, the whole point of services like Hometown was to provide web authoring abilities to users who lack knowledge of the alphabet-soup of low-level Internet machinery.

A user named "Gloria" was more typical:

What happened to my web page on my husband, Bob ——, that took me many years to put together on his career and which meant a lot to me and to the aviation community. I noticed with 9.0 I lost the left margin and the picture of him exiting the X-1. I need to restore it to the internet as it is history. Please tell me what to do. I will be glad to retype it, I just don't want it lost to the world.
I need help.
    Gloria—

AOL member "Pat" was even more distraught:

Well I am also so surprised to see all our work is gone, why didn't they notify everyone on the update through email I never even knew this was going to happen to even get a chance to save my webpage..Also is anyone getting any answers as to where or how we can get our work back..there has to be a way and something saved on there end. AOL not for nothing this was an awful decision to make and you have hurt many people who cherish there pictures, there life stories and just plain old happiness . . . It like stealing our hearts and souls without our knowledge . . . I WANT MY WEBPAGE INFO BACK I never gave you permission to destroy it.. we should all file one big lawsuit against you for this. ANY LAWYERS OUT THERE THAT CAN HELP..EMAIL US ALL for one class action..or we get a second chance to get our work back.

And then there was the unfortunate case of "Alice":

It is so sad that I have lost all my saved all pages from my daughter. That's all i had left all her memories now I have nothing at all. I lost my daughter 2 years ago, and I needed those pages. I beg you is there any way I can get them back pleaseee. It will be very much appreciated.

In all, nearly 30 user comments were posted that day and the next, and then the comments abruptly ceased.[2] One person said, "You gave us ample notice," though that may have been sarcasm. Most comments complained of receiving no notice at all.

AOL posted no response at all to the comments. As of this writing, a Google search of the string "http://hometown.aol.com" still produces more than 9 million hits. Most of these are links to content once found on Hometown. None of them work. Nor, ironically, does the so-called permalink

---

[2] A Google search will reveal many similar messages posted elsewhere on the web.

that AOL thoughtfully included in their original termination notice.[3] Instead, at least at this writing, the link (and, apparently, all other Hometown URLs) redirect to a newer AOL service called Lifestream. We're sure they will do better this time.

In the meantime, staff blogger Kelly was busy elsewhere on the system. On December 2, 2008, she filed the post, "Ficlets Will Be Shut Down Permanently," and the next day she posted, "Circavie Will Be Shut Down Permanently." It's hard to deduce what "Circavie" was; apparently it allowed one to create timelines of events and embed them on other web pages. An interesting idea, though few users took the trouble to protest its disappearance. Ficlets, however, was another story. This was a place for sharing works of very short fiction, and it clearly meant a great deal to some AOL users. In the comments attached to AOL's announcement of Ficlets' demise, "Brebellez" wrote:

> ****SOBS!!!!****
> What? This is the only place that I'm on CONSTANTLY!! Its the only 'happy place'. could you please give me one thing? tell me, why. why is this horrid, horrid thing happening!!??

And a user named Alexa said:

> I feel like I lost a family member. Or several.
> I'm completely overwhelmed by my shock.
> I just . . .
> I just really hate this.
> Kevin, thanks for creating the one thought-provoking, creative site on the Internet and the only decent thing AOL has ever brought me.
>   AOL—a pox on your house.

"Kevin" is Kevin Lawver, the actual developer of Ficlets, who posted a comment himself, which began:

> I knew this was coming, I just didn't know the day. I tried, with the help of some great people, to get AOL to donate ficlets to a non-profit, with no luck. I asked them just to give it to me outright since I invented it and built it with the help of some spectacular developers and designers. All of this has gone nowhere.

Kevin revealed that he had exported all of the contributions and has led a volunteer effort to reestablish the Ficlets community elsewhere. And he added, "I'm disappointed that AOL's turned its back on the community, although I guess I shouldn't be surprised."

---

[3] "Permalinks" are a web convention for specifying web page addresses that will never change. We are writing this with a straight face.

Forever Is a Long Time

In fairness, sudden suspensions of service are not unique to America Online. And, at least these were "free" services. The same cannot be said in the case of on-line e-book retailer Fictionwise, who, in January 2009 (shortly before being bought by Barnes & Noble), announced that its customers would lose access to certain texts they had purchased because one of the company's "digital rights management" providers had gone out of business, leaving the encrypted products orphaned. Many customers had interpreted their user agreement to mean that their Fictionwise e-books would remain on their virtual bookshelf "forever." In its FAQ, the management of Fictionwise helpfully observed: "Forever is a long time."

One month earlier, Google had shut down its scientific research service Google Research Datasets (although, in this case, at least Google had followed its common practice of labeling the service as "experimental"). In an online article on the shutdown, *Wired* magazine noted that "the service was going to offer scientists a way to store the massive amounts of data generated in an increasing number of fields," but that "the dream appears to have fallen prey to belt-tightening at Silicon Valley's most innovative company." Then, in rapid succession, the company killed Google Video, Google Catalog Search, Google Notebook, Google Mashup Editor, and Jaiku, a rival of the Twitter microblogging service, among other "side" projects. Explaining the closings, one of the search giant's product managers said, "At Google, we like to launch early, launch often, and to iterate our products. Occasionally, this means we have to re-evaluate our efforts and make difficult decisions to be sure we focus on products that make the most sense for our users."

Welcome to the future.

We do not mean to be overly harsh on the businesses cited in these stories. After all, they are only corporations trying to do what corporations are legally required to do: Maximize return for their stockholders. But, these experiments from the early days of the web are reasonably accurate harbingers of how we comport ourselves today, and their outcomes portend what we may expect in the future.

Of course "information interruptus" isn't caused solely by changes in corporate policy. There are other factors, like the small matter of bugs. Late in 2008, certain models of Microsoft's Zune music player simply stopped working thanks to a leap-year glitch in the device's internal clock driver. Did what was then the world's largest software company offer an official fix? Yes. Owners afflicted by the problem were instructed to run the battery all the way down and then wait until after the New Year to turn the device back on.

The fact is that we're babes in the woods of information. Computing complexity is already far beyond the ability of most normal people to manage, and we've scarcely gotten started. You used to be able to go into your grandparents' attic and find the photo box full of family images. Now everybody takes pictures with perishable cell phones that they don't know how to sync. When they do use a full-fledged digital camera, they store the pictures on perishable hard drives that almost nobody ever backs up.[4] Whole lifetimes of personal history vanish every day. What happens when popular "free" media-sharing sites like Flickr or Picassa or YouTube stop producing value for their owners' stockholders and get taken down?

Sterling companies like Yahoo! and Google wouldn't do that, you might say.

They most certainly would, we reply. Not just "would"—*will*.

Or how about just catastrophic accidental data loss? It can't happen to companies that big, you might believe. Really? On May 14, 2009, 14 percent of the users of "the Internet's biggest property" lost Google Search and other core services for a full hour when the company made a technical networking mistake, and it wasn't the first time.[5]

My New Plasma TV
By Pete

I recently bought a new plasma television. It was nothing fancy, a middle-of-the-line product with a well-known brand. It was beautiful and didn't cost that much. I plugged it in, and the picture was gorgeous. I was thrilled.

Two days later the screen froze. The picture, which moments before was beautifully flowing on the screen, was now a still image. I picked up the remote, pressed the channel button, and nothing happened. I pressed the power button, and nothing happened. I began to press buttons randomly. Nothing at all helped this problem. I was no longer thrilled.

Angrily I walked behind the set to the wall, unplugged the device and plugged it back in. This "hard reboot" worked.

Everything was fine for another two weeks, then the freeze-frame process repeated itself, requiring another trip to the power cord. It's become a routine drill ever since. Sound familiar?

If you're primarily a user of TV sets, my story is probably not familiar at all. If you spend a lot of your time on computers, you might consider this incident not worthy of notice. From where I sit, though, it appears very much worthy of attention, for it is a reliable tracer of a trajectory that is leading toward nothing good.

While flipping through the moderately thick owner's manual that came with the TV, I discovered on the very last page something called a "GNU Open Source License Agreement," a page of fine-print

---

[4] We will get to the state-of-the-art alternative of "cloud computing" a little later.
[5] Such incidents have become so commonplace that our originally planned litany of such examples has become superfluous.

legalese included in compliance with the terms of said license. This may or may not mean anything to you, but it means something to me. It means that the engineers building this device went out to the Internet and found pieces of "free" software (most likely having to do with the complexities of high-definition image processing) and saved what was no doubt a significant amount of money by using that software, rather than writing it themselves, or licensing some commercially available professionally produced equivalent.

Where did this software come from? Who wrote it, and how did it come to be free-for-the-taking on the Internet? The answers to these questions and their consequences are matters that we will explore in some detail. Briefly, however, this software was very likely written by a college student, motivated by a complex mix of altruism, camaraderie, political activism, and hacker macho.

A great deal of such software is available; much of it—by the standards of the computer industry–is pretty good. But the standards of the computer industry are not the same thing as the traditional standards of the consumer product industry. For a long time now, we have been used to turning on TVs and having them operate until we turn them off

again. And if there is a power flicker, we are not used to lengthy waits while we stare at messages that say "Starting up. Please wait. . . ." (Figure 3.1).

Perhaps we can come to get used to such things, if we really want to. Maybe that is just the way life is at the top of our particular mountain. But as we begin the climb up Trillions Mountain, this won't be so easy. When the world has a trillion computing devices, it would be good if they worked more like 1950s TVs than like PCs—or my fancy new plasma set.

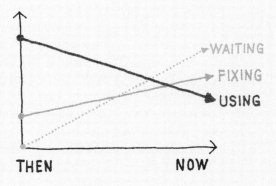

Figure 3.1 *When scenarios like Pete's TV occur, it makes you wonder how much time we spend using, waiting for, and fixing our technology. We imagine it looks something like this.*

The Dark Side of "Convergence"

The suspension of various services does not make America Online a special villain in the computing landscape. They're just another company making it up as they go along—which is, of course, the problem. Still, there's special symbolic significance when AOL drops the guillotine on its users because the company was once the poster child for a phenomenon called "convergence." AOL's merger with Time Warner in 2000 (consummated in 2001, just in time for the dot-com collapse) was trumpeted, by its champions, as the beginning of a new era of human experience in which knowledge, entertainment, and commerce would be "synergistically" fused together by digital information technology and networks. Even at the time, however, some observers were not particularly sanguine about it. Commenting on the merger before its rapid collapse, Lawrence Lessig wrote:

> Though I don't (yet) believe this view of America Online (AOL), it is the most cynical image of Time Warner's marriage to AOL: the forging of an estate of large-scale networks with power over users to an estate dedicated to almost perfect control over content. That content will not be "broadcast" to millions at the same time; it will be fed to users as users demand it, packaged in advertising precisely tailored to the user. But the service will still be essentially one-way, and the freedom to feed back, to feed creativity to others, will be just about as constrained as it is today.

This, Lessig went on to say, was the "future of the Internet" that we seemed to be choosing (or that we were having chosen for us): "Take the Net, mix it with the fanciest TV, add a simple way to buy things, and that's pretty much it." As it turned out, AOL's merger with Time Warner was a catastrophic failure. That's one face of the dark side of convergence: the inevitable vagaries of highly speculative business dealings. Even if publicly traded companies were not bound by law to put shareholder value above all else, there would still be an obvious conflict in conducting the core affairs of humanity's information-future in the volatile milieu of competing board rooms.

The increasing flakiness and frustration of computerized products are another glimpse of the dark side. Televisions didn't freeze and need to be rebooted before "convergence." Why are we going backwards? The simple answer is that we're incorporating badly designed complexity into virtually everything. Most people's experience will jibe with this statement: "Computerizing any device makes it far more complex than it was before, and the predictable side-effects of that complexity are that the device becomes harder to use and its reliability goes down." But most people have not yet experienced, or imagined, a world crippled by the uncountable interactions among trillions of improperly complex and thus unreliable devices.

The Complexity Cliff

There is strong temptation to assume that minor annoyances like a frozen plasma TV represent the last few bugs that need to be squashed before we perfect the wonderful new technologies that will make life in the twenty-first century a thing of beauty and a joy forever. The thesis of this book is *precisely the opposite*. These examples of information interruptus are merely the first dim glimpses of looming disaster.

Put bluntly, we are heading, as a civilization, toward a cliff. The cliff has a name, but it is rarely spoken.

Its name is *complexity*.

Computing is making our lives vastly better along certain dimensions but noticeably worse along others. We're like the frog in the pot of water on the stove with the temperature going up one degree at a time. By the time the frog feels enough discomfort to think about jumping out, the frog is scalded. In five years, people won't think any harder about rebooting their phones and TVs—even their household heating plants–than they think today about rebooting their PCs. Only 20 years ago, rebooting a TV or a phone or a furnace was unthinkable. Today, our time and attention are drained daily by products that force consumers to understand technical things they shouldn't have to think about. And it's about to get much worse. We tell ourselves that this goes hand in hand with progress. It doesn't, but manufacturers with quarterly profit targets need us to accept that story. The human beings are babysitting the machines, playing handmaiden to tools that aren't good enough to get along in the world on their own.

Today, the price of underestimated and ill-managed complexity is usually only inconvenience or annoyance—mild words that don't capture the frustration and lost productivity of a really bad day in the digital revolution. To make the same point in another way: There is an unspoken reasoning behind deciding how "good" to make usability; that it depends on the "cost" of failure or an error. Something like annoyance is near one end of the cost spectrum and death is at the other end. So, historically, the first human factors studies were done for military aircraft cockpits. But is there a point where countless annoyances become equivalent to one death?

The time is not far off when the price of undesigned, ill-managed complexity will be much, much higher than inconvenience or annoyance. It's not the worst thing in the world that a brand-new plasma TV locks up and won't respond to its controls. We could live with it, though we shouldn't have to. But how about the same scenario in a city's traffic control system? How about waiting ten minutes for an ambulance to reboot? With current ways of thinking about computing technologies, we could easily "brick" all the lights in a next-generation skyscraper that uses wireless systems to control illumination. Or the elevators. Or the ventilation. It is quite within the realm of possibility that such a technical glitch could render a modern smart building—or an entire campus of such buildings—uninhabitable for months.[6]

If we're going to embrace, in blind faith, the limitless extension of our current technologies, then we have to consider the possibility (among many others) of people dying in skyscrapers because some pervasive, emergent, undesigned property of a building's systems—or an entire city's systems—starts

---

[6] If this seems overblown, try the following math exercise: How many light switches and fluorescent fixtures are there in an 80-story skyscraper? How long would it take if each of them had to be manually removed and reinstalled?

a chaotic cascade of failures. To some readers these dire hypotheticals will ring of Chicken Little. But they're quite reasonable extrapolations of what we know today—if only we'll admit that we know it.

And all this before we've even mentioned malice. Every day brings another story of computer systems and infrastructure under attack. The vulnerability that makes these attacks so easy is largely due to our thoughtless use of unnecessary and badly designed complexity, usually for no better reason than that it's cheap or "free." But complexity is never free. In fact, it's quite expensive indeed. Among many other liabilities, it gives attackers plenty of vectors in, and plenty of places to hide and operate once they are in.

We are about to meld superminiaturized computing and communication devices into the very fabric of the physical world, ushering in the age of Trillions. This will create a planetary ocean of awareness and intelligence with the potential to transform civilization. We're not going to "decide" whether or not to do this. The process, as we have seen, is already well underway. Obviously, it will make us vastly more dependent upon digital technology than we are right now. More importantly, the technology itself will be vastly more dependent upon the core design principles and engineering intelligence of its creators.

We're heading into a world of malignant complexity, the kind that grows like cancer from flawed architectural principles—or from none at all. But we can still choose not to go there. Complexity itself is inevitable. Dysfunctional complexity isn't.

THE KING AND THE MATHEMATICIAN

This steady creep of increasing complexity has been quietly feeding on itself, and soon it will hit its exponential inflection point and lift off like a rocket. If we wait until then to change our relationship to information technology, we'll be engulfed by the explosion of our own creations and their interactions with each other.

Now, we do understand that this will sound completely ridiculous to many readers. There you are, wirelessly trading securities on your laptop, searching the web for any information your heart desires, meeting up with everybody you've ever known on social networks, streaming feature films on your mobile phone. And we're saying that information technology is seriously broken, that we're headed for technology dystopia if we don't rethink it. Yes, on its face that sounds absurd. Exponential growth is counterintuitive, and counterintuitive things often seem nonsensical until, like boomerangs, they come circling back around to hit you in the head.

The salient feature of exponential curves is that for quite a while they look just like ordinary, tame, linear ramps, and then suddenly they bend upwards and go almost vertical. In the early phases of such growth, it's basically impossible for people to believe that the pleasant warmth they're feeling will suddenly burst into a firestorm and incinerate them.

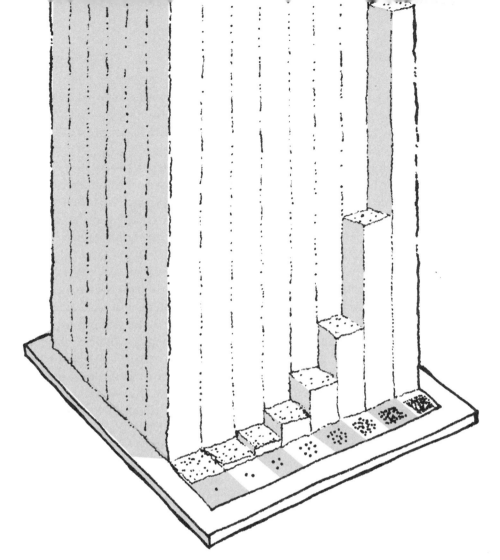

Figure 3.2 *Grains of rice on the King's chessboard*

To illustrate this phenomenon, one of your math teachers may have told you the story of the king, the mathematician and the chessboard. A king offers his court mathematician a reward for something good that he's done. The mathematician can have anything he wants, but he asks only that one grain of rice be placed on the first square of a chessboard, two grains of rice on the next square, four grains on the next, and so on—simply that the grains of rice be doubled for each successive square (Figure 3.2). The King bursts out laughing. He thinks the mathematician is a fool but for his own amusement he orders that the request be fulfilled.

About halfway through the chessboard, the King isn't so amused anymore. All the rice in the palace is gone, and the King has had to send out for more. A few more squares later, the King realizes that there aren't enough grains of rice in his entire kingdom to fulfill the mathematician's simple request. "Actually, Sire," the mathematician informs him, "there aren't enough grains of rice in the universe." Depending upon which version of the story you hear, the mathematician then marries the King's beautiful daughter or gets his head chopped off.

On the great chessboard of information and computing, we haven't reached the halfway mark yet, and so it seems laughable that our presently dependable systems could suffocate on their own proliferation.

Every time we hang a fancy digital TV, or stop our work to reboot a crawling laptop, or waste half a day trying to get a wireless network running, or lose the precious contents of a computer hard drive, we are experiencing the leading edge of an imminent, full-scale collision of unimaginably complex systems with ordinary people who don't have—and never will have, and shouldn't need to have—the ability to cope with complexity of that sort.

When our world literally doesn't work for people anymore, we'll be ready to make changes. Unfortunately, that's going to be tough. We'll be stuck because the number of embedded, networked microprocessors controlling and sensing the physical world and all its processes will have multiplied like the grains of rice on the mathematician's chessboard. But these grains of computing will be connected to each other, interacting and producing incalculable *network effects*. It will be the most complex system ever created by human beings—by a long shot—and when bad architecture rears its head in a structure like that, the potential for catastrophe is something we don't even know how to talk about.

If complexity is our destiny, and ill-designed complexity is the death of us, what does well-designed complexity look like? It should look a lot like life. A trillion-node network is still unimaginable to most designers, but we have trillions of cells in each of our bodies. The rules that govern biological development—the genetic code—are simple, yet they give rise to fantastic (and highly functional) complexity and diversity. In life, limitless complexity is layered upon carefully constrained simplicity. John Horton Conway's *Game of Life* is built on the idea of establishing a simple set of rules, yet those rules create far-reaching consequences. Explore the *Game of Life* online at http://trillions.maya.com/Game_of_Life.

Unbelievable as it may sound, the very need for such a principled, designed architecture for civilization's information systems has not yet occurred to the thought leaders of high-technology. They're too busy remaining "competitive" as they go about their local hill climbing. But the systems themselves are growing exponentially, even in the absence of good architecture, and by the time we admit that the foundations are bad, we'll be living in a technological dystopia more bewildering and jerry-rigged than a Rube Goldberg cartoon or Terry Gilliam's film *Brazil* with its ubiquitous wacky computers and metastatic ventilation ducts.

The message of this book is not that we're helplessly doomed, and it's certainly not that technology per se is bad. The message is that we are indeed headed for a complexity cliff, but there's a better path into the future, and we're still free to take it. To get to rational complexity in information systems, certain fundamental things about the technology need to be redesigned. We'll discuss those things in detail later in this book. But the real challenge is not the technology itself. After all, the chessboard obeys understandable rules.

The real challenge is the laughing King.

LINKS TO NOWHERE

If you examine the bibliography of any scholarly book published in the last few years, the odds are very high that, in addition to citations pointing to traditional paper documents (which routinely stay live for hundreds or thousands of years), it will also contain references in the form of web URLs. This, of course, is symptomatic of the obvious fact that the World Wide Web has very rapidly become nearly the sole source of important public information for global society. It is interesting to consider the following simple question: Fifty years from now, what percentage of these web references will still be operational?

We will be very surprised if the answer turns out to be greater than zero.

The reason is simple: URLs are fundamentally different from traditional references on ontological grounds. Traditional citations refer to published information *as such*. That is, if you cite, say, *Moby-Dick*, everyone understands that you're not referencing a particular instance of that book. Any of the millions upon millions of more or less identical replicas of Melville's words will (for most purposes) do equally well. A URL, on the other hand, points not to a web page that has been massively replicated like a published book but rather to a specific place in the structure of a specific server (or at best, in any of a relatively small number of redundant servers under common management) where that web page might (at the moment) be found. Such a pointer will remain relevant only as long as the owner of that "place" possesses the resources and the will to maintain the pointer. And we all know that this will not be forever. Sooner or later, all links on the World Wide Web will go dead.[7]

Heads in the Sand
By Mickey

When I started making the point about the ephemeral nature of web pages during speaking engagements, I was surprised to receive a fair amount of push-back from certain—mostly technical—audiences. The comments generally go something like this: "Well, we'll just make lots of copies of the things that are really important; Google and Amazon have lots of servers with copies of things."

I like this. It sounds believable. I wish it were true because it would give

(Continued)

---

[7] Many of the web references included in first drafts of this book have already gone dead and have had to be replaced. No doubt, others will have done so by the time you are reading this. Our apologies.

me comfort. Unfortunately, such thinking misses the point along a number
of dimensions. First of all, how can we
know today what will be important tomorrow, and who gets to decide? Do we
want our grandchildren to know us by our
adorable cat videos and our painstaking
documentation of celebrity scandals?

Secondly, Amazon and Google may
have plenty of copies of all of the data
in their care, but there are no copies
of Amazon and Google. No, their competitors don't count, since in the current
market, competitors generally don't store
the same data, and users generally don't
sign up for redundant services. There are
many potential vulnerabilities—technical,

economic, and criminal—that could
threaten all of the replicas that are stored
in a single system, no matter how much
redundancy that system has.

Finally, and most importantly, the
status quo places the ultimate decision
of how long any given information object
is worth saving in the hands of a single,
typically corporate, entity. Maybe I'm
missing something, but I can't think of
any scenario in which their decision will
be "we will store it forever." Even if that
were their decision, and even if they were
an entity intending to "do no evil," forever
is still a long time. In the scope of things,
their attention span and their will to hold
to that decision is as fleeting as a mayfly.

And yet, web URLs with a half-life of only a few years have become the
primary way that knowledge workers around the world document their thinking and their research.

Have we completely lost our minds?

This is no way to run a civilization. We are not the first to make this observation, and there have been sporadic efforts toward data preservation. The
solution to the problem, however, does not lie in acid-free paper, the archiving
of floppy drives, or any of the many other schemes focused on preservation
of media. Paper books have proven to be a wonderfully robust and reliable
medium, but not fundamentally because of their physical longevity, admirable
though it may be. The reliability stems from the fact that they are deployed
as part of a bibliographic system that relies on distributed ownership and
massive replication. Paper books are liquid, in the sense that they can flow
freely from publisher to printer to bookseller to first purchaser (individual or
library) to resale shop to giveaway shelf. In the process, the contents of the
books are scattered to the far corners of the earth such that destroying the last
copy—whether by natural disaster or by censorship—is in most cases nearly
inconceivable. And most importantly, any single copy suffices to "resolve the
link" found in a citation. None of these things is true of web information, or
for that matter, any of the other information found in the many petabytes of
data "safely" stored away in the world's databases. We need an entirely new
information architecture that is designed from the bottom up to support the
key qualities that our paper-book system gave us: namely, information liquidity
and massive replication.

THE WRONG CLOUD

The interesting thing about cloud computing is that we've redefined cloud computing to include everything that we already do. I can't think of anything that isn't cloud computing with all of these announcements. The computer industry is the only industry that is more fashion-driven than women's fashion. Maybe I'm an idiot, but I have no idea what anyone is talking about. What is it? It's complete gibberish. It's insane. When is this idiocy going to stop?

—**Larry Ellison, CEO, Oracle**

Something Vague and Indistinct, Up in the Sky

A few years ago, computing marketers started touting the great benefits of something they were calling "the cloud." The industry must have needed a shot in the arm because pretty soon you were nobody unless you had a big reference to the cloud on the home page of your website. Even Apple, Inc.—not often a follower of industry fashion—got into the act. Apple's wildly successfully iPhone can keep some of its data in sync with computers if the devices share information in the Apple cloud. These days, phones and computers can do this wirelessly from arbitrary locations, which contributes to the vapory imagery.

The web retailer Amazon.com had the cloud even before Apple did. Amazon's cloud dispenses not books and music but data storage-space and computation cycles, both by the pound, so to speak. You can buy as much or as little of each as you want at any given moment, enabling you to build expanding and contracting virtual computers.

Facebook and Microsoft have clouds of their own, of course. So does Salesforce.com and Google and Yahoo! and, one assumes, any other company worth talking about. Naturally, these clouds are all of proprietary design and built to compete with each other, not cooperate with each other. No corporate cloud possesses the inherent ability to interoperate with other clouds. And yet they're all called "the cloud." Strange. If their purveyors feel like allowing it, the clouds can sometimes conduct feeble interactions by means of cobbled-together "web services" and APIs that you can spend a lot of time researching and learning if you enjoy that kind of thing. Don't memorize them, however; they will change.

Customers who know what's good for them just choose one incarnation of "the cloud" from one vendor and stick with it.

It's beginning to sound familiar, isn't it? It turns out that all these clouds are what we used to call servers, and those smaller entities hurling their astral bodies up into the cloud were once known as clients. Yes, cloud computing is the same old client-server computing we've known for years, except pretending to be intoxicatingly new and different and liberating.

There are both technical and commercial reasons that the web has evolved this way. We will explore the technical reasons later. The commercial ones reduce to a deeply held belief on the part of content providers of all kinds that the simplest way to make money from information is to keep it tightly locked away, to be dispensed one piece at a time. This belief is correct, as far as it goes. It *is* the simplest way to monetize information resources. The problem, as we shall argue, is that this simplistic strategy is fundamentally incompatible with the world of Trillions. If the world is going to become one huge, vastly distributed information system, don't we need one huge, vastly distributed database to go with it? It would be a lost business opportunity of monumental proportions if we were to use these incredible new computational capabilities in a way that perpetuates patterns of information access that evolved in a time when computers were large, expensive, centrally controlled, and few.

Today's so-called cloud isn't really a cloud at all. It's a bunch of corporate dirigibles painted to look like clouds. You can tell they're fake because they all have logos on them. The real cloud wouldn't have a logo.

Once There Was a Real Cloud

A very long time ago, back in the 1990s, whenever somebody wanted to represent the Internet in a diagram for a brochure or a slide show, they would put in a little cartoon of a cloud. Countless presentations to venture capitalists featured little pictures of desktop computers, modems, and hard drives, all connected by wiggly lines to the cloud cartoon. In fact, for a few years there, the entire global economy pretty much consisted of nothing but images just like that. When people needed money, they would just draw a diagram where everything was connected to a cloud, and take it to the bank. Those old pictures seem quaint and naive by today's standards, but the truth is that the cloud in the 1990s dot-com business-model diagrams was vastly better than the cloud we have today.

One of the main virtues of the old cloud was its singularity. It was a single cloud—the Internet—not many as we find today on the web.

When it appeared in a diagram, it instantly conveyed an extremely important idea: If you went into this cloud, you were automatically connected to everything else that was in the cloud. This idea has been completely lost today, but back then it was considered a beautiful thing.

This point is so important that it is worth repeating in a different way: The very heart of the miracle that is the Internet is that it is able to establish virtual connections between literally any two computers in the world such that they can communicate directly with each other. This is a truly amazing ability, and our current usage patterns of the Net have barely scratched the surface of its potential.

The other main virtue of the old cloud was that nobody owned it. It wasn't the Microsoft Cloud or the Apple Cloud or the Google Cloud or the Amazon Cloud. It was just the Internet. The one and only Cloud of Information, property of Humanity.

Those were the days. It's getting hard to remember them now, it being almost 20 years ago and all. But let's think back, as our vision gets all wavy and blurry. . . .

THE DREAM OF ONE BIG COMPUTER

It was the heyday of a programming language called Java, when people were excited about things like "thin client" and "applets" and "zero-footprint." The Net was going to be One Big Computer. PCs would be supplanted by "network appliances" that would have no local "state" at all. There would be nothing to configure because these machines wouldn't have anything "in" them. Instead they would be "in" the information—in the cloud. You could walk up to any appliance and log on, and via the magic of the cloud, there would be your stuff.

The machines wouldn't have anything "in" them because they wouldn't have any storage of their own. There was an important reason for this particular detail. High-capacity hard drives were expensive and not very reliable back then. The advantages of a thin client were several, including convenience and ease of maintenance, but the key advantage was cost savings. Computers with no disks would be significantly cheaper, and thus you could have a lot more of them.

But then, all of a sudden, disks got absurdly large and cheap. Almost overnight, the world was awash in disk space. The thin client idea started to seem silly. Why should we rearrange the world in such a fundamental way just to save the now-trivial cost of local storage? Plus, along with CPUs boasting meaninglessly faster clock-speeds, "bigger disks" were one of the few motivators we had to get people to trade up their PCs every couple of years.

So there went the idea of network appliances.

Hard drives kept getting bigger and cheaper, but once everybody had ripped their CD collections it got harder for people to understand why they would want even higher-capacity disks. The only obvious answers were (a) to store really big files, like digital video; and (b) to move to a peer-to-peer world where every machine could be a client and a server at the same time, and participate in a global scheme of data integrity via massive, cooperative replication. Both of those activities made a great deal of sense, culturally and technically.

Unfortunately, both were also political landmines.

THE GRAND REPOSITORY IN THE SKY

Nonetheless, it was around this time that advocates of peer-to-peer (P2P), including our team here at MAYA Design, began to talk seriously about extending the Internet "cloud" metaphor to storage. We meant a genuine "cloud of information" that you and your devices could be "in" no matter where you were. In MAYA's technical literature we half-facetiously called it GRIS—the Grand Repository In the Sky. But we thought of it not as a mere metaphor, but as something that could actually be built, or at least approximated—a vast, disembodied information space built out of P2P and massive data-replication. With the essential support of visionary clients, we started making plans to build it. The system intended to implement GRIS is called the Via Repository and is part of a larger project called Visage. Another project dating from this period sharing a similar vision (although a very different technical approach) is the OceanStore project from UC Berkeley.

This vision has many of the virtues of the thin client idea, with the additional virtue of being able to take advantage of all that ever-cheaper disk space. In this model, devices have local storage all right, and plenty of it. Arbitrarily large amounts of storage will enable more and more data replication, which means that GRIS will just keep getting better and better as its many nodes add terabytes. However, unlike the thin client idea, which is still a species of client-server computing, the GRIS model is based on radically distributed computing in which all network nodes—peers—are both clients and servers that transact with each other directly.

Like most successful complex systems, it works in a way that compares well to nature. Information rises from devices the way water vapor does and forms local clouds. Those clouds can easily fuse together to form bigger clouds with even more potential for sustaining precipitation. The digital equivalent of the Gulf Stream moves the cloud-stuff around the world. The many peers on the ground can store enough data-precipitation to survive local droughts if cloud-connection is ever interrupted, as it surely will be from time to time. And every component is a part of a sustainable ecosystem. The real cloud has the deep virtue of being able to bootstrap from zero infrastructure while remaining scalable without bound.

Exactly which information ends up being stored on which disk drive is controlled by no one—not even the owner of the disk drive. You don't get to decide which radio waves travel through your house on the way to your neighbor's set—your airspace is a public resource. In this vision, the extra space on your disk drive becomes the same kind of thing. This might be controversial if all that extra disk space wasn't essentially free—but it is, and is all but guaranteed to become more so as Moore's law ticks away.

The real cloud is made of information itself, and computing devices are *transducers* that make information visible and useful in various ways.

FUD AND THE BIRTH OF THE IMPOSTOR CLOUD

The computing industry loves to toss around the term *paradigm shift*, but (naturally and understandably) its established interests aren't so excited when the real thing comes along. And the vision of a truly pervasive information cloud was the real thing. So, even though such "network computing" clearly represented increasingly irresistible advantages in terms of usability, convenience, and lowered costs, the industry countered with classic FUD (Fear, Uncertainty, and Doubt) about this scary, decentralized phenomenon called peer-to-peer (P2P) that could only result in the wholesale theft of intellectual property and The End of Life As We Know It.

And the client-server paradigm survived yet again.

Finally, someone in the industry had a Big Idea: All those cheap disks didn't have to go into laptops. They could be used to build huge disk farms that would let companies offer a new service called *network storage* that promised the marketing equivalent of magic: It would tether users to a proprietary service, just like always, yet it would convey a vaguely "distributed" feeling that suggested openness and freedom. It worked, and soon ever-cheaper CPUs were similarly lashed together to offer remote computation as well as remote storage. The marketing fairy godmother waved her wand over the whole "new model" and pronounced it Cloud Computing.

The Rise of the Computing Hindenburgs

Earlier in this chapter, we quoted an exasperated Larry Ellison as he declared cloud computing to be nothing but empty hype. What we didn't quote was Mr. Ellison's next remark. After dismissing the phenomenon as ludicrous, and damning the entire industry for its triviality, Oracle's CEO went on to say, "We'll make cloud computing announcements. I'm not going to fight this thing."

We'll let you draw your own conclusions from that. Meanwhile, as we watch Oracle enthusiastically enter the fray, we're reminded of something else about all these corporate cloud-balloons: their remarkable fragility. The sight of them bobbing around up there brings to mind the massive stateliness of the *Hindenburg*. Like the infamous exploding zeppelin, today's cloud computing looks substantial but it's really a very delicate envelope of ether. All is not heavenly in the heavens. The client-server cloud uses architecture that is vulnerable to assault, and yet, as Mr. Ellison's remarks about fashion suggest, the greatest threats may come from within. Corporate takeovers and plain old changes in business strategy bring down "web services" every day, even from the biggest names in the business. Chances are, you know about it all too well already.

Let us be clear about this: Perhaps you are enough of an optimist to be willing to assume that all of the headlines about technical, economic, and criminal vulnerabilities of these new centralized services represent temporary growing pains and that the industry will mature to the point at which these become acceptable risks. Fine. But the bottom line is that as long as you choose to trust all of your data to a single commercial entity, those data will remain available to you no longer than the lifetime of that entity and its successors. Is that good enough for you? Well, before you decide, consider the following quote from *Bloomberg Businessweek*:

> The average life expectancy of a multinational corporation—Fortune 500 or its equivalent—is between 40 and 50 years. This figure is based on most surveys of corporate births and deaths. A full one-third of the companies listed in the 1970 Fortune 500, for instance, had vanished by 1983—acquired, merged, or broken to pieces. Human beings have learned to survive, on average, for 75 years or more, but there are very few companies that are that old and flourishing.

Yes, most companies have successors, and often they try to do the Right Thing. But when the Right Thing ceases to make economic sense, their ability to continue to do it becomes extremely limited. This is no way to run a world.

The radically distributed networking of a P2P cloud is a whole different vision altogether. P2P at the hardware level—in some forms known as *mesh networking*—is self-adjusting and self-healing. Its lack of central control may make it seem ethereal (it's really a cloud, remember), but that's what makes it so resilient. Every time a node appears or disappears, the network automatically reconfigures, and, of course, if properly designed, it scales forever. And like the Internet itself, nobody owns it. Not only can the real cloud withstand attackers, it can't be shot down by its own proprietors either.

Today's "cloud computing" claims to be the next big thing, but in fact it's the end of the line (or rather "a" line). Those corporate dirigibles painted to look like clouds are tied to a mooring mast at the very top of PC Peak, which we conquered long ago. There's nowhere left to go within that paradigm. The true P2P information cloud hovers over Trillions Mountain—the profoundly different and vastly higher mountain of the real information revolution.

Having said all of this, though, it is important not to succumb to guilt by association. Not everything going under the rubric of "cloud computing" is ill conceived. Amid all the hype can be found some genuine and important innovations. Of particular note is the emergence of a cluster of service-oriented business models, with names like Software as a Service (SaaS), Platform as a Service (PaaS), and Infrastructure as a Service (IaaS). These models amount to a kind of outsourcing in which generic but difficult-to-manage aspects of IT infrastructure are purchased as needed, rather than being provided in-house. This approach is particularly effective at lowering barriers to entry for new players. If you're just starting a business and are trying to focus on what you really do well, pay-per-service can be a prudent and cost-effective way to manage your affairs. Further, it levels the playing field, democratizing the tools of business and allowing new entrants to keep up with their more mature competitors. The current crop of social media startups could not have become so successful so fast without this sort of business innovation.

We do not at all disparage these developments. It is just that absent the principle of data liquidity, the platforms upon which the innovations are being delivered constrain the evolution of the marketplace in dangerous ways. It is quite possible to embrace these important new business models using technical approaches that also make long-term sense.

THE CHILDREN'S CRUSADE

Basically, a lot of the problems that computing has had in the last 25 years comes [*sic*] from systems where the designers were trying to fix some short-term thing and didn't think about whether the idea would scale if it were adopted. . . . It was a different culture in the '60s and '70s; the ARPA (Advanced Research Projects Agency) and PARC culture was basically a mathematical/scientific kind of culture and was interested in scaling, and of course, the Internet was an exercise in scaling. . . . Once you have something that grows faster than education grows, you're always going to get a pop culture.

—Alan Kay

The Demise of Software Engineering

A plumber will never install a faucet that dips below the highest possible water level in a sink basin. Why? Because if the faucet were to become submerged, it could conceivably siphon contaminated basin water back up into the fresh water supply.

An electrician will never install a circuit breaker panel in a space unless the opposite wall is at least 36 inches away from the front of the panel. Why? So that if some future electrician were to ever inadvertently contact a live circuit while working in the panel, she would have enough room to be thrown back out of harm's way, and thus avoid electrocution.

A building contractor will never build an emergency exit door that opens inward toward the interior of a building. Why? Because in an emergency, a panicking crowd might surge forward toward the exit with enough force as to make it impossible to open an inward-swinging door.

A computer programmer, faced with a mission-critical design decision—such as a mechanism for providing network access to the control systems of a municipal waterworks—will do, well, whatever pops into his head.

So, what's the difference? The difference, in a word, is *professionalism*.[8] And we don't mean the professionalism of the computer programmer. Plumbers, electricians, and builders are all members of mature communities of practice. These communities are participants in a complex ecology that also includes architects and other designers, standards organizations, insurance companies, lawmakers, enforcement bureaucracies, and the general public. One of the essential roles of communities of practice of all kinds is to serve as reservoirs of the accumulated wisdom of their communities. This is accomplished in many ways, but in the case of the building trades, the process is centered on a set of wholly remarkable documents known collectively as building codes. Maintained by various trade and standards organizations, these manuals essentially comprise a long litany of "thou shalts . . ." and "thou shalt nots . . ." They don't tell us what to build, and they don't place significant constraints on the process of building. What they do say is "if you are going to do thus, *this* is how you shall do it." They do so with remarkable clarity and specificity, while also recognizing the realities of the job site. For example, the electrical code is very specific about what color wires are to be used for what purposes. But, they also allow substitutions, provided that the ends of the nonconformant wires are wrapped with the correct color of electrical tape. These documents are masterful examples of practical wisdom.

Building codes do not themselves have force of law (although they are often included by reference in municipal building laws and regulations).

---

[8] *Professionalism* is not actually quite the right word. Plumbing is a trade, not a profession. But, interestingly, the analogous word does not seem to appear in English. *Tradecraft* comes to mind, but that term has come to be closely tied to the espionage trade.

However, apprentice tradespeople are trained from the beginning to treat them with sacramental reverence. They are not matters of opinion, and tradespeople don't argue about whether or not a given rule is "stupid." You don't question them; you don't even think about them; you just do them. This training is reinforced by tying the process of obtaining an occupancy permit to a series of inspections by government bureaucrats. If you go to the electrical panel in your basement, you will find a series of initialed and dated inspection stickers that were placed there by a county or city building inspector at certain well-defined stages of the construction process. Although (as in all large-scale human activity) there is a certain amount of give-and-take in this process, and the exchange of cash is not unheard of, for the most part the system works remarkably well.

We doubt that very many computer professionals have ever even seen a building code. The thought processes that these codes reflect are alien to their way of doing business. Computers have long since become an essential part of our built world, and that part most certainly has health and safety implications. So, why isn't there a National Computer Code? Perhaps it is just a result of the immaturity of the industry—after all, we are at the early stages of computerization. Well, maybe. But, here's a data point: The first National Electric Code was completed in the year 1897, 15 years after the opening of the first commercial power plant—Edison's Pearl Street Station in Manhattan.

And yet, as we enter the second half-century of the Information Age, one would be hard-pressed to point to *any* widely honored standards of practice governing the deployment (as opposed to the manufacture) of computerized devices. No inspectors come around with clipboards to verify that a piece of software is "up to code," even though a great deal of programming is as directly relevant to public health and safety as are the creations of civil engineers.

It is not that nobody thinks about such things. Our own Carnegie Mellon University hosts a Department of Defense (DOD)-funded center called the Software Engineering Institute, which routinely develops and promotes standards and practices of a very high quality. More generally, researchers from areas ranging from academic computer science to industrial engineering do excellent work in this area. And, of course, there are a great many well-trained and highly skilled software engineers in the industry. What is lacking is any kind of organized professionalism out in the field.

Why? For starters, this is an area of activity to which there are almost no barriers to entry. Anybody can play, and so anybody does, and the field is full of amateurs with no engineering training or experience. Yes, you might have some trouble getting a full-time job as a coder in a major corporation without some kind of a college degree—preferably one involving some programming courses. But a large and increasing amount of the code that finds itself in computerized products (remember Pete's Plasma TV) comes from the so-called open source community. Their standards for entry are somewhat lower.

The open source movement romanticizes this democratization of computer code in much the way that the culture at large romanticizes the lack of training or proficiency among musicians in punk rock bands. "Anybody can play." The difference is that punk rock is a folk art, and software development is—or should be—an engineering discipline. Its purpose is the creation of machines made of code that run on networked processors. The future of humanity is quickly coming to depend upon the reliability and interoperability of such networked code-machines.

In this Internet era, the creation of software is now one of the most far-reaching and consequential of all human activities, yet it's not a profession or even a trade. It's much closer to a free-for-all. Personal computing pioneer Alan Kay says flatly that we no longer have real computer science or real software engineering. "Most software today," Kay commented in 2004, "is very much like an Egyptian pyramid with millions of bricks piled on top of each other, with no structural integrity, but just done by brute force and thousands of slaves."

It wasn't always this way. There was a time when computer science was taken seriously by work-a-day developers, and software development was as rigorous as any other branch of engineering. Thirty years ago, the world ran on minicomputers that booted in seconds, not minutes, and ran flawlessly from power failure to power failure with no memory leaks or performance degradation. It is true that they didn't have fancy graphics and they couldn't stream CNN, but for most routine textual and numerical work they were every bit as good (and from the user's perspective, as fast) as what we have today. Every academic science and engineering lab depended upon them, and if you had to reboot one of those machines due to an operating-system bug, you'd consider it a professional disgrace, and you wouldn't stand for it. Today, the phenomenon of a laptop slowing to a crawl if it has been up too long doesn't even bear comment.[9]

As computing moves forward on certain fronts, its ill-managed complexity is causing it to regress on others. In the "professions" of computer science and software engineering, almost all the rules have somehow devolved into matters of opinion. As the screenwriter William Goldman famously said about Hollywood, "Nobody knows anything." Practitioners have wars about the most basic assumptions of the field. If you log onto a discussion forum and make the least controversial statement possible about any aspect of computing, some practicing "professional" from somewhere will surface to tell you that you're stupid. You might be instructed in the wisdom of "creative waste," and you will probably be reminded that cycles are cheap but programmers are expensive and that you don't understand the future and that you had best get over it.

The Internet itself was designed so that it would scale gracefully—that is, grow arbitrarily without deforming or breaking its architecture. It could do that because its architecture was rigorously modular and because its designers

---

[9] We are well aware of the argument that these machines were orders of magnitude simpler than today's PC, but is that a *bad* thing? We will argue that much of the additional complexity is gratuitous, and that it is quite possible to deal with the complexity we do need in ways that do not doom us to perpetual flakiness.

did the math before they wrote the code. But the Internet era has now passed into the hands of a pop culture that is neither formally trained nor intellectually rigorous, and doesn't particularly care whether its "solutions" have a rigorous engineering basis—as long as they accomplish the task at hand. Programmers have been pampered by Moore's law for their entire working lives, and have every reason to believe that this will continue. As the herd stampedes from one social networking site to the next, for example, it's abundantly clear that fashion and other superficial, self-regarding considerations are the real drivers of technology adoption in this era.

Many authors have discussed the sensations of power and control that coding can confer upon anyone with an inexpensive PC and the patience to master the syntax of a programming language. Programmers are the gods of the microworlds they create, and this status, along with the puzzle-solving appeal of the work itself, has produced a global culture of devotees who hunger for influence and approval, and who know just enough to create code that others find useful.

Software Pop Culture and Bad Abstraction

Software designer/programmers currently have unprecedented power, since they have craftsperson-like control over products that are destined for mass production. Programming is like a craft in that design decisions tend to be made by individuals with access to a wide range of alternatives, and their choices are often idiosyncratic. But it's unlike a craft in that the resulting product is often mass-produced, and typically has extremely high lifetime support and maintenance costs. These costs are perhaps comparable in magnitude to the upfront tooling costs that help motivate careful design in traditional manufacturing, but, since they mostly occur *after* the product has shipped, they are insidious and lose their power to motivate a sense of engineering discipline. This pseudocraft character of programming does much to account for the poor quality of much production software: In handicraft, the origin of quality lies in repeated production and gradual perfection of the product. In mass production, the high cost of upfront tooling and commitment to large production runs motivates discipline and investment in design. Programming has neither. It is fair to say that a large percentage of production software comes into existence via a process that shares many of the worst aspects of both traditional craft-based production and of serial manufacture. Most software is produced by a small group or even an individual, with little separation between conception and realization. But it shares with serial production the fact that, unlike the craftsperson, the programmer tends to produce a given product only once.

Thus, we have the worst of both worlds: Lacking the rigor of careful a priori designs that the requirements of toolmaking and production engineering impose, the producer of software is free to behave like a folk artist, melding design and production into a single creative act. But, unlike handicraft, this creative act is not expected to be repeated until mastery is attained. A working piece of code is almost never reimplemented from scratch the way a potter repeatedly throws ceramic vessels on a wheel. Computer programs are certainly *modified* incessantly: Errors will be corrected (and new ones introduced), features may be added (but rarely removed), interfaces updated. But rare is the software product that has the occasion for even a single complete rewrite, far less a long tradition of iterative refinement and perfection.

In this regard, software is more like literature than like a physical artifact: Its quality varies widely with the talents of the individual creator. But unlike literature, the result of such an effort is a *product* that is destined to be used over and over again by an end user whose motivation for its use is typically not recreational. Indeed, software often runs without anyone's conscious choice; it's just part of what happens in the world.

Ask a software "engineer" to tell you the minimum number of bytes of memory necessary for her latest program to run, and she will look at you like you're crazy. Coders are generally completely unaware of the low-level computing resources needed to make their creations run. They've been spared all that. Real engineers, however, know these things. Buckminster Fuller was fond of noting that the designer of a sailing vessel could tell you almost exactly how much a new ship weighed. Why? Because it *mattered*. Today's software developers don't think about the analogous aspects of their creations because too many things about the systems they work in have been hidden from them in order to make their lives easier. Abstraction can be a powerful tool, but it can also lead to heads buried in the sand.

In many facets of the industry, most notably web development, software development no longer even pretends to be engineering. Nothing is specifiable anymore. Supposedly, Moore's Law makes such "compulsiveness" unnecessary: Computation and bandwidth are now "approaching free," and we can just use as much of them as we want. If these resources really were free, then there might be some truth to this position. But they are not. As we have seen, the use of these resources implies the creation of complexity, and complexity is never free. Moore's Law simply gives us more and more rope with which to hang ourselves. Or, if you will, more and more acceleration toward the complexity cliff.

It would be an exaggeration, but not a great one, to claim that the premier technologies of our time are in the hands of amateurs. A loose federation of teenaged hobbyists is on the verge of running the world. They are writing the codebase of humanity's future. Worse, they're doing it in an ad hoc, arbitrary manner that many people romanticize. These children are not scientists or architects, or artists for that matter. They are not trained, experienced, seasoned, or even necessarily very disciplined. They are good at math and have an appetite for coding, and this is their credential and the source of their authority. The world has handed them the keys because the need for the services that they offer is boundless, and real engineers are scarce and expensive. The children often work for free.

The Cathedral and the Bazaar

If the open source movement has a single sacred text, it is a 1997 essay by one Eric Steven Raymond titled "The Cathedral and the Bazaar." No other document of comparable length will provide a better understanding of the mind-set that drives the open source zealots. The title refers to a comparison between two styles of building software. They can, says the author, be "built like cathedrals, carefully crafted by individual wizards or small bands of mages working in splendid isolation, with no beta to be released before its time" or, they can be built in the style of a bazaar: "No quiet, reverent cathedral-building here—rather . . . a great babbling bazaar of differing agendas and approaches . . . out of which a coherent and stable system could seemingly emerge only by a succession of miracles."

Citing numerous open source "successes," most notably the Linux project (a re-implementation of a 40-year-old operating system called Unix), the author proceeds to account for such miracles, offering such pithy advice as "given enough eyeballs, all bugs are shallow." The gist of the argument is that since Linux and its ilk are such obvious successes, and since they are results of the open-source process, then it is clear that the "great babbling bazaar" will outperform the disciplined drudgery of traditional engineering process every time.

The problem with this argument is not so much with the conclusion as with the premise: that these projects are "successful." It is almost certainly true that the bazaar process will be faster and cheaper than the cathedral process, but only if you want to end up with a bazaar rather than a cathedral. Cathedrals focus communities, lift spirits, inspire greatness of many kinds, and for centuries were a driving force in the advancement of building technology. Bazaars just go on—essentially without change.

So, in the end, the matter comes down to one of aspirations. No one would argue that Linux and other products of the open source process aren't useful. And useful combined with free is nothing to sneeze at, especially in periods dominated by the consolidation and perfection of the radical innovations of a previous generation. But this is not the kind of period we are facing. Navigating the foothills of a new mountain will require leadership more akin to that of the builders of cathedrals than that of the denizens of bazaars. We, at least, aspire to more than seeing our children live in a bazaar.

Geek Culture Doesn't Care about People

In many respects, the world of the computer avant-garde is exotic and wonderful in ways that are little understood or appreciated outside the fraternity of its initiates. The digerati and geek culture are the vanguard of a computer-dominated future[10] in which technology is a pleasurable end in itself. They live with a passion for computing machines and their possibilities. The term *hobbyist* scarcely does it justice. They see digital devices not as tools for accomplishing tasks but rather as the quintessentially malleable, infinitely flexible devices that, in fact, they are. Grasping their power and their possibilities can forever alter one's perceptions of life and work. How can you be content to use a computer like a typewriter when it could do *anything*? The digerati are like the star child at the end of Arthur C. Clarke's *2001: A Space Odyssey*: "For though he was master of the world, he was not quite sure what to do next. But he would think of something."

We understand the romance and the futuristic thrill of computing machines. We know how the digital adepts feel about the limitless potential of their skills. We're technologists, too. We just happen to be technologists who put people first and technology second, because that's the way it ought to be. We get the enchantment of computing; we just don't expect our neighbors or our children's classmates' parents to get it. We get excited by the prospect of all of *them* coming to the conclusion that these machines are less trouble than they are worth.

The geeks actively desire to live in a technical milieu. They *like* the obscurity of technologies that sets them apart from the masses. But ordinary people have no such relationship with technology. Though the worldview of the digerati is fundamentally unlike that of "ordinary" users, their worldview drives the agenda for everyone. Walt Mossberg of the *Wall Street Journal* has written of the widespread phenomenon of technology columns that are written by geeks for geeks. How about geeks restructuring the whole world only for other geeks? That's the world we're heading into.

But computers aren't really the point. Complexity is. The real agent of change is not computers per se but rather the computation that we are installing into even the most mundane constituents of our everyday surroundings. As we have seen, we are at the point that it is now often cheaper to manufacture digital information processing into an object than it to leave it out. Microelectronics permit even trivial products to be deeply complex and connectible—and that is both the promise and the problem.

That complexity is the domain of the machines. People cannot directly cope with it. Therefore, it should be the job of the machines to shield humans from machine complexity rather than mercilessly exposing them to its harsh glare. That is precisely what we mean by *taming complexity*. You don't have to dumb down machines and sacrifice their potential to make the future work. Nor should you expect people to smarten up in ways that are not human. The alternative? Design the whole thing much better than we do today.

---

[10] As opposed to a "human-enabled" future, which will be a lot more interesting to many of us.

Open Source Is Not the World's Salvation

The undeniable success of the open source movement in facilitating collaborative software projects has led many people to believe that it changes the rules of the game for technological innovation, and maybe everything else that human beings do, too. This belief is incorrect and represents a misunderstanding of the phenomenon.

Open source can be a wonderful, surprising, even magical way to grow and deploy ideas that are already well understood and accepted. But it is emphatically *not* a good way to create new ideas or to promote genuine innovation. Almost without exception, the highly touted success stories of the open source process represent derivative re-implementations of existing successful designs.[11] One is hard-pressed to point to significant cases where the open source process *as such* resulted in the *creation* of something genuinely new.

Open source is widely perceived as a radical, paradigm-shifting phenomenon. There's some truth in this, but the innovations are primarily economic and political, not technological. Technologically, open source is inherently conservative. Its efficacy lies in forwarding sustaining technologies, not disruptive ones. Open source has been disruptive in the marketplace, but not in the technological landscape. Further, the promulgation of "free" versions of mainstream tools—Linux for Unix, MySQL for Microsoft SQL Server, and so on—reduces the economic incentives for people to attempt disruptive innovation. Thus even the market mechanisms of open source tend to reinforce the status quo.

There *have* been a small number of truly significant innovations coming out of the open source community. One that we consider particularly important is Guido van Rossum's Python programming language. It is absolutely true that the open source status of the Python project has provided dramatic amplification of van Rossum's efforts. But our reading of the long and complex history of the project leads us to the conclusion that the true innovations associated with Python are in almost all cases traceable back to the vision of van Rossum himself, and not the open source process as such. This is a pattern that we believe characterizes the few other examples of true innovation coming from the open source community. It is worth noting that van Rossum ended up working for Google, under terms that permit him to spend half of his time on Python.

Open source is characteristically about herd behavior and local hill climbing. There *is* such a thing as the wisdom of crowds, but it is an inherently conservative wisdom. A crowd can tread a meandering cowpath into a highway. What it will never do, however, is decide to dig a tunnel through the mountain to shorten the path, or to leave the mountain altogether for a better one.

---

[11] Indeed, many of the proponents of open source do not pretend otherwise. It is worth noting that the mother of all open-source projects, Richard Stallman's exhaustive effort to re-implement Unix bears the self-consciously ironic moniker "GNU," which is a self-referential acronym standing for "GNUs Not Unix!"

THE PEER-TO-PEER BOGEY

Occasionally, an important new technology for one reason or another gets off on the wrong foot. Nuclear technology, for all of its revolutionary medical and scientific applications, is forever burdened by its initial introduction in the form of the atomic bomb. Stem cell research is currently entangled with reproductive politics. Similarly, peer-to-peer (P2P) communications architectures have been sullied by their association with the theft of music recordings and other intellectual property.

Actually, it isn't quite right to characterize P2P as new. The term refers to communications patterns characterized by symmetrical transactions among more-or-less equally privileged entities. That is a bit of a mouthful, but the concept is simple and extremely common. Two humans carrying on a conversation—in person, via telephone, or writing letters—are engaged in P2P. The interlibrary loan system is a P2P network. Nor is it new or unusual in the context of computer networking. The aforementioned beaming capability of Palm Pilots was P2P. The World Wide Web as it was originally conceived was arguably P2P. The Internet itself is, of course, P2P. And not just in some theoretical sense. The file transfer protocol (FTP) is one of the oldest tools in the suite of basic capabilities of the Net. Using it (or its more secure successors), any two PCs for which this capability has not been explicitly blocked, can copy any files from each other's hard drives. There is no need for Napster, BitTorrent, or any pirate website in order for two consenting adults to share computer files.

So, what is it about Napster and its successors that so terrifies the entertainment industry? The answer is *convenience*. This is no small matter. It is true that most people are basically honest and don't tend to steal each other's money. But that doesn't mean that it is a good idea to leave piles of unwatched cash on your front porch. In the view of the record industry, that is just about what Napster was forcing them to do. Their response—and that of other powerful holders of IP—was predictable. They have done everything they can think of to obfuscate, cripple, demonize, and criminalize all things P2P.

This impulse is at the core of many of the most familiar aspects of the contemporary computing landscape. It is why the web evolved away from P2P and toward the antiquated client-server model. It is why home Internet connections are engineered to be asymmetrical—with most of the bandwidth devoted to incoming data while the ability of consumers to be a source of data is crippled, if not outright prohibited. It is why you can't use your iPod or iPhone as a generic container for exchanging information with your friends.

Books quite a bit thicker than this one have been written on the difficult legal, economic, and ethical issues underlying this response and we are not about to enter the fray—at least not here. But whether one assumes that our current approach to compensating for creative effort needs to be rethought, or conversely that existing IP rights need to be protected at all costs, one conclusion seems to us to be inescapable: Attempting to solve the problem by outlawing P2P is doomed to failure.

We will see in the following chapters that the wholesale avoidance of the P2P communication pattern is quite literally unnatural. Life on Trillions Mountain simply cannot be made to work without the embracing of a fundamentally decentralized mode for many kinds of routine local communications. There are solutions for the protection of information in a P2P world—even if you believe in the status quo with respect to IP issues. But attempting to stop the evolution of a peer-to-peer world amounts to spitting into the wind.

The Web That Almost Was
By Pete

My wife Diana spent most of the 1980s and early 1990s as a member of a small community of researchers studying the then obscure field of hypermedia. As in most scientific disciplines, those researchers gathered once a year for a professional conference. "Hypertext'91" was held in San Antonio in December of 1991. Diana was presenting a poster session (a one-on-one format used for presenting preliminary research not yet ready for a full paper) at the conference, so I decided to tag along to see what these folks were up to.

As I wandered among the card tables set up so that poster presenters could give informal demos, one poster caught my eye. It was titled "Architecture for Wide Area Hypertext." I sat down across from the presenter, who gave me a demo of his system—which he called W3—on one of Steve Jobs' cube-shaped NeXT Machines. The presenter was one Tim Berners-Lee, and W3 as it turned out was short for "World-Wide-Web."

But the system that Berners-Lee showed me (and the computer tape he kindly sent me afterward) bore little resemblance to the web as we know it today. Specifically, his implementation of the web was not a browser. Rather,

to quote the official W3C history of the web it was a "'what you see is what you get' (wysiwyg) browser/editor with direct inline creation of links." That is to say, it was in many respects a *peer-to-peer* application. Berners-Lee showed me how a user on one computer could edit a draft of a paper, or change the phone number in his or her address book entry using the browser/editor, and users on other computers would immediately see the changes. This was a far cry from the world of huge, corporate-controlled "websites" that we know today.

Berners-Lee's original vision of a user-to-user web was clear and compelling. I can still remember the excitement in his voice as he described it to me. But in the short run, it was not able to withstand the pressures of the vested interests that preferred short-term profits to long-term disruption. Had his vision prevailed, we would today be a good distance further along on our climb up Trillions Mountain than in fact we are. For all its wonders, today's World Wide Web is ill-suited for the coming revolution of vastly distributed devices and data. There is much damage to be undone as we resume the climb.

CHAPTER 4

How
Nature
Does It

The proliferation of microprocessors and the growth of distributed communications networks hold mysteries as deep as the origins of life [and] the source of our own intelligence. . . .

—GEORGE DYSON

You arrive in Utah and set out on a hike in early October. You fill your back-pack with some fruits and veggies, a bottle of water, and a snack bar or two. You put on your hiking boots and set off into a glorious stand of trees that are glowing in the still morning light. A few hours later, having worked up a good sweat, you shed your jacket and stop by a stream that bubbles through the rocks below. You lean against one of the trees and just listen to the sound of the forest. It is fall, and the leaves are turning. As you look around, you notice something odd. It seems as if the entire forest has gotten the idea to change colors all at the same time. As far as you can see, all the leaves are a particular shade of yellow. You are surrounded by Nature with a capital N. In fact, you are in the midst of one of the world's most massive living organisms.

Say hello to Pando.[1] It is a male quaking aspen and it has been your companion since you set out this morning. It has been thriving here for over 80,000 years, just waiting for you to stop by. Pando is an example of what Nature can do when she feels like showing off. This stand of trees is called a monoclonal colony. Pando propagates using something called a rhizome, which is an underground horizontal stem of a plant. Beneath the surface of the forest floor is an extensive network of these rootstocks spreading out for miles and miles. What look like individual trees are shoots sent up by Pando's rhizal network.

It is believed that in times of great fires, when other types of trees were destroyed, Pando's rhizal network survived under the soil. Destroying a quak-ing aspen turns out to be very difficult. Experiments that employed a rototiller dragged three feet beneath the soil to chop up the roots failed to kill an aspen clone.

Quaking aspens aren't the only plants to benefit from rhizal networks beneath the soil. It turns out that an estimated 80 percent of land plant spe-cies employ a related mechanism known as a mycorrhizal network. The word *mycorrhizal* comes from the Greek words for fungus and roots. These networks transfer nutrients from the soil into nearby trees that would suffer if left to their own devices. You can also find them digging veins into the earth to access trapped water and free up nitrogen.

THE INTERNET OF PLANTS

Mycorrhizal networks have been shown to move water to areas of drought, confer resistance against toxic surroundings or disease, and even support inter-plant communication. The fungi often benefit by getting access to carbohy-drates, while the plants are supplied with a greater store of water and minerals such as phosphorus that the fungi free up from the soil. Carbon has been shown to migrate, via mycorrhizal networks, from paper birch to Douglas fir trees.

---

[1] *Pando* is Latin for "to spread out, stretch out, extend."

There is evidence that inoculating degraded soil with a mixture of mycorrhizal fungi leads to more robust long-term growth in self-sustaining ecosystems. Finally, scientists have discovered that some species of fungus in certain mycorrhizal networks act as hubs interconnecting various species. While we often hear of parasitism (good for one, bad for the other) or commensalism (good for one, does no harm to the other) in symbiotic relationships, these networks are classified as examples of mutualism (good for one, good for the other, too), where each member in the community benefits from the relationship.

These patterns represent one of Nature's grand experiments in building a massively connected, diverse, sustainable, resilient, and mutually beneficial social network.

NATURE HAS BEEN THERE BEFORE

When contemplating the trillion-node network, it's easy to become overwhelmed by the sheer scale of the undertaking. We haven't solved the problem of Trillions, but Nature has gotten a head start. The human body has many trillions of cells. And yet we can expect to live for the better part of a century without a catastrophic system failure. Unlike the current crop of computing devices, humans don't have to be rebooted every few weeks. Nature is the most advanced and resilient system for managing information that we can find.

If you want to accomplish something particularly difficult, a good first step is to find people who have already succeeded at something analogous, and to study how they did it. We are not claiming that Nature has all the answers to the design of our computational future, but we are claiming that Nature is a very good place to begin looking for clues.

Humans are really just beginners when it comes to understanding information systems. It was only in 1948 that Claude Shannon first provided a rigorous definition of the term *information*. It was around 1440 when Gutenberg first provided us with the technology for reproducing an unbounded spectrum of information using a limited set of parts—moveable type (Figure 4.1). Counting even primitive writing systems, humans have been encoding, storing, displaying, and manipulating information for, at most, tens of thousands of years.

But Nature has been running mature, ultracomplex, resilient information systems for *billions* of years.[2] And, as far as we can tell, all of this magnificent work has been based on a single, incredibly simple but vastly expressive information architecture.

In this chapter we will explore design patterns found in Nature that we believe are necessary to the building of a resilient, successful, and sustainable trillion-node world.

---

[2] The fossil record for living organisms has recently been pushed back to almost 3.5 billion years ago.

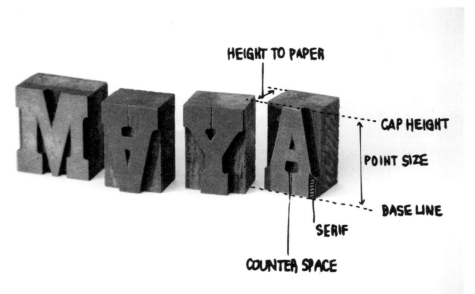

Figure 4.1 Movable type

Atoms Get Identity for Free

In Chapter 2, we introduced the idea that we should imbue unique identity to every digital object we create. While we'd like to claim credit for this idea, the Universe beat us to it. There is an example of this sort of identity in Nature. It can be found in a principle of physics called Pauli's Exclusion Principle.

Down near the foundations of the Universe, we find protons, neutrons, and electrons combining to form atoms. In 1925, Wolfgang Pauli formulated the principle that no two fermions (protons, neutrons, and electrons are examples of the class of particles called fermions) may occupy the same quantum state simultaneously. While it is not our intention to pursue a diversion into quantum mechanics, suffice it to say that one of the consequences of this principle is that no two atoms can occupy the same place at the same time. As a result, each particle has a unique path through space-time. In effect, that unique path *is* the particle's identity.

This turns out to be very convenient if you are trying to build things, or refer to things, or express relations among things. For instance, if you and I are discussing a can of cola that is on the table in front of us, we generally have confidence that we are talking about the same can of cola. Two different containers can't be sitting there in the same place and time. How we *experience* an object may be very different. I may be sitting farther from the table than you. From my distant perspective the soft drink may look like a little rectangular blob of color. From your perspective, sitting right at the table, it may look like a cylinder with a logo on it and some text. But we both know that we are talking about the same thing. Everything made out of atoms has a unique identity, and this "contract" with the Universe is rigorously enforced. No two atoms can exist in the same place at the same time, period.

Thus, in the world of atoms we get identity for free. In the world of bits, however, things are different. Consider an "information object" like, say, *Moby-Dick*. What exactly are we talking about when we refer to *Moby-Dick*? Do we mean the story encoded in the book in my hand, my copy? Or do we mean the (not necessarily identical) one stored over there in your library, your copy? Or the copy from the 1960s that had those amazing illustrations? Or do we mean all copies of *Moby-Dick* everywhere? Or, do we mean the "idea" that there is such a book? Or, do we mean the words themselves?

These are serious questions if we are to have a trillion devices capturing and sending out uncounted numbers of messages about every aspect of our world and our lives. If we take Trillions Mountain seriously as a place where information will not be stored "in" the computers, but rather where computers, people, and devices will be embedded "in" the information, we need to have a plan for how we are going to consistently identify those free-flowing information containers, for determining whether we have the current version (or even what counts as "current"), for resolving conflicts, for maintaining security and privacy, and for fostering collaboration.

Consider the familiar fable of the blind men and the elephant (Figure 4.2). A group of blind men are asked to describe something sitting in the king's court. The first one grabs the tail and shouts, "Ah, it's a snake!" The second holds one of the legs and says, "No, it's not. It's a pillar." "What?" the third exclaims, "This is surely a wall before us" as he pushes on the elephant's belly.

Figure 4.2 Exploring the elephant

While the story is well trod, it highlights deep questions. How do you collaborate when you're not even sure you're talking about the same thing? How do you find important patterns in a sea of information when a global, top-down view is impossible? Many arguments that people have turn out to be confusions about identity. They think they are talking about the same thing. But they're not.

Gravity Isn't Open-Sourced
By Mickey

You are a 16-year-old computer geek who likes to hack. One day Loki, the Norse trickster god, wanders into your room. He tells you that he's been paying attention to your hacking and is very impressed. You have certainly made a name for yourself in the open source community. You have real moxie. He'd like to make a deal. If you'll do a little work for free, he'll give you access to something that has never been open-sourced before. He'll practically hand you the keys to the kingdom. He'll let you hack gravity itself. Ignore all those wet blanket physicists who decry that the code for gravity was developed during the Big Bang and that the source code is long gone.

Having spilled hot coffee in your lap twice in the past month, you proceed immediately to write in an exception to gravity in the case of containers having hot stuff in them. If they ever spill, you'll just make the liquid hover like magic.

Having just gotten grounded to your room for the fifth time this month for driving recklessly, you also insert a bit of code that lets you snap your fingers three times, step out of your window, and fly. You are basically a superhero.

Meanwhile, Loki has been busy.

He not only visited you today, but also 10,000 other kids willing to do a little

work for free in exchange for access to gravity's code.

Natasha wants to be able to show off feats of strength and comes up with a hack that lets her "double-click" the bumper of a car and pick it up as if it were light as a feather.

Slim just added a feature that lets him change the direction of gravity by thinking the word *bingo*!

Marc thinks he can make millions by selling a hack that reverses the effects of age on tired faces by secretly pulling up with the same force at which the world pulls down.

Each of these little tweaks is extremely handy. Soon the open gravity movement is gaining steam—people start committing various fixes to gravity behaviors that had always bothered them—they are on their way to saving the world from thousands of senseless deaths and accidents.

But here is the thing. What we've gained in convenience, we have lost in consistency. The rules have suddenly gotten very complicated. It isn't obvious at first. Coffee bistros start having a really hard time pouring cups of coffee, so they try heroically to turn it into fun with newly designed vacuum bubble cups. But then buildings start to collapse, and fires can't be put out. The world starts to notice. When the lack of consistent gravity starts to upset our basic processes of biology, it turns out to be too late.

The laws of physics are free to all of us, and yet they are not open source. Their code has been burned. These points of stability not only help us cope with a complex world but give us structure to push (and build) against. Instead of open source, we might want to start considering open, but stable, components.

The Architecture of Chemistry

Pauli's Exclusion Principle underpins another pattern found in Nature that has widespread consequences for pervasive computing. Those atoms with the universal identity form the basis for a higher-level architectural framework called chemistry. If you think of an architecture as the blueprint for how to define all the constants and variables in a system, you can find no better example of the power of architecture than the Periodic Table of the Elements. Dmitri Mendeleev is credited with drawing one of the first versions of this "map" of chemistry's territory in 1869.

He inferred that atoms of different elements fall into a repeating pattern and that by formatting the pattern as a table he could predict the existence of undiscovered elements—sometimes decades before they were proven to exist in Nature. His chart, unlike other attempts by his peers, left some places blank in anticipation of future discoveries. He also at times ignored the most obvious way to order the atoms (by their weight) but rather grouped them by similar properties. As scientists learned more about the nature of atomic structures, they found that Mendeleev had ordered his elements by atomic number (which denotes the number of protons in an atom's nucleus)—a concept that didn't even exist when he did his work. One of the powerful things about architectural frameworks like this is that they confer predictive powers and help us *future-proof* our endeavors. When he found an empty square in his table, rather than forcing the next element to "fit," he left it empty. Not only that, he made predictions about the weights and properties of these missing elements and gave them placeholder names.

For example, in 1869 he predicted the existence of a then-unknown element, which he called "eka-silicium," which he said would have a high melting point, be gray in color, and would have an atomic mass of 72 and a density of 5.5. When the element—now called Germanium—was isolated in 1886, it was demonstrated to have an atomic mass of 72.61, a high melting point, was gray, and had a density of 5.32.

The periodic table gave us a way to think about the basic building blocks of chemistry. More importantly it enabled us to understand the physical world and use that knowledge to figure out how to combine atoms in new ways to discover, understand, and build all sorts of amazing new composite materials. In essence it gave us *generativity*, which is an example of what we call beautiful complexity.

Life's Currency

Of course, the real payoff of all this architecture is this: Implicit in the structure of the periodic table is the potential—actually, the inevitability—for the formation of molecules. But for this, we would live in a world built exclusively out of 92 discrete elemental chemicals—a situation reminiscent of those 51 noninteracting application-level protocols we find in today's Internet.

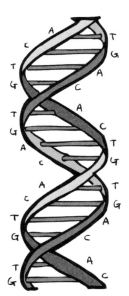

Instead, the real world contains an unbounded number of chemically distinct molecules, setting the stage for the emergence of one epochal macro-molecule called DNA. DNA is found inside just about every cell in your body.[3] The information about what makes you *you*, is largely stored in that DNA. The building blocks of life are encoded in this molecule in the form of genes on chromosomes. It is Life's way of not only encoding critical information, but also copying it, moving it around, and experimenting with new ways to use that information. A chromosome is a "container" for genetic code. In fact, it is not just the container for what makes you and me what we are as humans; it is *the* standard information container for all life on Earth.

That container has some remarkable properties. Its contents are not immutable—they can be changed. Information can be added and removed. This process is called mutation. DNA can also be copied through a process that nearly all cells have the machinery to perform. Consider: An information container that is standardized across literally all life forms; that can be mutated and extended; and that can be copied and stored by simple (for a cell) mechanisms. Sound familiar?

The evolution of a universal container for storing information—one that could be readily replicated and extended—was a very big deal. In Nature, this drove vast experimentation within huge spaces of possibilities. Nature did get locked-in, eventually, on certain powerful patterns, such as bilateral symmetry, but only after life went through the Cambrian Explosion where all kinds of alternatives were explored.

Consider the parallels between genetics and a liquid economic system. One member of a species combines genes from another and creates an entirely new unit of "value" in the form of a unique offspring. DNA is Nature's information container but it is also Life's idea of liquid currency. We don't call it the Gene

---

[3] Mature human red blood cells do not have a cell nucleus or DNA.

Pool for nothing. This is information liquidity writ large. Nature's "blueprints" are stored in lots of these little, recombinable boxes of information, replicated in unimaginable numbers, recomposable in unpredictable permutations, flowing freely across space, time, and generational boundaries. Moreover, even the inevitable errors inherent in this process prove to be essential, genetic transcription errors being the primary engine of evolution.

Today we are reaping the benefits of this liquidity using a technique called *transgenesis*. Scientists now routinely combine genetic materials from various species to create new variants, such as goats that produce human drugs in their milk. Recently, students at MIT created transgenic E. coli (a kind of bacteria found in our digestive system) that had genes from plants. When the E. coli was growing, it smelled like mint, and when it was mature it smelled like bananas. Vaccines for hepatitis B have been built this way, and there are a number of trials in progress looking at ways to use these techniques to cure debilitating diseases. If every kind of organism stored its information in some unique format, we wouldn't be here, and none of those advances in science would be possible.

Resilience

As we build the trillion-node network, resilience will be ever more important. A number of patterns can be found in Nature to handle the challenges of resilience. We will discuss two of the most valuable ones.

First of all, Nature employs massive redundancy as a universal principle. A newt can regrow an amputated toe because the structural pattern for newt toes resides in the DNA of each of its cells.

With this information (and a bit of biological processing magic that humans lack) a lost toe can be regenerated. Memory is cheap in Nature, so the structural patterns that describe what we are can be stored in every cell. Every one of us stores the information equivalent of 200 volumes of the proverbial Manhattan-sized phone book in each of our cells.

Secondly, Nature uses peer-to-peer (P2P) networking. We've already discussed the prevalence of mycorrhizal networks in plant life. Obviously, there is no one central "server" in these networks. Imagine how brittle and short-lived life on Earth would have been if there were single points of failure in such massive networked systems.

When cells communicate, they mostly communicate with their peers. When they replicate, they carry a copy of all their information with them. That information turns out to be very handy when things go wrong. Consider when you get a cut on your skin. Almost immediately a cascade of events begin at the location of the wound. First blood platelets produce inflammation and begin to aggregate at the site to aid in clotting. As healing progresses, new blood vessels grow into place, collagen is used to form scaffolding, and finally new skin cells proliferate and mend the wound. The skin cells on your toe don't talk to the skin cells on your ear.[4] The cells in your body don't ask some central server for permission to repair, replicate, process, or exchange information. That isn't to say that at higher levels of complexity there aren't also more centralized control mechanisms. Beyond cells and organs, there are components that do overall coordination. These include the nervous system for fast-paced responses and the endocrine system for more long-term modulation of activities. Even those more centralized functions benefit from this pattern of massive redundancy. There are countless cases of patients with some form of brain damage going through rehabilitation and regaining some level of function via another part of the brain.

Before the advent of the Internet, society had already learned how to use peer-to-peer networks. As we have already mentioned, good old-fashioned libraries are a nice example. The information stored in libraries is massively replicated in the form of books. Literary citations don't point to individual copies—any copy of *Moby-Dick* will resolve a link request. Copies are stored in a vast number of independent places. And any library can request a copy of some missing volume through the interlibrary loan network, and some other library will almost certainly be able to serve it up. Books have been a common currency of information for many hundreds of years, and they, like DNA, have been promiscuously replicated and distributed throughout the world. We couldn't get rid of *Moby-Dick* if we tried.

Biological systems and world-spanning ecologies have much to offer the student of Trillions. Our efforts at biomimicry for information systems have only really just begun. We'd like to highlight four patterns that recur in

---

[4] In the popular conception of the Internet of Things, many people believe that everything will talk to everything else. If Nature is our guide, we would beg to disagree.

different guises throughout the remainder of this book, all found in Nature, all valuable to our future.

THE QUALITIES OF BEAUTIFUL COMPLEXITY

Earlier we referred to *beautiful complexity*—a made-up term to distinguish good complexity, the kind of complexity we want to foster, the complexity that provides power, efficiency, and adaptability without standing in the way of usability or comprehensibility. We can recognize this beautiful complexity because it is built on a few powerful structural (or "architectural") principles. These include hierarchy, modularity, redundancy, and generativity.

Hierarchy

We are inspired by the lessons of atoms and chemistry, but the devil is in the details. The power comes when atoms are put together to make molecules, and how those molecules make cells, and how cells make organs, and organs systems, and those systems make you, and how you and I and others make us. Each level can be described and modeled without reference to its use in any higher level. This is what we mean by the term *layered semantics*. The levels below don't need to "know" how they will be used by the layers above or what those higher layers do.

Hierarchical composition is the most fundamental quality of beautiful complexity and the one we mention most often and with the most variations. In a hierarchical design, parts are assembled into components, which become the parts of larger wholes, and so on. It is a revelation to discover the extent to which hierarchical organization pervades the natural world and complex systems in general, but not in itself a particularly useful revelation. The natural advantages do not result from simply dividing things into parts. The boundaries between parts and wholes must be arranged in particular ways or the hierarchy doesn't achieve beautiful complexity.

Consider a bucket of fried chicken. Choosing pieces from the bucket—looking for your favored white meat—casually chewing on the bones in a moment of reflection—you become aware that the "chicken" represented by this bucket of pieces makes no obvious sense. Instead of wings, legs, breasts, and so on, the pieces look as if some insensible hand had randomly cleaved the bird into roughly equal-sized pieces. And it is difficult to understand how these pieces could be reassembled into a whole chicken (Figure 4.3).

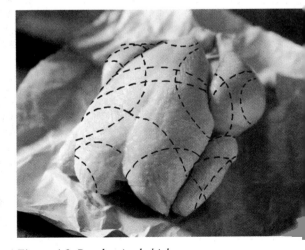

Figure 4.3 Randomized chicken

The joints between bones are the boundaries that define the architecture of a chicken—in life and on the butcher block. Similarly, in the design of complex systems, one of the important, and often difficult, tasks is to identify the best boundaries between the layers of the hierarchy—to find the natural joints. In naturally evolving systems, the boundaries emerge over a long time in response to functional needs, such as the requirements of replication or growth. Military units and ranks evolved in response to the pressures that war places on command. The assembly we call an automobile engine (which is simultaneously both a component and a complex system) evolved, of course, in response to the needs of its mechanical function, but also to the constraints of material properties, manufacturing limitations, and the geometry of assembling and servicing all those many, many parts.

The important lesson from these systems is that, over time, hierarchical layers and their boundaries become well established when they support the system's survival—its creation, its modification or adaptation, its performance. Whether we are talking about squads, battalions, and armies—or crankcases, valve trains, and fuel systems—the stability of the boundaries is important to the evolution of better subsystems. If every time we wanted to develop a better fuel delivery system (e.g., fuel injector versus carburetor) we had to redesign all the way down to the level of pistons and bearing journals, evolutionary progress would be stymied.

Simon's Tale of Two Watchmakers

Our late colleague at Carnegie Mellon, Nobel laureate Herb Simon, was a pioneer in the study of complexity in natural and artificial systems. In his groundbreaking book, *The Sciences of the Artificial*, he presented the following parable:

There were once two watchmakers, named Hora and Tempus, who manufactured very fine watches. Both of them were highly regarded, and the phones in their workshops rang frequently—new customers were constantly calling them. However, Hora prospered, while Tempus became poorer and poorer and finally lost his shop. What was the reason?

The watches the men made consisted of about 1,000 parts each. Tempus had so constructed his that if he had one partly assembled and had to put it down—to answer the phone, say—it immediately fell to pieces and had to be reassembled from the elements. The better the customers liked his watches, the more they phoned him, and the more difficult it became for him to find enough uninterrupted time to finish a watch.

The watches that Hora made were no less complex than those of Tempus. But he had designed them so that he could put together subassemblies of about ten elements each. Ten of these subassemblies, again, could be put together into a larger subassembly; and a system of ten of the latter subassemblies constituted the whole watch. Hence, when Hora had to put down a partly assembled watch in order to answer the phone, he lost only a small part of his work, and he assembled his watches in only a fraction of the man-hours it took Tempus.

Simon's tale suggests that hierarchical composition, and the systematic decomposition that it permits, is important not only for understanding, describing, and working with complex systems, but it also affects, in a fundamental way, their very viability. Through hierarchical means, complex systems can evolve—part by part, level by level—to adapt to changing conditions and shifting needs. And in designing to this advantage it is important to consider, not just the hierarchy itself, but the number and size of the layers, and to get the boundaries between layers in the right places.

As a cautionary note, Simon also highlighted something interesting that he found in exploring complex systems. Not only were they often hierarchical in nature but they tended to be "nearly decomposable." That word, *nearly*, is an important one. He specifically didn't say "completely" decomposable. There are times when no matter how hard you try to turn things into little black boxes, they show some effects from other components in the system. Not everything is hierarchical, and you can't assume that systems can be completely decomposed without losing some critical essence. Effects can leak through hierarchical containment. For instance, if you're building a physical system, you can make a box, but the box isn't going to hide the mass of the stuff inside, or prevent it from radiating or absorbing heat. These *unmodeled* effects often give rise to unexpected, hard-to-predict, emergent properties. In the world of software systems, there are many examples of unmodeled effects like CPU usage, memory requirements, consumption of stack space, and shared mutable state.

Software designers often build centralized services to mitigate these side effects. Such services allow them to "cheat" their way around the inconvenient aspects of strict modularity. Yet if we are to build the trillion-node network, the demands of arbitrary scalability will require more sophisticated solutions. Unlike Mendeleev's peers who just put things together without leaving places for future discoveries, we have to plan for unbounded complexity.

Hierarchy gives us a very powerful tool for understanding and building complex systems, but emergent properties and unintended consequences remain a challenge for the design of the trillion-node network.

Modularity

Modularity is sometimes confused with hierarchy—they're not the same thing. Modules may be arranged in hierarchies, but not necessarily. And hierarchic layers may be modular, but again, not necessarily.

Generally, a module is a standardized part or unit that can be used to construct a more complex structure. But in the field of design, the word also carries an implication that a unit can be added, deleted, or swapped out with minimal impact on the overall structure or assembly. That is, the designer need not modify the underlying structure in order to add a module or as a consequence of removing a module. Thus, you can plug a coffeemaker into your kitchen outlet, or unplug it, or exchange it for a toaster without making any modifications to either appliance or to your kitchen wiring. This example is so simple and common that we don't think of it as an example of modularity, but it does capture the feature of modularity that makes it significant to achieving the beautiful complexity that is our goal.

Note that for all its *local modularity,* you wouldn't be able to take your toaster from your kitchen in the United States to a kitchen in Sweden and plug it in so easily—you'd have to find an adapter. Adapters are, of course, possible as a means of correcting for failures in modularity. But we never *want* to resort to them. They ruin the beauty of the complexity. Eventually, it becomes a question of how far to push the boundaries of local modularity. Context matters in this regard. This question is one that will become increasingly important with the spread of pervasive computing. What makes modules so significant to beautiful complexity is not just standardization of independent units, but in particular the standardization of the interfaces where one module meets another or adds on to the underlying structure.

Recall that in Chapter 2 we referred to Legos as an everyday example of a system with fungibility. Get out your Legos again and look at the interface aspects of the toy. It's all about the bumps. It works because of the particular size, shape, and spacing of the bumps on the tops of the blocks, and the shape of the hollow on the bottoms of the blocks. Pretty simple. Works great with little brick like shapes. But can it do more than that, more than what the originators of Lego had in mind?

A look in any toy store confirms that the answer is yes. Beyond the general-purpose Lego blocks, which maintain the basic integrity of the system, kits are available, including specialized parts of limited (not general) utility—like rolling wheels with tires, spacecraft fins, miniature doors and windows, and *people.* It all works because the designers of the system have been absolutely scrupulous about the details of the interface—where part meets part, or module meets module. Examine one of the people closely: Their hands and feet are shaped to grip the bumps. The top of the body ends in another standard bump that fits into a variety of heads. And all the heads are the same shape, so that they can be printed with a variety of faces. Finally, all the heads are topped with a bump that fits a variety of hats. A system with few distinctly shaped parts enables a vast variety of distinct creations.[5]

Redundancy

The core meaning of redundancy has to do with the inclusion, in an object or system, of information or components that are not strictly necessary to its meaning or function. Complex hierarchical systems generally have a great deal of redundancy.[6] Yet redundancy as such is superficially thought to be a symptom of inefficiency. But in a real, entropic world, redundancy is the safety net of life. It keeps things going when some of the details fail or are ignored. In engineering, redundancy provides backup capability in case of the failure of components or the unexpected exceeding of environmental assumptions. In languages, redundancy is the extra information that protects meaning when part of an expression is vague, corrupted, or simply missing.

Human communication via natural language uses far more words than are strictly necessary to convey the meaning of a sentence or utterance. We repeat ourselves, but we learn through repeated hearing—and by repeating we can carry on a semblance of a conversation even in a noisy bar. In the printed word, our letterforms themselves are full of redundancy. A common demonstration in basic typography courses shows students the importance of letter shapes and word shape by covering the bottom half of printed words. In most cases, especially with lower case letterforms, the text is still nearly perfectly readable[7] (Figure 4.4).

Symmetry is a kind of redundancy that deserves special attention because of its conceptual origins in the physical and perceptual dimensions of our world. Symmetry provides additional information about the form, structure, or action of some physical object—natural or artificial. If you have seen one side of a car, you can be pretty sure what the other side is going to look like;

information

Figure 4.4 *What is this word? How much of the word is actually there?*

---

[5] And the story doesn't end there. A product line called Lego Technics extends the architecture to support active electrical and mechanical components—including bumps containing electrical contacts.

[6] This is often where we encounter the *nearly* decomposable quality of complex systems. But just as *nearly* can frustrate decomposability, by relying on redundancy across layer boundaries, we can arrange to separate the layers without losing information. Looked at another way, this redundancy places a limit of the semantic isolation in semantic layering.

[7] Interestingly, the trick doesn't work nearly as well if you cover the top half of the words. This demonstrates that most of the information is located in the top halves of the letterform shapes.

all that's needed is your memory of the side you see, plus a spatial "mirror" transformation that our brains perform quite easily, as long as the image isn't too complicated. We aren't generally conscious of performing such symmetry operations in everyday life, but they *are* going on at a deeper level, and we notice them in a jarring way when our mental predictions are not met—as in a car that is different on each side or in the *Batman* character Two Face.

Though the bilateral or mirror sort of symmetry is the one that first comes to mind, there are other symmetries that are common to physical/perceptual experience. The terminology varies, but three other fundamental symmetries are generally known as rotational, translational, and dilatational symmetry. Sometimes repetition is included as a fifth type (Figure 4.5).

At their roots, all these symmetries do the same thing. They reduce the information that we need to process in order to recognize, describe, or construct a complex physical object. But we are discussing the design of a world where physical objects and digital objects exist in concert—information architectures, connected experiences, relationships among people and information devices—we need to be aware of symmetries and other kinds of redundancies in these circumstances as well.

We are already familiar with a sort of intermodal redundancy in user interfaces that pair icons with descriptive words. It's repetition with a difference, where one mode supports the other. In a world of ubiquitous information

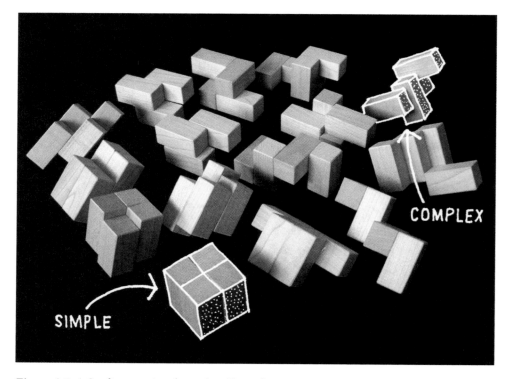

Figure 4.5 A Studio exercise about the effect of symmetry on perceived complexity

devices, how will we accomplish similar enhancements of usability—perhaps a word coupled to a gesture, or a vibration coupled to a feeling of heat, or a texture coupled to an odor?

In Chapter 3 we discussed the current instantiation of "the cloud" and how it often excludes the sorts of redundancy found in Nature. We noted that this lack of redundancy could be not only damaging but catastrophic. Redundancy may seem inefficient at some level, but it turns out to be a critical optimization if your goal is long-term resilience. In the pervasive computing community one sometimes encounters the phrase *creative waste*. We are not fond of the term—redundancy is not waste at all.

In the world of Trillions Mountain, redundancy will become an even more important path to beautiful complexity than it is today. In a world that is international and intercultural; in which our possessions are informational as well as physical; and where we interact with one another across widening gaps of space, time, and intention; designers of connected systems will need, more than ever, to pay conscious attention to this aspect of beautiful complexity.

Generativity

Generativity is qualitatively different from the other aspects of beautiful complexity. Hierarchy, modularity, and redundancy are concepts that describe and qualify the *states* of things. By contrast, generativity is fundamentally about *processes*. Of course we can speak of a process as being hierarchical, but it is more likely that we are actually talking about a structure—or organization, or its state—which gives rise to the process we describe as hierarchical. The notion of generativity entered the design profession by way of linguistics. Generative grammar, developed and promoted in the 1950s by Noam Chomsky and others, is a type of grammar that describes language in terms of a set of rules, called transformations, which operate within a hierarchy of cognitive levels, to generate an unbounded number of possible sentences from a limited number of semantic primitives, word parts, and possible sounds.

A prior approach, known as phrase structure grammars, tried to account for human language by proposing what amounted to sentence templates, with the various parts of speech at their appointed places in the templates, waiting for the speaker to fill in the template with actual words. It was a view of language that owed more to the methods by which scholars analyzed speech than to an understanding of how ordinary people speak.[8] Phrase structure grammar was ultimately inadequate because it seemed to require far too much preplanning on the part of the speaker.

The importance of generative grammar was that it accounted, in a reasonable way, for our human ability to concoct an apparently endless stream of

---

[8] Those "sentence diagrams" they made you do in fourth grade were essentially exercises in phrase structure grammar.

complex sentences out of a very limited range of semantic, syntactic, and pho-nological means. That is, through generativity, it doesn't take much to say a lot.

Soon after the notion of generative grammar was in the wind, other exam-ples of generative systems were quickly proposed in other realms of creative production.

Architectural theorists proposed generative "form grammars" by which they characterized practicing architects as generating building forms through a set of hierarchical rules. While no working architect may admit to consciously invoking generative rules, the notion of an architectural form-generation pro-cess maintains its viability. After all, no speaker necessarily admits to invoking generative rules in speaking either, but the evidence that it's happening, uncon-sciously, is too strong to be disregarded.

A simple generative system—much simpler than the grammars proposed for natural language—can be illustrated using a set of possible combinations expressed in a matrix. Imagine a matrix for generating snacks; four rows by four columns (Figure 4.6). The rows represent the "outside of the snack," and are labeled "chocolate," "peanut butter," "bacon," and "hot peppers." The col-umns are similarly labeled, but represent the "filling inside."

Now if the rule is "choose the intersection of one row and one column, and describe the snack at that intersection," you find you can generate 16 dif-ferent snacks. Granted, some may not be very interesting, like the intersection

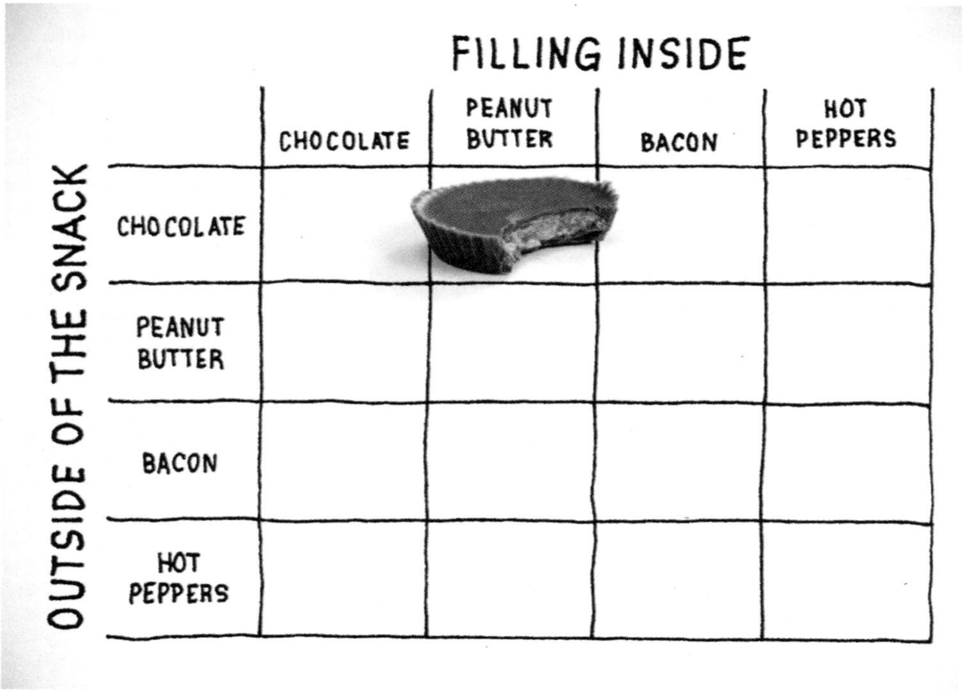

Figure 4.6 A matrix for comparing snack foods

of chocolate/chocolate—unless you're a chocoholic. And some may not be very appealing. But you do generate a Reese's Cup, which is good, but already exists. And you also generate peanut butter outside, with a chocolate filling inside. A sort of Inverse Reese's Cup, which doesn't exist, and might be pretty good if you could find some way to structurally stabilize peanut butter. Fortunes have been made from these kinds of experiments in generativity. The concept of generativity is very broad, found even in the elementary processes of visual design (Figure 4.7).

Generativity makes it onto the list of qualities for beautiful complexity specifically because of the needs we see arising in the land of Trillions. Not only will there be trillions of nodes—trillions of devices—but similarly large numbers of opportunities for satisfying human needs and desires—the needs and desires of billions of individual and subtly different people who may each claim their fair—and individualized—share of the digital resources of the planet.

The well-worn practice of designing just *states* (products, devices, messages) will not do to satisfy such a demand. We will have to also get good at designing *processes* by which people author and tune the digital environment in which they live. Imagine a world in which purchasing a product, or an app, or a service becomes more like the process by which you buy a home, or gather

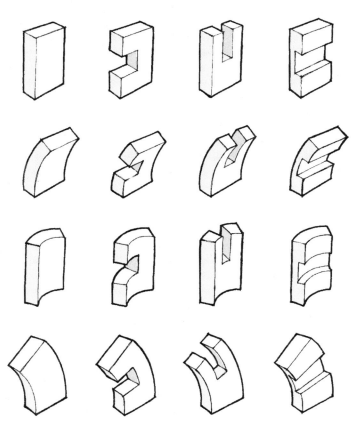

Figure 4.7 *Generative Sketching: Combinations and permutations are used to generate a large number of unique shapes from a few simple rules.*

your circle of friends around you. It's not just about price or features, but has a lot to do with personal identity, preference of lifestyle, comfort, and familiarity. Maybe it sounds complex, but if it works, it will be rich and beautiful. There is no better route to beautiful complexity than to seek generativity in the things we design.

AT THE INTERSECTION OF PEOPLE AND INFORMATION

The reader may note that to this point we haven't mentioned many of the actual physical *things* that humankind has copied from Nature. We haven't mentioned the rise of biomimicry that has driven new inventions in artificial limbs, airfoils, adhesives, or living quarters. We didn't talk about geodesic domes or seashells.

While we think these efforts are all well and good, our focus is not on the design of things per se, but on the discovery and application of design patterns and processes that can be applied at the intersection of information systems and people. As Tolkien taught us, we are not merely copiers, we are subcreators—we need to understand the rules that give rise to the systems we create.

In the next chapter, design itself will take center stage as we explore ways in which we can use the building blocks of the natural world along with practices honed over decades—in some cases centuries—of deliberate creativity to drive thoughtful systematic change.

CHAPTER 5

How Design Does It

The role of the designer, as the humane and aesthetic conscience of industry, is that of a surrogate for the consumer. He senses the pattern of evolutionary factors in manufactured products and directs the object toward the perfection of its typeform.

—ARTHUR PULOS

You are a 32-year-old scientist, jobless, broke, and considering suicide. A pandemic is growing across the country and around the world. Your daughter is a victim. You blame yourself for your child's death. No doctor or researcher has yet found a cure. When you consider the state of the world and your failure to protect your child's precious life, you begin to drink heavily. You are living in low-income public housing near the shores of Lake Michigan. One day you decide you have had enough and begin to walk out onto the beach and into the water. You are chilled but just keep walking. As the waves break across your chest, one last idea occurs to you. As a scientist you can't stop teasing at this idea and soon have formulated an experiment. It will be the next and last one you will ever run.

You decide to run an experiment to find what a "human of average size, experience, and capability . . . could effectively do [to] . . . lastingly improve the physical protection and support of all human lives. . . ."

Your name is R. Buckminster Fuller and you will ask that your epitaph read, "Call me Trimtab." But the headstone will have to wait more than 50 years because you've got an experiment to run.

Buckminster Fuller, scientist, engineer, architect, futurist, and designer, was born in the waning days of the nineteenth century and would live to the age of 83. During his time he would focus on the challenges facing all of the inhabitants of Spaceship Earth. A structure that he designed to shelter humanity, the famous geodesic dome turned out to embody a design pattern identical to that found in a particular molecule of carbon whose atoms are arranged on a perfect sphere (Figure 5.1). When scientists in the late twentieth century discovered these surprising nanoscale soccer balls, they officially named them buckminsterfullerene, and universally refer to them as "buckyballs."[1]

While patterns found in Nature inspire us and give us ideas for how to build things, they are not the end but rather the beginning of the story. Design, as a practice, continues the tale.

Bucky's phrase "Call me Trimtab" refers to an elegant piece of nautical engineering based on an understanding of fluid dynamics. A giant ship like the *Queen Mary* has a rudder to help it change directions, but on that rudder is a small device known as a trimtab—it is the rudder's rudder. By changing the angle of that little device, just enough turning force is created to counteract the

---

[1] In 1996, Robert F. Curl, Jr., Sir Harold W. Koto, and Richard E. Smalley were awarded the Nobel Prize in Chemistry for their discovery of buckyballs in 1985.

Figure 5.1 *The Montreal Biosphère, a geodesic dome originally built as the United States Pavilion at Expo 67, designed by R. Buckminster Fuller*

direction of the ocean current and keep the ship moving at the intended bearing. The realization that he was just one small part of a very large system, but that he could change the world by consciously applying design techniques to solve problems at the point of greatest leverage, was profound, and for Fuller, life saving. When asked what he was, rather than answering with a typical discipline descriptor such as engineer, or architect, he liked to say, "I am not a noun, I seem to be a verb." These two quotes begin to explain the value of design as a practice.

BIRTH OF INDUSTRIAL DESIGN

Soon after Buckminster Fuller walked the shores of Chicago contemplating the future, the world was plunged into the Great Depression. One little-mentioned factor that helped America emerge from the devastating downward spiral was the emergence of the profession of industrial design.

Figure 5.2 Norman Bel Geddes with a model of his ocean liner concept

Source: Courtesy of Edith Lutyens & Norman Bel Geddes Foundation and Harry Ransom Center, The University of Texas at Austin.

The industrial designer emerged out of the financial chaos to become a consumer advocate with a carrot rather than with a stick—representing the consumer's interests in the corporate boardrooms, and rewarding the attentive industrialist with increased market share and increasing profits.

In the late 1920s and early 1930s a few dozen men (they were virtually all men)[2] more or less drifted from other careers—mostly in various of the visual arts—to meet the demand being created among manufacturers by advertisers and economic recovery theorists for help in creating, through an essentially craft tradition, aesthetically and functionally improved products. A smaller number proved to possess the right combination of skills—technical, aesthetic, diplomatic, organizational and promotional—to build large nationally known design organizations. Most prominent of the latter group were the big four designers: Norman Bel Geddes, Walter Dorwin Teague, Raymond Loewy, and Henry Dreyfuss.

It is notable that "fine" artists founded none of the early full-service industrial design organizations. Bel Geddes and Dreyfuss were successful stage designers, while Teague and Loewy had had careers in commercial art. Goaded by their advertising agencies, who felt increasingly helpless in attempting to convince depression-weary customers to purchase tired old merchandise, and encouraged by enthusiastic articles in trade and business journals—most notably *Fortune*—manufacturers increasingly sought out designers, whose employment started out as something of a fad and eventually became institutionalized as a part of standard business practice in many industries.

The personalities of these early designers, and their views on the relationship among technology, design, and society, were markedly diverse. Bel Geddes (Figure 5.2) was a showman and a visionary, with a reputation as "the man who, when asked to redesign a product, went on to design its factory." Consistently ahead of his time, he was the least successful of the big-name designers in terms of commissions actually produced, but he excelled at promoting industrial design as a consequential and glamorous profession and at popularizing streamlining as a uniquely American design style.

---

[2] In 1959 Cary Grant famously fell in love with a female industrial designer while traveling *North by Northwest* in an inspired bit of scriptwriting meant to hint at a certain *élan* and untapped resourcefulness.

"Gentlemen, I am convinced that our next new biscuit should be styled by Norman Bel Geddes."

Source: *New Yorker*, 1932. © Kemp Starrett/The New Yorker Collection/www.cartoonbank.com.

In contrast to Bel Geddes' flamboyance, Teague (Figure 5.3) was by temperament reserved and understated, more the businessman than the artist. Politically conservative, he was trusted and liked by the businessmen who were his clients because he was like them and trusted in their enterprise and the cumulative wisdom of their enlightened self-interest to bring about social progress.

Raymond Loewy had a simpler view of the role of design in human affairs. Eschewing the more extreme claims of functionalist determinism, and avoiding, for the most part, extravagant visions of technological utopias, Loewy's passion as a designer was simply to make the technological world, and the lives of the people who inhabit it, less abrasive and more pleasant. Loewy (Figure 5.4) characterized his early efforts to sell his design services as a personal crusade to convince America's industrialists that improving people's lives by improving the design of the products they used was not only possible, but was also profitable. Although Loewy was temperamentally reserved, throughout his long career he was an indefatigable promoter of himself and of his profession, and was by no

Figure 5.3 (left) Walter Dorwin Teague in his New York City office. (right) The Kodak Bantam Special Camera, designed by the Teague office in 1936, part of a long-term designer-client relationship with Kodak

Source: Courtesy of TEAGUE. Copyright TEAGUE.

means hesitant to stretch a fact for the sake of rhetoric. However, there is no reason to doubt that a modest quest for elegance and style was the motivating force in both his personal and professional lives. Loewy coined the acronym, MAYA, that we use as our company's name, for that optimal zone that balances the <u>M</u>ost <u>A</u>dvanced design that is <u>Y</u>et <u>A</u>cceptable for normal consumers.

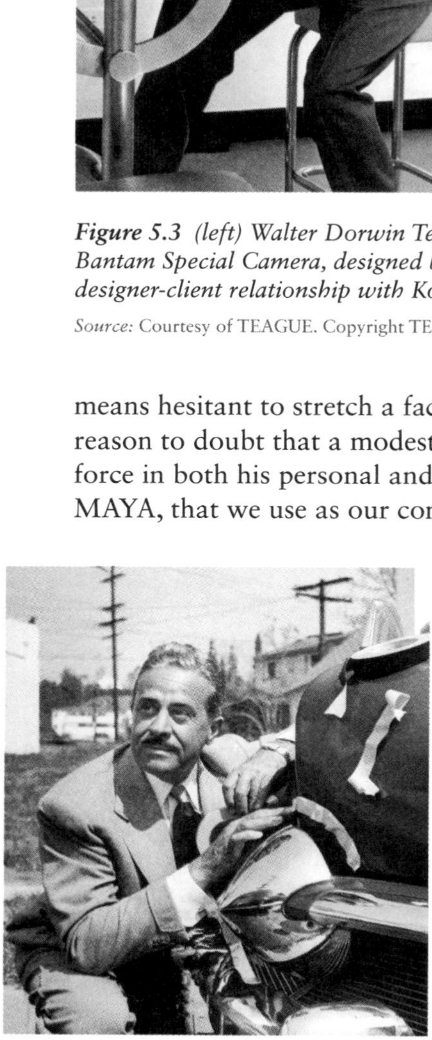

Most modest of all in his aspirations for the profession, Henry Dreyfuss (Figures 5.5 and 5.6) devoted his career to an effort to mold the products of technology to the needs of people rather than the reverse. Dreyfuss was educated in the tradition of the Society of Ethical Culture to the belief that the highest moral imperative was to direct one's efforts toward the improvement of society and to a broadly conceived concept of "progress." Claiming no mystical wisdom and embracing no grand designs, Dreyfuss believed that the role of the designer was simply to, first, understand the needs and characteristics of users as individuals and as groups and, second, to make products more useful—and therefore more saleable—by applying such understanding to

Figure 5.4 Raymond Loewy posing with a Studebaker of his design

Source: Bob Landry/Getty Images

improving their usability, safety, and aesthetics. As part of its product design regimen, the Dreyfuss office accumulated voluminous statistical data about the physical and perceptual characteristics of the population. As a result, Dreyfuss became recognized as one of the founders of the discipline of ergonomics.

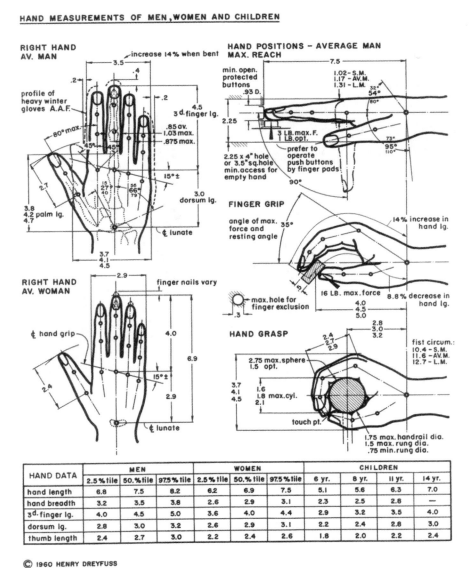

HAND DATA	MEN			WOMEN			CHILDREN			
	2.5%tile	50.%tile	97.5%tile	2.5%tile	50.%tile	97.5%tile	6 yr.	8 yr.	11 yr.	14 yr.
hand length	6.8	7.5	8.2	6.2	6.9	7.5	5.1	5.6	6.3	7.0
hand breadth	3.2	3.5	3.8	2.6	2.9	3.1	2.3	2.5	2.8	—
3d. finger lg.	4.0	4.5	5.0	3.6	4.0	4.4	2.9	3.2	3.5	4.0
dorsum lg.	2.8	3.0	3.2	2.6	2.9	3.1	2.2	2.4	2.8	3.0
thumb length	2.4	2.7	3.0	2.2	2.4	2.6	1.8	2.0	2.2	2.4

Ⓒ 1960 HENRY DREYFUSS

Figure 5.5 *Hand anthropometrics from Dreyfuss's* The Measure of Man, *a landmark compilation of human factors data for designers, stressing usability*

For all their diversity, these and other successful early designers evolved remarkably similar methods of operation and, by the end of the 1930s, represented a genuine movement in the annals of American industry. Teague once accounted for the fact that all of the well-known designers developed such convergent methods by observing that "those who did not, simply did not last." More explanatory, however, are a number of common themes that emerge from an examination of their careers and of their writings.

One such recurring theme in each of their stories was a rejection of superficial "surface" design. In the pre-industrial design era manufacturers often hired artists and craft-oriented designers to "beautify" products by applying surface decoration prior to mass production.

Source: U.S. Library of Congress, U.S. Department of the Interior, National Park Service, Historic American Engineering Record.

In contrast, the founders of the major design offices unanimously rejected this approach in favor of an "inside out" functionally driven approach. Dreyfuss often repeated the story that early in his career the Bell Telephone Company selected him as one of 10 commercial artists to be offered a thousand dollars each to provide sketches of an improved telephone set. Dreyfuss declined the offer, insisting that a successful product design could not be completed under such circumstances, but must rather be carried out in close collaboration with the company's engineers. A year later, Bell returned to Dreyfuss, admitted that the submitted designs proved impractical, and hired him in a consultant relationship that lasted throughout the rest of his career (Figure 5.6).

Figure 5.6 *Dreyfuss (L) and William H. Martin (R), an engineer and Bell VP, with studies from their work with ATT*

Source: Eric Schaal/Getty Images.

NOVELTY, BEAUTY, RITUAL, AND COMFORT

Soon after design was recognized as a profession, it was further specialized into narrower concerns—product design, graphic design, communication design, interior design, sound design, fashion design, and even further specialized into product categories such as automotive design, furniture design, and, more recently, interface design and web design.

These specialties were born of the human love of novelty, beauty, ritual, and comfort; they were raised in the arts and enabled by engineering and technology. They have grown to be powerful resources employed in the service of building brand, stirring desire, and "fitting" products and services within our human-scale world.

For a brief period there was uncertainty whether the teaching of design belonged in schools of engineering or schools of art. In our opinion, it should have remained balanced precisely at the intersection of the two. But Academe is notoriously bad at such interdisciplinary balancing acts, and, so in the event, it ended up for the most part in art colleges or university departments of art or architecture. Graphic design typically grew out of painting programs, industrial design out of sculpture programs, and interior design out of architecture. And the method of instruction was typically through the imitation of masters, with scant analysis or reasoning to back it up.

Over time, the various flavors of design have evolved significant methods and rationales. They have been enormously successful at tapping the cultural streams that determine human reactions to our designed and built environment—reactions of desire or satisfaction; a sense of beauty, of pride, of place, of ownership. Structured methods have been developed for sensing problems, defining problems, and solving problems. But they also help us with elements of drama, surprise, and satisfaction. And because many of these specializations rely on the visual language of design, they are spatial and holistic at their core. Many of the methods and techniques used in these areas have proven to be effective at describing design problems between and across diverse disciplines beyond their traditional borders—tapping into the perceptual powers that all players in the product development process—engineers, mathematicians, social scientists, writers, business executives, financial analysts, and policy specialists—bring to the table.

HEARING HISTORY RHYME

There have been three fundamental technological revolutions in human history. Eight thousand years ago was the agricultural revolution. Roughly 200 years ago the industrial revolution began. But then, no sooner had that revolution run its course than we found ourselves in the midst of the information revolution. In human history, only these three developments have made a fundamental, permanent difference in the lives of ordinary people. And of course the increasing time-compression of these periods—8,000 years, 200 years, and 50 years—has been remarked upon countless times.

The industrial revolution brought unprecedented, world-changing power but it also foisted unspeakable mechanized ugliness and brutality upon human beings—not to mention on the landscape, the natural world in general, the planet itself. The so-called machine age crushed people both figuratively and literally. In its final stage, its technology impinged on the everyday lives of people in the form of inexpensive mass-produced products intended for mass consumption. But it also produced a transformation of the average person's daily environment from a pre-industrial state of relative order and integrity to an early-industrial state of noise, danger, squalor, and ugliness. "History doesn't repeat itself," as Mark Twain allegedly put it, "but it does rhyme." We founded MAYA Design because we heard history rhyming. The information revolution was echoing its predecessor.

Today, we are arguably on the cusp of a fourth revolution: the age of Trillions. No one disputes the evolving phenomenon itself, though some argue that it is merely a continuation of the information revolution. We think that pervasive computing represents a profoundly different relationship of people to information, and that eventually it will be understood as a distinct epoch of

The Great Exhibition
By Joe

It is the middle of the nineteenth century, and Great Britain is feeling its oats, being the dominant world colonial power and the leader in the industrial revolution that is sweeping the world. Queen Victoria has convened a Royal Commission, with Prince Albert as chairman, to oversee the planning and implementation of a great international industrial exhibition. It would come to be regarded as the first of a century-long succession of events that came to be known as World's Fairs.

On May 1, 1851, it opened in London's Hyde Park as the Great Exhibition of the Works of Industry of all Nations to the accompaniment of cannons, fanfares, cheers, prayers, and a performance of Handel's "Hallelujah Chorus." It was immensely popular right up to its closing in October 1851. In those six months, it became a benchmark of industrialized design and has remained so ever since. The nearly 15,000 exhibitors and their products—over a million of them—were certainly responsible for the Exhibition's popular success, but so was the Exhibition building itself—The Crystal Palace (Figure 5.7).

A closer look at the Crystal Palace and its contents provides insight into the recurring paradox of great technological revolutions: increased productive power coupled with a seeming loss of judgment about how to use that power—about making the right products. It's the historical theme we hear rhyming as we near another revolution.

The exhibition building itself, at least from today's perspective, was the brilliant breakthrough of the Exhibition. After months of bureaucratic delays with unsuccessful proposals from all the "proper" people, and with only 10 months to go until the scheduled opening, Joseph Paxton, a landscape architect with extensive experience in building greenhouses, stepped forward with plans for what would become known as the Crystal Palace. It is regarded as the first modern modular building, consisting of glass plates glazed into a framework of cast iron modular columns and just four types of support beams. The final building covered over 19 acres and was 65 feet high, with a 108-foot high cross vault that enclosed three

(Continued)

Figure 5.7 *Original Crystal Palace of 1851*

ancient elm trees. Paxton avoided traditional Victorian decorative elements; the building was meant to serve a specific function for a limited time. The visual impact was the result of only material, color, light, and, of course, sheer size. The building was so successful that, after the closing of the Exhibition, it was dismantled, enlarged by nearly 50 percent, and moved to South London's Sydenham Hill, where it served a variety of public purposes until it was destroyed by fire in 1936—a temporary building with a life of 85 years. Many of the details of the Crystal Palace can be found in a comprehensive book published by John Tallis and Company.

By comparison with the building, the contents of many of the exhibits are remembered as being somewhere between crass and silly (Figure 5.8). Granted, the exhibits of industrial machinery and manufacturing processes showed the best engineering and machine design of the era. In contrast, the products of that manufacturing—what we would call consumer products—amounted to a compendium of Victorian excess. Even given the prominent legitimate role that surface decoration played in Victorian sensibilities, the amount of decoration was excessive and lacking in sophistication. The focus of Victorian pride had shifted to an ability to industrially imitate—at low cost and high volume—traditional decorative themes, but in the materials of industry. Floral and animal motifs had for centuries been painstakingly refined, by hand, in materials like wood

Figure 5.8 A work table displayed in the Crystal Palace

tiles without regard for appropriateness or the relationships among material, process, and form.

The mid-twentieth century designer, Charles Eames, accounted for this problem—an eternally recurring problem in his mind—in terms of *constraint* and *restraint*. He believed that one or the other was a necessary condition for good design. With Paxton's exhibition building, there were so many constraints—short time, immense size, construction difficulties, and so on— that there was no creative energy to be wasted on pointless decoration or empty symbolism. But for the manufacturers displaying their wares, constraints had been removed. Productivity was up, dependence on human skill was down; it looked like an unbounded variety of goods would be available to all. The problem now was to find a substitute for scarcity as a source of value. They settled on unconstrained decoration. This is the point when, as Eames argues, restraint must enter into conscious design problem solving. When the question of "how to make" has been answered, the important question becomes "what to make."

and stone. Now they were being copied in cast iron and machine-loomed tex-

human history. As an intrinsically networked phenomenon, it will also continue the historical trend of acceleration. A decade in the era of pervasive computing will bring unimaginable changes.

INSTABILITY AS THE STATUS QUO

One of the changes that we—business people, designers, consumers—are already dealing with is the recognition that good design decisions are increasingly

Painting, Palettes, and the Art of Systematic Experience Design
By Bill Lucas

Before the Industrial Revolution, fine arts painters worked within color constraints that were set for them by the natural world. The natural pigments constituted a set of *constants* that artists could extend by mixing them to achieve *variations*. Their portrayals of reality were confined to the spectrum afforded them by these constants and variables.

The Industrial Revolution gave rise to synthetic pigments and a corresponding wave of chromatic complexity. In response, many painters embraced the discipline of setting a limited palette for themselves. Before putting brush to canvas, they deliberately narrowed the spectrum of colors to a small, yet potent, assortment. The specific values they chose may have been utterly different from those offered by Nature, but they functioned in the same way: restricting the artist to a limited, comprehensible color world that could be fully and meaningfully explored by mixing the components.

In the age of pervasive computing, coordination of constants and variables is the central act of pattern making in everything from visual arts to computer engineering. As we pursue systematic experience design, the interdisciplinary teams at MAYA embrace the discipline of setting limited palettes. We deliberately narrow the full range of possibilities to a small, yet potent, assortment of elemental attributes. Like skilled painters we choose our palettes wisely and then draw from them to create user experiences formed by information technology—compositions of remarkable diversity, with an automatic harmoniousness that we got for free, you might say, from the well-chosen limitations of our constants.

In Nature we get physics for free. You might call it the automatic harmoniousness of the world. As interaction designers we create virtual physics for the interfaces that users experience. We determine a fruitful set of constants and variables. We come to understand that the natural world, paintings, and software interfaces are all information designs. They all get their diversity and harmony, their variety and coherence, from the interplay of constants and variables in both appearance and behavior.

Bill Lucas (no relation to Pete) served as Director of MAYA's Visual Design Group from 1996 to 2001, then becoming the inaugural member of MAYA's Professional Practice Fellowship Program.

influenced by the need to be context dependent and dynamic. Context dependency has always qualified the "goodness" of design decisions. The addition of dynamic considerations, giving us a *dynamic context*, makes for a tricky scenario—an inherent and persistent instability.

Experts who deal routinely with potentially dangerous dynamic situations have evolved elaborate procedures and protocols that are worthy of study as examples of complexity design. Rock climbers employ highly structured sets of telegraphic calls and acknowledgments for reliably communicating the state of a climb to the belaying partner on the other end of the rope. Similarly, military pilots and astronauts revert to a highly drilled set of terse commands and responses when communicating on noisy channels under the pressures of flight.

Space flight provides an interesting example of how dynamic systems can require constant reevaluation in light of new circumstances: Throughout the American space program and up until the Apollo moon landings, the act of deciding whether to continue or to abort a mission was termed a "go/no go" decision. However, just a few months before the Apollo 11 landing, mission planners realized that this term, which had served well in all previous circumstances, suddenly became ambiguous and potentially confusing once the lunar module touched down on the surface of the moon. As a result of this insight, the terminology was quickly changed to "stay/no stay." What constitutes "good design" is always contextual, and never more so than in the case of complex, rapidly changing systems.

The above examples—climbers, pilots, and astronauts—all share the common characteristics of operating in highly dynamic situations involving limited bandwidth. That is, compared to most human communication situations, the quantity of information that can be passed back and forth in a given amount of time is limited. This is true both because verbal communications is often carried out over noisy or otherwise "weak" channels, and also because such situations are often impoverished in terms of the various nonverbal cues that are so important in more normal human communications. Both of these same impoverishments—limited bandwidth or attention span and lack of nonverbal cues—also characterize the kinds of human-machine communications that are the essence of user interface design.

Design has *consequences* that can go far beyond matters of appearance and personal preference. The annals of technology are littered with examples of disasters attributable directly to designs that inadequately coped with dynamic complexity.

POST-INDUSTRIAL DESIGN

From today's perspective, the early pioneers of industrial design might seem to have been pursuing a shallow and sometimes crassly commercial role in industrial America. But they were on the right track. They learned how to learn. And many of the major elements of a post-industrial design were there: an integrative position situated between industry and consumer, the collection and application of explicit design data and design methods, the persuasive power of aesthetics, and collaborative methods for integrating the expertise of a broad range of disciplines.

When we founded MAYA Design in 1989, the basic idea was perfectly simple: We proposed to do the same thing for post-industrial design.

We were hearing in the burgeoning computer industry the unmistakable echo of the industrial revolution's impact on human beings. The information revolution wasn't spewing smoke and steam from "dark satanic mills" or shattering tranquility with the cacophony of heavy steel, but it was placing significant stresses upon people—all the more insidious, one could argue, for not being ear-splitting or suffocating or glaring.

Computers were by then well into a metamorphosis from rare and precious tools for trained specialists to a major constituent of the everyday environment. For the first time in human history, highly complex systems were in the hands of ordinary people—systems that had nothing to do with natural human life. Their complexity stemmed directly from the ultraminiaturized electronics they were built from, a profound mismatch with human senses and cognition and interests. This was something genuinely new in the world. It demanded new approaches to design. But for the most part, the computer industry was making no real distinction between design and engineering. Indeed, engineers often were the sole designers of computing machines intended to be sold to and used by people who knew nothing about engineering.

Post-Industrial Design = Complexity Design

Humanizing technology, shielding ordinary people from the inhumane impacts of machines, creating and expanding markets for well-designed products—this was what industrial designers were supposed to do. But the profession was not rising to the challenges of the information age as it had risen to the social and business needs of the machine age. There were certainly specific individuals with vision in this regard, but in the final decades of the twentieth century, industrial design (ID) as a whole had abdicated its leadership in the development of usable, safe, pleasant, attractive, and otherwise marketable high technology products.

The vacuum created by this abdication of responsibility by the ID profession was certainly recognized at the time. In an effort to fill it, a new discipline came into existence, calling itself Human Computer Interaction (HCI). Unfortunately, with only a few important exceptions, its early practitioners were trained either as engineers or as academic psychologists—both highly relevant disciplines, but ones that almost entirely lacked access to the 50 years of accumulated methodological wisdom in human-centered design that formed the foundations of the profession of ID. As a result, the HCI community was attempting to reinvent Design out of whole cloth.

No one involved in high-tech product design was addressing or even talking about the central issue raised by the proliferation of computing and electronically transmitted information: the collision course of ordinary people and complexity.

It is significant that the icon of that moment in American technological history was not a computer per se, but an *inexpensive computerized device* that could be found in almost every home—the VCR flashing "12:00" in red LED numerals all day. This ubiquitous machine had become so commoditized that you could buy one for less than $100, yet it was so complex to operate that most owners could not figure out how to set its clock.[3] The few who managed it probably went on to learn how to program the machine to record a TV show unattended—one of the primary reasons for owning the device (and something you couldn't do if you couldn't set the clock). But in the end their VCRs flashed "12:00" too, because the stupid things lost their hard-won settings with every power outage, and it just wasn't worth the effort to constantly re-figure-out how to fix them.

It did not take a genius to see that the day would come when every home in the United States would contain 10, 15, 20 such devices, each of them a source not of pleasure and satisfaction but of frustration and anger, even fear (Figure 5.9). And then there was the personal computer. PCs were young adolescents at that point, still a special, expensive purchase, hardly found in every household. That would take another decade or so. But it was pretty clear that we were soon going to have a mess on our hands.

A world full of microelectronics was going to need design redemption in the worst way, but it wouldn't come from any community of designers already in existence. Once again, a new profession would have to tame the beast of a new era. If Industrial Design humanized the Industrial Revolution, it stood to reason that the Information Revolution needed Information Design. In the end we chose the even more encompassing term *complexity design*, but information design is a big part of what you do to achieve complexity design.

The need to humanize information technology wasn't apparent to most people back then, and a passing glance at

Figure 5.9 *April 29, 1991: Usability awareness makes the cover of* BusinessWeek

---

[3] In fairness to those owners, it is probably less accurate to say that they couldn't figure it out than that they found it just too ridiculously complicated to be worth the trouble.

computer culture today will confirm that for the most part it still isn't. Like fish that can't see the water that surrounds them, we aren't fully conscious of the milieu we live in. Computing today (by some measures, but not others) is the best it's ever been, so we have nothing to compare it to. Nothing high-tech, that is. We certainly do have something *non-high-tech* to compare computing to—namely, the long stretch of human life before computing.

But many technologists treat all of that as if it were now somehow completely irrelevant. Their implicit assumption is that people—after eons of adaptation to the physical world—should now completely change their behavior to accommodate machines that are based upon developments five or ten years old. If users want to benefit from the brave new world of cyberspace, they are expected to pull up stakes, sign onto a wagon train to the life digital, and wave goodbye to their old lives. The designers of the new world force technical complexities upon users, burdening them with the intricacies of whatever arbitrary designs pop into their heads and forcing them to suppress their natural gifts for functioning in the real world—the accumulated endowment of a million years of evolution.

Becoming "Human Literate"

When Nintendo designed the controller of its Wii game machine to be swung through the air like a golf club or a tennis racket, they may have been leaving hard-core gamers behind, but they were embracing real human beings. We can't overstate the importance of that lesson.

Like anything else immature, high technology tends to be amazed by itself and to want to call constant attention to its own wondrous powers. The powers *are* wondrous, but they are also supremely ugly—ugly because they continue to demand that human beings become computer literate when, by all that is right and just, computers should be becoming human literate.

What is technically possible is virtually always attempted sooner rather than later. Thus the early tangible result of new technologies is inevitably chaotic, unplanned, and often counterproductive—almost by definition not-by-design. Such times of revolution must equally inevitably be followed by more deliberate, more evolutionary periods during which the technologies are tamed, the possibilities are explored and sorted out, and mastery is sought and attained. It is during such periods that design assumes center stage.

Taming complexity will always increase the size of markets for the simple reason that frustratingly complicated products are just not salable to a significant segment of the population. For every early adopter who prizes the aura of the Next Big Thing and revels in mastering a challenging new interface or platform, a hundred ordinary people[4] will give wide berth to digital products if perceived complexity even slightly exceeds perceived value.

---

[4]Let us be clear here: The segment of the population in question does not comprise the "dumb" ones—people too slow to cope with innovation. Quite the opposite, these are the people smart enough not to waste their precious time with tasks that insult their intelligence.

The Interdisciplinary Dimension

There may still be people in the world who can claim the title of Renaissance Person, but there are certainly not enough of them to save us from the deluge

Consumer Feature Overload

One of MAYA's earliest commercial design projects involved the development of a coordinated family of on-screen displays for the products of a well-known Pacific Rim manufacturer of televisions and VCRs. On our first trip to the client's Asian headquarters, it was explained to us that while televisions routinely sustained healthy double-digit profit margins, VCRs were barely profitable. "What's the difference?" we asked. The answer was telling. Our client patiently explained that it is easy to "upsell" televisions, since they are differentiated along a number of dimensions that consumers value, such as screen size, premium sound, and so on. The market, on the other hand, views VCRs as utter commodities—the only important differentiator is price. "But VCRs have many different features," we naively observed. "Yes," explained our hosts, "but our customers don't care. They tell us that they are uninterested in paying for new features until they figure out how to use the ones they already have."

of the coming revolution. The necessary disciplines have become far too numerous and demanding for us to expect even exceptionally talented individuals to attain adequate mastery in more than a few. Rather, design today must be seen as fundamentally and essentially a collaborative enterprise.

None of this will come as a surprise to anyone—engineer, designer, or business leader—who has ever seriously attempted to create a powerful product or service with ease of use as a primary goal. Our understanding of the process has increased dramatically in recent years, yet there are few great success stories of brilliant usability design in the computer industry. This helps to explain why the few that exist—Apple products being the obvious recent example—make worldwide headlines, and drive new forms of value.

By now, the notion of interdisciplinary design has become commonplace. *Interdisciplinary* and *innovation* are often heard in the same sentence. But sadly these ideals are more often than not honored in the form of faddish, cookbook exercises or, worse, as bureaucratic hoops to be avoided when possible and jumped through otherwise. Sometimes a group of engineers—mechanical, structural, civil—is called interdisciplinary. Perhaps that's strictly true, but functionally it's not much of a stretch. Sometimes the group's work is passed sequentially from one specialist to the next—procedurally, that's not very *inter*. So, after the first blush of enthusiasm, we hear such groups expressing something less than excitement for their interdisciplinary experiment. Not surprisingly, real interdisciplinary practice is hard, and the reason is simple: The specialization of professional fields, while essential to their mastery, militates against such an overarching vision of design.

Why Interdisciplinary Collaboration Is Hard
By Pete

Interdisciplinary design doesn't just happen to be hard. It is hard *by definition*. After all, what, exactly, *is* a discipline? What it amounts to is some particular definition of what is important. So, if you are a disciplinary expert, somebody has sent you to school for years and years with the express purpose of beating into your head some particular definition of what's important. This, in turn, means that if you bring together members of different disciplines and assign them to the same project, you by definition are going to find yourself with disagreements about what is important. This, of course, is exactly what you were trying to accomplish, but it is rarely pretty.

We wish that we could report that we at MAYA have found some miraculous methodological trick for getting around this, but sadly, we have not. All of our project teams without exception have representatives from all relevant disciplines, and these designers are expected to represent their various disciplinary perspectives with vigor and force. As a consequence, design sessions at our offices are often—shall we say—lively. After almost a quarter-century of trying, the best we have been able to do by way of mitigating this liveliness is this: We hire designers who are not only experts in their chosen fields, but who value doing great work more than they value winning arguments. We never do quite come to understand why our cross-disciplinary colleagues insist on obsessing on the things they do, but we have seen the positive results of their obsessions often enough that we are able to suspend disbelief so as to ensure that each disciplinary perspective gets its due.

Draw What You Mean

A truly interdisciplinary approach to a problem will not be the most apparently "efficient" one. Further, few businesses possess the means to build, nurture, and support interdisciplinary teaming. However, one of the most effective methods is almost too simple to be taken seriously—draw what you mean. If you are, say, an interaction designer and you ask, say, an engineer to draw, rather than tell you, what is in his head, you can decode the jargon almost instantly. Drawing can serve as the lingua franca of thinking. You can immediately map what the engineer has drawn into your own worldview, you can see how the engineering discipline structures the problem or solution, you can note what isn't drawn, you can treat the

Figure 5.10 *An interdisciplinary session in action*

drawing as a communications medium by adding your own parts to the picture, and most importantly, you can identify critical gaps in your collaborator's thinking that your discipline can fill in. We often wonder if a simple metric based on the number of square feet of drawing surface (in the form of papers pinned to walls, whiteboards, etc.) in use *between* disciplines within an organization would be a reliable indicator of true interdisciplinary teaming, collaboration, and innovation. Effective teams share images. If a day goes by where you don't hear "draw what you mean" at least a few times within and between teams, it's likely that deeper sharing and integration is not happening either. Our prediction is that on Trillions Mountain everyone involved in building new experiences, new services, new connected things, and new business models (not just designers but business leaders and even customers) will draw as a basic literacy of collaboration (Figure 5.10).

Only one of the original founders of MAYA, Joe, has a traditional design background. Pete is a cognitive psychologist who would not be thought of as a designer by most people. Jim Morris, the third founding partner of MAYA Design, is a computer scientist who played a role in the birth of the modern PC at Xerox PARC; he typically wouldn't be considered a designer either. But by insisting upon a fusion of traditional design, the human sciences, and engineering, we have been consistently able to practice design in a rigorously interconnected manner.

When we started MAYA in 1989—one computer scientist, one cognitive psychologist, and one industrial designer, and with yet other disciplines entering the mix—we set aside time to explicitly break the disciplinary

VISUAL DESIGN
Form & Function

ENGINEERING
How Things Work

HUMAN SCIENCES
How People Think & Behave

Superior User Experiences

barriers. We tried explaining design concepts in each other's languages. We summarized for each other the classic works of our individual fields. We shared each other's reading lists. In short, we committed time and money to making interdisciplinary collaboration work. And over the decades of MAYA's existence, we have developed other practices and traditions that continue to contribute to the richness of our process.

The Value of Real Estate

One example of our cultural practice in this regard is something called MAYA Neighborhoods. Our workplaces are arranged, not by disciplines—an engineering section, a marketing section, or a visual design section—but rather in interdisciplinary groups of six to eight people. These neighborhoods do not represent fixed teams that necessarily work together on the same project. A given client project will most often draw from a number of neighborhoods. But avoiding clumping neighbors by discipline has both symbolic and practical impact. In addition to being a constant reminder of what we value, maintaining intimate physical proximity among disciplines leads to uncounted serendipitous synergies as eavesdropping neighbors chime in with unexpected contributions of data and ideas. By recognizing the high price we pay for such real estate, and the high cognitive and perceptual value we can receive by sharing it across disciplines, we increase the bandwidth, the agility, and speed of collaboration (Figure 5.11).

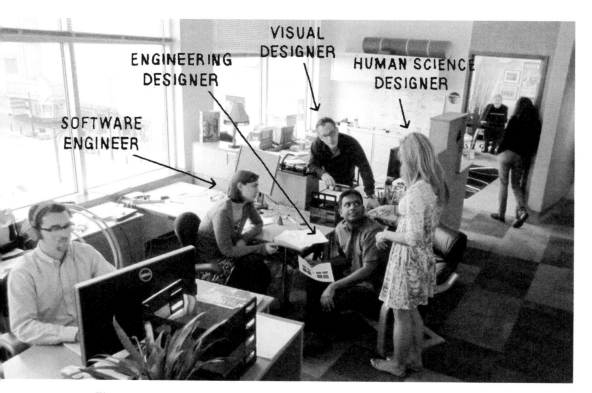

Figure 5.11 An impromptu meeting in one of MAYA's neighborhoods

People, Things, and Information
By Joe

Though I, like all of us, live and work in a technologically intensive world, there is something about my early life[5] and interests that attracted me to a more "craft" view of design. I don't mean craft as a focus on the *things* of craft such as pottery or jewelry, but on the *ways* of craft, the essential nature of "making" and the intense concentration on the properties of materials, the integrity of joints between parts, and the subtle trace of the process by which a designed thing comes into being. And the big payoff is that things that are designed and made in this craft-conscious way provide immense satisfaction, both for the maker and, more important to this discussion, to the people who own, use, and live with the designed thing.

When we began the company, I expected that the things we designed, the projects we worked on, would be about equal parts material objects and immaterial information. Though materiality has always played a part in our work, it soon became clear that the hard problems, the interesting problems, the added value we were positioned to give were all dominantly immaterial or at the intersection between the physical and digital world. In spite of the clear understanding that craft wasn't just about stuff, I experienced a dissonance between design as I had known it and design as it was coming to be. The guiding notions of craft, while not overtly threatened, were certainly under question—by myself if by no one else. Even though those notions felt comfortable and natural to me, I began to be bothered by them. "Am I becoming a closet Luddite," I wondered, "just an old fart"?

I've come to understand that something entirely different, something unexpected is happening. As the objects of design become increasingly dematerialized and share richer connections between people and information—as we find ourselves designing software objects, or processes, or experiences—we find ourselves discovering higher principles and find that, in part, they are derivatives of principles we learned and internalized as designers in the traditional material world.

The basic human urge to design, to shape one's environment in a way that favors desirable outcomes, is certainly as old as humanity itself. But unlike the other traditional liberal arts and sciences, design was not quick to be singled out as a field of study, or what we would today call a discipline. The earliest conscious attention to design occurred in the context of building, or of making or crafting things.[6] But even there it is subsumed

(Continued)

---

[5] I was born before electronic television was first demonstrated at the New York World's Fair and, while we did have telephones and airplanes, the first telephone I used was one where you picked up the receiver and waited for the operator to say, "Number, please," and I remember the day during World War II when my Uncle Frank showed me the first picture I ever saw of an airplane without a propeller! He said it was called a "jet."

[6] The earliest reference to a specific designer that I've found is in the Bible, Exodus 31: 1–5. After God has given Moses the specifications for the tabernacle in the wilderness, He says "I have called Bezalel ... and I have filled him with divine spirit, with ability, intelligence and knowledge in every kind of craft, to devise artistic 'DESIGNS'..." in order to make all that He had commanded."

under a focus on the thing being built: a mason's structural guidelines for a *building*, a potter's proportions for a storage *vessel*. During the European renaissance we begin to see the emergence of artists, like Leonardo da Vinci, or builders, like Filippo Brunelleschi, who gained fame for their ability to generalize and apply design principles across a broad spectrum of the built environment. Then eventually in the early twentieth century we see experiments in formalizing and explicitly teaching design—its principles and application—as a professional discipline.

The downside of this coalescing of a discipline with abstract principles was a very gradual retreat from the intimate association with making concrete objects. Soon there was a fascination with design theory and design methodology, which, though it tried to stand on its own, got pretty wobbly in the knees when the act of making was sidelined. Furthermore, as we began designing dematerialized objects we inevitably trod on the turf of other arts and sciences. For example, in designing a user experience, we draw methods and principles from the long-established practices of religion, the theater, tourism, business organization, and even politics.

We are finally seeing a turn to the aspects of design that we hold dear: In essence, they are *interdisciplinary experiments in making*. It isn't what you could call a movement yet, but the most advanced schools of design and the most successful technology firms are re-immersing themselves in the challenging but satisfying discipline of making, and using this experience as the glue that bonds the interests of people from across a variety of disciplines. I attribute

this to the leap in scope and interconnectedness that is being recognized in contemporary design problems combined with the radically lowered costs of prototyping complex products—and not just the form, but prototyping those actions, behaviors, and component relationships that represent the joint efforts of several disciplines. Achieving a fleet of fuel-efficient cars requires not only new automotive design, but also a new fuel supply infrastructure, new legislation, and, as we're experiencing presently, a reorganization of the businesses needed to realize our desires.

Making Things Out of Atoms and Bits

As the circumstances we design for and the materials we design with become increasingly blended between the physical and the metaphysical, between space and cyberspace, it at first seems inevitable that an environment of making will become harder to achieve and less important to achieve. Well, perhaps it will be harder—our cognitive wiring may be less well-suited for modeling formless information than it is for making physical models of material objects—but it is definitely not less important. The virtues and flaws of a material object—a new item of furniture, a new communication device—are at least partly understandable through direct manipulation (does my back feel well supported, do my fingers find the enter key?). But immaterial objects usually don't give us immediate feedback through sensations such as the fear of falling or the threat of pain. Instead, the immaterial design reveals its virtues and vices through the experience of use or through exposure over time. Only then do we come to realize our sense of confusion, our vulnerability, or our loss of privacy. So we have rediscovered making; we have made iterative prototyping, and testing those prototypes, and simulating the intersection of people and information, into an essential part of our design process for the trillion-node network.

It is essential that prototyping not be put off until the conceptual design is complete. Fortunately it is possible to partially isolate some aspects of a design solution—the appearance of a graphical user interface from its behavior, for example, or the development of back-end capabilities. We call this method *parallel prototyping*, and it works marvelously well as long as the designer remembers two things: that parallel prototyping is iterative with incremental gains in knowledge and understanding, and that, eventually, parallel prototypes have to give way to a holistic prototype of the entire designed experience (Figure 5.12).

Does It Fit?

We have acknowledged for a long time that the forms that objects take are a mirror to the culture—beliefs, values, technologies, and enterprises—that

created them. Were that not true, the reconstruction of history through the analysis and understanding of artifacts would be impossible. One indicator of good design is a sense of wholeness or integrity in the experience. That sense comes with the realization that, in many ways, the whole experience "fits." It fits with the values of the individuals who own it and use it. It fits with the collective goals of the culture in which it was made. It adheres to contemporary notions of beauty. It makes good use of the technology of its time. And, most importantly, it fits with itself; its various parts or aspects are mutually informative; the whole has integrity.

We have to re-learn this concept and apply it anew to the things we design in the age of pervasive computing.

For many years Bob Lepper was a fixture of the industrial design program at Carnegie Mellon University—and Carnegie Tech before that. In my many years there I never actually took a course from Bob, but everyone there learned from him indirectly. In the 1960s and 1970s, when industrial design was working out its present position vis-à-vis other creative, constructive disciplines, there was a lot of talk—if not thought—given to defining industrial design, or design generally. "What *is* industrial design?"

Figure 5.12 Stages in the design process from sketched prototypes to a production prototype

(Continued)

Many of the definitions grew into convoluted, intractable pseudo-philosophies. In the midst of these circular discussions, one of my colleagues passed along Bob Lepper's refreshingly simple way of thinking about it: "If it's about the relationships of things to things, it's engineering; if it's about the relationships of people to people, it's the social sciences; but if it's about the relationships between people and things, it's design."

So when we get into the new area of designing for the trillion-node network, problems look new in some ways—mostly in ways having to do with scale or connectedness. But in other ways it's the same old problems and questions: Does the form of the solution grow naturally out of the materials and processes of the solution? Is the design sustainable, and are valuable resources preserved? And mainly, are people better with or happier having the design at their disposal than they were without it?

Reflecting on the way we built MAYA, there was an essential understanding of who we are and what we do, and that each contributes out of his or her own particular expertise. We draw a three-ring Venn diagram to denote our intersecting disciplines and often look for people to hire that are at the edges rather than the centers of those rings. It is a realization of our corporate concern for the wants and needs of people. Those wants and needs are multifaceted and subtle. The engineering tribe, the human (social and cognitive) sciences tribe, and the visual (product, graphic, film, brick-and-mortar architecture) design tribe all sit together, work together, depend on each other, and rub each other's corners off, and sharpen our collective wisdom.

Violent Agreement and the Opposable Mind

I've often been asked, "How do you create a culture that is *actually* conducive to innovation?" While that topic deserves a book in its own right, there is one aspect that I believe deserves particular attention at the dawn of the pervasive computing era. You have to begin by recognizing that different views of reality can be simultaneously valid and must be allowed to jostle each other and intersect. This is not something that happens once a year at a corporate retreat. That doesn't create a culture. It's something that needs to happen every day, backed up by the unyielding resolve to believe in the process and stick to it.

F. Scott Fitzgerald said, "The test of a first-rate intelligence is the ability to hold two opposed ideas in the mind at the same time, and still retain the ability to function." Roger Martin, dean of the Rotman School of Business, has noted the same quality in great leaders. He called this sort of ability the Opposable Mind and noted that just as humans evolved to have an ability to grasp things more dynamically with opposable thumbs, some people have evolved the ability to grasp new ideas with opposable minds.

When it comes to collaboration, it would be hard to do better than *Star Trek's* Vulcan method of sharing thoughts. So you might think of this theory applied to teams as the Opposable Mind-Meld. Having a team prosper under this sort of relentless pressure is hard, and it never gets easier. Practitioners often gravitate toward a given field of study in the first place because they have a very specific cognitive style and perspective. You can imagine—and may have even experienced—an example of a time in which two strong-willed innovators are at each other's throats. They encode and process and present information differently. But what you discover when you work at this form of collaboration is that those supposedly great differences are actually superficial. If the group acknowledges that interdisciplinary collaboration is just going to be hard, they almost always find their way to a deep, fundamental agreement that has been masked by different languages and descriptions. Once they get past that, their underlying concepts are compatible and often mutually enhancing. They find they can combine their ideas to make a deeper, rounder, and more enduring worldview. It's a phenomenon we've seen time and again, but it demands an investment. Interdisciplinary teams will argue about something for hours, days, or even weeks, and then suddenly one of the team members will say, "*That's* what you meant? Of *course* I agree with that!" We think of this as "having a violent agreement." Analogues

to such moments are also found in the actions of great leaders, whose actions usually lead, not to the dismissal of one view or another but the discovery of a third way.

The most important (and perhaps least obvious) benefit of this cathartic process is that those seemingly impossible meetings of the minds very often produce unique and unexpected value for customers.

When smart people from different disciplines hang around with each other, share ideas, teach each other, and solve problems together, it exercises collaborative muscles and creates a professional context that you learn, over time, to trust—because it works. A rigorously interdisciplinary setting gives people the potential to detect valuable patterns that more vertically oriented teams might not see. One reason is simply that they experience and learn to appreciate many points of view and are thereby exposed to many more samples of reality. This form of pattern recognition will become increasingly important as the amount of noise in the world increases exponentially.

The Future Is Already Here

William Gibson—our cyberspace prognosticator from Chapter 2—once quipped, "The future is already here, it's just unevenly distributed." No one understood this better than Raymond Loewy. He loved to tell the story of redesigning the Sears Roebuck Coldspot refrigerator.

For this assignment, he ended up using a new material for the shelving—sheets of perforated aluminum—that he had discovered in a previous project involving the design of an automotive grille. It would never have occurred to anyone inside the refrigerator industry to use that particular material for shelves. No one in refrigeration was aware it existed. But it had precisely the right combination of light weight, durability, good looks, and resistance to corrosion and rust. The perforated aluminum shelves became a marketplace differentiator and a selling point for the new Coldspot design. The product sold nearly five times as many units as its predecessor.

Nothing could have made Loewy happier. He was famous for insisting that his work be not only elegant and innovative, but also attractive to consumers and commercially viable. The purveyors of locomotives, automobiles, refrigerators, and vacuum cleaners needed him, but he needed them too, and he worked for them with affection and respect. Some of his more theoretical (and briefly more famous) counterparts eventually went out of business by conceiving futuristic designs that couldn't be built, but Loewy's firm prospered for many decades thanks to his insistence upon measuring his own success by the success of his clients in the marketplace. If a Loewy design failed to inspire consumers to buy, he had failed. In many particulars, the design industry has left Loewy behind, but in terms of basic goals and motivations, the underlying patterns remain. The designers who will really matter in the age of Trillions are the ones who figure out how to apply Loewy's commercial sensibilities in the context of a thoroughly decentralized world—a world in which commercial transactions will be absurdly numerous and yet seemingly just out of reach.

Yesterday, Today, Tomorrow: Data Storage

Like the foundations of a building, data storage technologies have little glamour. Yet, they are the base upon which the edifice of modern computing is built. One of the major theses of this book is that many otherwise obvious innovations have been rendered impossible due to inadequate data storage architectures. It is worth a closer look at the evolution of these architectures.

YESTERDAY

We have long since come to think of computers as containers for information, so it is a bit surprising to note that an entire generation of commercially viable computers operated with essentially no persistent storage at all. Typical of this era was the IBM 1401 (see Figure I2.1). Introduced in 1959, and sold through the early 1970s, this extremely successful low-end machine brought electronic data processing within

Figure I2.1 *IBM 1401 computer circa 1961*

Source: Ballistic Research Laboratories, Aberdeen Proving Ground, Maryland

reach of thousands of small businesses. And yet, it had no disk drive or other digital storage of any kind. Each power cycle was essentially a "factory reset."

How was such a device useful? The key was a complete reliance on external storage, typically punched cards. Bootstrapping the 1401 involved placing a deck of cards into a bin and pressing a button labeled LOAD. Each of the 80 columns of punches on each card was interpreted as a character of data and copied into main memory and then executed. What happened then was completely dependent on the particular deck of cards that one had chosen. Thus, for example, a programmer might type (on a "keypunch machine") a program in the Fortran programming language and stack it behind a pre-punched deck containing the Fortran compiler. Finally, additional cards containing the data to be processed would be appended to the end of the deck, which would then be fed into the card reader. When the user hit LOAD, the cards would be read and, if all went well, a few seconds later the massive, noisy 1403 line printer would cheerfully spew out the desired results. Then, the user would step aside, and the next programmer in line would repeat the operation with his or her own deck.[1]

Even larger machines that *did* have mass-storage tended to use it only for supervisory purposes, and this general pattern of external storage for user data persisted well into the time-sharing era. A well-equipped college campus of the 1970s, for example, had "satellite" computing stations consisting of a row or two of keypunch machines, a card reader, and a line printer, connected to the campus mainframe via telephone wires. Except for the fact that the Fortran compiler was probably stored centrally rather than in cards, the user experience at these self-service stations was practically unchanged from that of the 1401 days.

---

[1] In MAYA's offices, we maintain a little museum dedicated to the history of technology, design, and culture. Among its holdings is a card deck that, if fed into a 1401, will churn out a staccato rendition of "Anchors Aweigh" on the line printer. Assuming that there are no remaining operational 1401s in the world, it is an interesting philosophical question whether that deck still counts as a representation of "Anchors Aweigh."

During the 1970s and 1980s, this usage pattern was slowly supplanted by timesharing systems, in which the satellite card readers/printers were replaced by "robot typewriters" (and later, CRT terminals) with which users "talked" to the mainframe using arcane "command line" languages. Since such devices had no card readers, this mode of interaction required the development of "file systems:" conventions for persistently storing and editing what amounted to images of card decks on remote disk drives. This card image model of storage was, at first, taken quite literally, with editors limiting each line of text to the same 80 columns of data found on punch cards.[2] Often, the storage of binary (i.e., non-human-readable) data was difficult or impossible.

Dealing with this deficiency was key to the development of early online interactive systems, most notably the SABRE airline reservation system. Such systems were barely feasible given the hardware of the era, and so required a great deal of exotic optimization. As a result, their storage systems tended to be different animals from the largely textual file systems familiar to timesharing users. Such efforts took a big step forward with the development of what came to be known as the Relational Model—the first mathematically rigorous approach to data storage. Relational databases promised (and eventually delivered) a dramatic increase in storage efficiency, one that was badly needed given the impoverished hardware of the day.

Such efficiency, however, was purchased at a great cost: The "relations" after which the approach was named are in fact large tables of identically formatted data items. This works very well when we are dealing with "records" of many identical transactions (such as airline ticket sales) whose structures are fully specified in advance and rarely change, and that are under the control of a single agency. It is not so good if the structure of the data changes frequently or if we want to routinely pass around individual records from machine to machine and from user to user as one might in a pervasive computing environment. But such requirements were not even on the radar, so all was well.

As mainframes gave way to minicomputers and then to personal computers, the relationship between users and their data evolved as well. Instead of files being a remote abstraction kept on the user's behalf on some remote machine, they became more tangible and local—more like personal property. One kept them first on floppy disks, and then on hard drives backed up by floppy disks. This is how we came to think of data as being *in* the PC. Gradually, "computing" started to seem incidental. Essentially, PCs came to be seen as containers for data: a place to keep my stuff (where "stuff" first meant words, but quickly evolved to include pictures, games, music, and movies). This is where things stood at the dawn of the consumer Internet.

---

[2] Indeed, the aforementioned "glass teletype" CRT terminals almost universally were designed to display 24 lines of 80 characters each. Old habits die hard.

TODAY

Given the above trajectory, one might have expected that adding the Internet to the mix would have had a predictable result: Users' stuff would begin to flow from machine to machine in the form of files. Services would emerge permitting users to find things on each other's disks. File systems would become distributed (i.e., they would span many machines). The boundaries among machines would start to blur. Cyberspace would come into focus.

In the event, of course, nothing of the sort happened. Despite a number of large-scale efforts in that direction—most notably CMU's Andrew Project (headed by MAYA co-founder Jim Morris)—no such public information space has emerged. It has long since become technically easy to move files from machine to machine (e.g., via e-mail attachments), but such transactions, while not uncommon, are peripheral to the workings of the Net, not central to it.

There are a number of reasons for this, but perhaps the most basic one has to do with the management of the identity of information. Strange to say, neither file systems nor database architectures have seriously grappled with this fundamental issue. In the system we have built, our ability to keep different pieces of information straight is *dependent* on the walls provided by machine boundaries. If we took down those walls, we would have chaos. To see why this is true, imagine if even two computers in your office had their disks merged. Even ignoring privacy and security issues, the experiment would likely produce disaster. Surely there would be instances where the same names were used for different files and folders. What if older and newer versions of the "same" file found themselves on the same disk? Worse, what if versions had diverged? Which one should prevail? And the situation would be no better if we attempted to merge "records" from relational databases. The identity of each row (its so-called primary key) is only unique within a given table. Unless we move the entire table (which is likely to be immense) and then carefully keep it separate from other such tables, chaos will ensue.

It is not that these problems are overly difficult. It is just that they are unaddressed. The industry has found it more convenient to keep the walls and instead to encourage users to stop thinking of their computers as data containers and to return to what amounts to the timesharing model of data storage—cunningly renamed The Cloud. And this has happened at a time in which the cost of local disk storage has become almost ludicrously cheap.

TOMORROW

However much the industry may prefer centralized data storage, such models make little long-term sense and certainly will wane. Nonetheless, the move to network-based storage will likely be successful at driving the last nails into the coffin of the file system as a storage model. What will happen instead, while clear, is a bit difficult to describe.

We are about to witness the emergence of a *single* public information space. This space does not yet have a name. As we mentioned in Chapter 3, we at MAYA call it GRIS, for "Grand Repository In the Sky." In articulating what GRIS *is*, it is helpful to first list some things that it *isn't*. It isn't a network of public computers. In this vision, the computers remain in private hands. It isn't the Internet. The Internet is "public" in the same sense that GRIS is, but the Internet is a public *communications utility*. It is made of wires, fiber optic cables, and switches. GRIS is made entirely of data. It isn't a collection of "free" (in the sense of "without cost") data. Much of it will be without cost and available to all—just like the web. But, also like the web, much information will be private and/or available only at a price. Finally, it isn't a huge database or data storage service that gathers together all the world's information.

Rather, GRIS is a massively replicated, distributed ocean of information objects, brought into existence by shared agreement on a few simple (very simple) conventions for identifying, storing, and sharing small "boxes" of data, and by a consensual, peer-to-peer scheme by which users—institutional and individual—agree to store and share whichever subset of these boxes they find useful—as well as others that just happen to come their way. Popular "boxes" will tend to be replicated in especially large numbers and thus be readily available almost instantly when needed. Obscure and little-used items, in contrast, might take some time and effort to track down. But, as long as there is any interest at all—even if only by archivists or hobbyists—the chances of any given bit of information being lost forever can be arranged to be arbitrarily small.

Once this system is in place, the idea of putting data in particular devices (be they removable media, disk drives, or distant pseudo-"cloud" server farms) will rapidly begin to fade. Taking its place will be something new in the world: definite "things" without definite locations. Because of this newness, we don't yet quite know how to talk about such things. These things will be quite real and distinct, but they will not depend on spatial locality for this distinctness. Asking where they "are" will be like asking where *Moby-Dick* is. They will be everywhere and nowhere—existing all around us in something that properly deserves the metaphor of cloud. "Tangible" isn't quite the right word to describe them, yet we will rapidly come to take for granted the ability to pull them out of GRIS on-demand, using any computing device that may be handy to give them tangible form and human meaning.

Most importantly, all of this will come without the need to cede control of our data (and thus our privacy) to any central authority, either corporate or governmental. We will no longer have to trade control of our own information in order to benefit from the magic of the Net. We will, finally, have a true Information Commons, part of the human commonweal and free to all. The stage will be fully set for the emergence of a true cyberspace. The real Internet revolution will have begun.

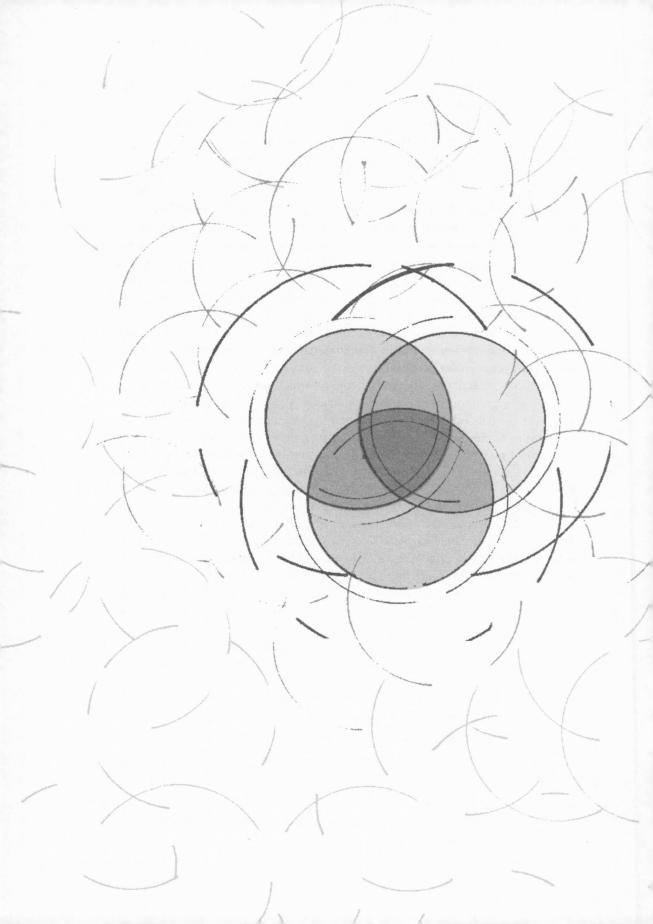

CHAPTER 6

Design Science on Trillions Mountain

We are as gods, we might as well get good at it.

—WHOLE EARTH CATALOG

If we are going to play god by creating an ecology of trillions of information devices, the first requirement is not hubris, but humility. Ecosystems are big complex things, and the ones we're familiar with have had millions of years in which to achieve the refinement that we see today. It is vitally important that we take our first steps into pervasive computing carefully and correctly because the processes we set in motion now will have huge implications later. The stakes are high. If pervasive computing arrives without adequate principles in place to guide it, it will quickly result in incoherent, unmanageable, malignant complexity, which is another way of saying "not much will actually happen that is good and some very bad things may happen as well." Among other important things, the viability of vast new markets is at stake. If, on the other hand, its development is guided by principled design science, technology and information will coalesce into a coherent, evolutionary, organic whole—a working information model of and for the world.

The foundations of this design science are largely in place. They come from a merging of the study of ecological patterns in Nature; from the long and evolved practices of the design professions; from the traditional sciences; and from a commitment to the search for underlying Architecture to provide structure. Yet the evolution of the discipline is not complete.

BEYOND DESIGN THINKING TO DESIGN SCIENCE

Design thinking is an *au courant* term used by business schools and corporations as some sort of Next Big Thing. Like most Next Big Things, it will most likely become an old obvious thing as soon as the next Next Big Thing comes along. In its present form, the methods and practices of design thinking are a far cry from those of the rigorous and well-defined methodologies of lean manufacturing and process engineering to which it is sometimes compared. It is more like a good marketing campaign to raise awareness of what designers have been working toward for some time, with the added insight that design shouldn't just be left to professional designers.

Facing the levels of complexity and dynamism toward which we are headed, intuitive, seat-of-the-pants approaches to design will no longer do. A genuine design science—along the lines of what Buckminster Fuller had in mind—will need to be put into practice. Fuller called his approach Comprehensive Anticipatory Design Science. And in typical Fuller form, each word is important:

Comprehensive means making sure that we are looking at the whole problem. Stepping back and seeing how all the elements interact. Thinking about the entire system, rather than some local issue. Fuller teaches us that if you understand the whole and also some of the parts, you will be able to infer more of the parts.

Anticipatory is about thinking forward in time so that we not only try to solve today's problem, but also solve for what happens tomorrow and the day after—future-proofing the solution so that it can resiliently continue to work as the world evolves.

Design is, as Herb Simon once said, about "[devising] courses of action aimed at changing existing situations into preferred ones." In other words, it is the systematic attempt to affect the future.

Science is about rigor, process, and repeatability. It involves interrogating Nature to discover her reliable laws. It produces a set of predictions that are subject to disproof, and can be used as inputs to generative processes for creating novel solutions. Put your trust in principles deriving from public, repeatable experiments, not clever ideas, opinions, or other flavors of superstition.

The natural sciences—physics, biology, chemistry, and astronomy—deal with what is. Design science deals with what might be. Its domain is human artifice in all its forms, the artificial world rather than the natural world.

This kind of science involves a systematic process of inquiry and exposition about all things made by human hands, a process that embraces the full range of human modes of thought—rational, intuitive, emotional, methodical—just as in the natural sciences. It implies the belief that there are objective design principles out there waiting to be discovered—analogous to the laws of physics. For some people, the term *design science* may evoke the image of a process in which the cultural, humanistic, and aesthetic components are stripped out until there is nothing left but sterile mechanism, devoid of human life and passion. Such thinking is wrong for two reasons. First, measuring something does not kill it. In coming to understand the structure and function of plants, the botanist need not lose sight of the beauty of flowers or the wonder of their relationships with the rest of the living world. Quite the opposite—the deeper the understanding, the greater the wonder. Similarly, our ability to precisely describe the process of creating artifacts is a token of our deepening understanding and appreciation of those processes. Second, in every science our knowledge is imperfect and limited. This is true even in the most mature of physical sciences. It is most certainly true in design science. As we apply science to the process of building, we inevitably reach the limits of what we know to be correct—often sooner than we would hope. At this point, the intuitions of the experienced practitioner, the passions of the artist, and the simple joy of creative desire find ample room to play their part. Human needs and desires defy simple classification, and no matter how rationalized it is, design is always for and about people.

Design science rejects a purely relativist view of traditional design thinking. In design science we avoid notions such as "liking" a design for personal or superficially stylistic reasons. There will always be a variety of good designs—some better than others; bounded rationality and the sheer diversity of problem situations suffice to ensure that. But there are also wrong designs. It's not just a matter of preference. Nor is it to claim that only mechanical experiments or design methods are valid ways of arriving at the right design. Intuitive methods have a place in all areas of science. But it *is* to say that, given a proper statement of goals and a sufficiently broad and careful consideration of the entire situation—technical, human, and market—it is possible to establish principled, professional, systematic techniques that rationally select some designs over others.

Not all design choices are objective—even in principle. One should consider the design process as one of using up degrees of freedom. At every stage of the process, one makes choices that embrace certain options and close off others. When one decides to commit to a new project for building, say, a refrigerator, one closes off the option of having the project be about washing machines. Deciding that the refrigerator will be propane powered ensures that it will be suitable for certain markets (say, recreational vehicles) but not others, and so on. Each such decision reduces one's options. A design scientist will seek, at each step of the way to provide principled, scientific answers to these questions whenever possible. However, rarely if ever will scientific methods alone fill in all the details of the territory. There are almost always degrees of freedom remaining after all objective criteria have been satisfied. There is room to spend these final degrees of freedom on the pursuit of novelty, pure aesthetics, and other aspects of the design team's artistic and creative impulses. Science and rationality should always come first, but they rarely have the last word.

The Whole, Messy, Hairy Problem
By Joe

Design science, unlike the reductionist traditional sciences, is prepared to look holistically at complex and highly interconnected problems. Indeed, without this view it would be a very long road, strewn with errors and false starts, toward anything like an ecology of information devices.

Workscape, an early MAYA project for Digital Equipment Corporation, was a fresh reconsideration of the paperless office concept. In order to have any chance of plowing new ground, we knew we would have to base the problem definition and subsequent design recommendations on something more than personal or local assumptions about what real people would want and need to work productively and comfortably when paper documents were no longer a part of the business scene. It was not a question of duplicating, digitally, the bits of paper that flow through an office, but of understanding the multiple purposes that those bits played in the lives of those who worked with them—tokens of information, location, comfort, authority, personal security, and so on.

Our approach was a multipronged and simultaneous application of field research, user studies, and digital prototypes. We had come to realize that we needed to understand the long-term ecology of our system—the interactions and dependencies among the people, the places, the papers, and the information they held. So during the project we turned all of MAYA into a mock-paperless office. We printed uniquely bar-coded cover sheets with check boxes for various options. We provided "scan" outboxes for each desk. If you wanted a paper document to appear in cyberspace, you attached a cover sheet, checked some boxes, and a short time later it would appear on the digital "part" of your desk. This was done not by some sophisticated robotic document-scanning system, but by tasking certain team members to roam the offices every hour, on the hour, collecting and scanning any and all documents that an office worker might place in that magic scan bin. They were to *be* the bridge between the papered and digital worlds. It was a simple, accessible, affordable way to simulate and test something we couldn't build for real at that stage.[1] The goal was to understand the whole ecology of people, places, documents, and information, and to model it early, before degrees of freedom had been used up in designing individual pieces of the system.

I cannot prove it, but I am utterly convinced that we could not have built this system—certainly not in the time we built it—if we had started with any one requirement and proceeded linearly toward an indistinct dream on the horizon. Making—through iterative, frequent, parallel prototyping—is a design method that turns indistinct dreams into tangible goals in record time. As a result of this project, MAYA was granted 11 patents, all of which were assigned to our client and created something that researchers at Xerox PARC, Intel, and Microsoft all cited as the first example of a three-dimensional layout of documents under user control. Our work was foundational enough that when Apple was recently required to defend its "Cover Flow" and "Time Machine" capabilities against an intellectual property suit, they asked us to serve as expert witnesses—explaining our prior art to the court.

MAKE THE RIGHT THING

The Crystal Palace exhibition of 1851 exposed the human weakness for celebrating what can be done with technology, with little thought about what *should* be done. We need to remind ourselves that even though we may have some prowess in *making things right*, we need to put equal emphasis on *making the right things*.

What goals, processes, and guidelines will lead us to the *right things— made right*? At this point in the book, readers may already have formed some

---

[1] But our engineering staff *was* able to develop scanning software to identify each cover sheet, read its barcode, and direct the associated document to the correct user—quite an achievement in those primitive days.

answers of their own. If we've been convincing, those answers will have drawn on the history of designing, the pervasive effects of technological revolutions, the inevitable and exponential proliferation of digital devices, and personal experience with information products, for better and for worse. We've argued that whether the reader's self-definition is as a "scientist" or not, there is reason to believe that scientific thinking, as embodied in the concept of design science, is a viable way to manage complex problems and generate solutions—products, environments, messages, systems—that are conducive to a good society in a deeply technological era.

A thorough and detailed description of how to design on Trillions Mountain is beyond the scope of any one book. Indeed, some of the design problems are yet to be discovered. We can, however, describe some qualities of design in a connected world. These descriptions emphasize process over product, and the evolution of process over the repetition of process. Through consideration of the process, qualities of the *practice* can be discerned. Design on Trillions Mountain will incorporate:

- Deeply interdisciplinary methods
- Focusing on humans
- Interaction physics
- Information-centric interaction design
- Computation in Context

Deeply Interdisciplinary Methods

We have already discussed the necessity of building bridges between disciplines in order to solve complex problems that reach simultaneously into the social, technological, physiological, and ethical dimensions of human life.

We have also acknowledged the inherent difficulty of interdisciplinary practice—the way it misaligns with the specialization and the narrow focus of traditional professional training. Indeed, this misalignment is one that contrasts design science with respect to traditional science.

Action at the Interstices
By Pete

I like to visualize all human knowledge as a giant jigsaw puzzle, where each academic discipline is a puzzle piece.

In some sense, there is only one picture, and the cuts that we made to form the puzzle pieces are artificial and arbitrary.

The place where biophysics ends and biology begins, for example, is simply a matter of definition. Although they may be arbitrary, the puzzle pieces do matter. They matter a lot. Among other things, they determine whom we go to school with, what courses we take there, what professional societies we join, and what journals we read. Most importantly, they determine who tends to judge the merit of our ideas. How these harsh facts affect the behavior of practitioners depends critically upon how talented they are. Specifically, those of average talent tend to huddle toward the center of their particular disciplinary piece. That is where they will find safety in numbers among many others who share the assumptions and values that they have all been taught. But this is not how the superstars behave. Rather, they migrate toward the very edges of their disciplinary puzzle piece. Why? Because they know that by doing so they will encounter other bold thinkers like themselves, exploring the unknown territory at the edges of other disciplines. So, the interstices between disciplines are always where the action is. It is where the best practitioners go to invent the future.

Interdisciplinary practice on Trillions Mountain will have to be *deeply* interdisciplinary. It will not be enough to occasionally bring separate specialists together for an interdisciplinary interlude. Depth isn't achieved by sprinkling on interdisciplinary fairy dust. It requires a thorough transformation of professional practice. And it will continue to require this transformation until our education systems find a way to integrate the generalized with the specialized in the core curriculum.

We will see a broad spectrum of professionals working together—not three varieties of engineers, or just 2-D and 3-D designers. We are already seeing this trend in companies that propel innovation. Their staffs include, yes, different flavors of designers and engineers, but also psychologists, anthropologists, sociologists, and game developers. And we should expect to see historians, biologists, economists, filmmakers, and more. It might be better to imagine a professional environment that maintains contact with not only narrow disciplinary organizations, but also mash-up organizations dedicated to cross-linking.

The Nature of Engineers
By Jeff Senn

"It is a very nice interface, but it cannot be built." We've heard these words (or variations on them) many times from our clients or their engineering partners. It's not surprising. I'm sure they have often dealt with designers hired to jazz up a

(Continued)

product, who provide sketches that are like concept cars: shiny and desirable, but technically impossible or commercially crazy.

The relationship between product engineers and designers (especially consultant designers) has always been rocky. It is in the nature of engineers to say, "No, it can't be done," until it is perfectly obvious to them that it can be. Engineers are the gatekeepers of technical sanity; if they didn't have this attitude, they'd be at constant risk of being led down a garden path of crazy ideas.

At Digital Equipment Corporation they told us that one thing or another about Workscape "couldn't be done," and defending the feasibility of our designs was a constant chore. We knew it could be done: We had a prototype of more than a hundred thousand lines of code that implemented a whole new way to render graphics, was based on a brand-new database architecture, and had a multitasking scripting language built in. This is not to say that anyone should ever have shipped a product based on that prototype code. We did not build it to be maintainable; we built it to prove a point—and not just a visual point, but also an architectural point about the operation of all of the internals.

And by "we" I mean a team of engineers, psychologists, and visual designers arguing and fighting for what they believed in and coming to difficult compromises—and in the process learning to trust each other. But, at the end of the day it wasn't our passions or our debating skills or even the trust that won the day—it was those 100,000 lines of code. They worked, and users loved what

they did. We did our homework, and the results spoke for themselves.

I recall another occasion in the early 1990s, at the end of a presentation to a major Asian electronics manufacturer. We had completed an on-screen menu design for their new low-end TVs. The American marketing division (who had hired us) was thrilled. We had delivered exactly what they wanted: a user interface that would break open the U.S. market for their competitively priced televisions. The Asian engineering team stood up and said, "A very nice interface. But it cannot be built."

I knew it could. The inexpensive chip they had chosen for the on-screen display functions was new. They had chosen it for price (the TV business being extremely sensitive to margins), but they didn't fully understand everything that this new chip could do. But I had called one of the chip's designers to verify some of its less well-documented features. As a result, I knew quite a bit more about this chip than did our client's engineering team. And then I worked carefully with our team's visual designer and interaction designer to give them all the creative latitude that this new chip would support. In the end, we were able to defend each and every detail of our prototype, and it was implemented exactly as designed, down to the last pixel.

This dialectic is key. The magic is found in those difficult conversations that bridge the gaps among disciplines. Many of the innovations for that breakthrough product were performed by visual designers who played with fonts in a way that looked impossible if you only followed the engineering documentation.

Jeff Senn is the Chief Technology Officer of MAYA Design.

Focusing on Humans

If we are going to design for Trillions in a way that is human-literate, rather than forcing people to become ever more computer-literate, we need to keep the human at the center of the process. We need a vision of how we will come to understand not just people and their needs and desires, but also how they will be affected by the myriad devices that will become intimate parts of their everyday lives. While laboratory user studies are standard practice in the current paradigm, Trillions will force us out of the laboratory and into the field. As the information itself takes center stage and the devices that mediate the information recede into the woodwork (sometimes literally), the user experience ceases to be a direct consequence of the design of individual devices. Instead, it becomes an emergent property—a complex interaction that is difficult to measure and even more difficult to design. Studying one product in isolation, unconnected from its "social life," will no longer suffice.

To add to the challenge, the range of potential products that have become technically feasible is becoming nearly boundless. Instead of being limited by the properties of materials and the realities of manufacturing, we increasingly find ourselves in a position in which we have the technical means to produce pretty much anything we can imagine. And, in the words of Han Solo, we can imagine a lot. Sizing up the market to decide where to invest one's efforts and capital has always been a core challenge of business, even when the range of possibilities was severely bounded. Now that so many of the bounds have been lifted, the challenge is that much greater. Remember the stuff *in* the Crystal Palace?

Both of these new challenges—designing for an emergent user experience, and identifying promising opportunities in an increasingly unbounded and unstructured space of possibilities—are challenges that are not likely to be successfully met by seat-of-the-pants methods. Fortunately, the range of systematic methodologies available to design professionals has kept pace with the need.

The word *systematic* in the previous sentence may raise red flags with readers from a certain background. In many industries, there is a regrettable tradition of treating usability and market research issues as simple matters of process engineering, in the same category as ISO-9000 certification or stage-gate model management techniques. Treated in this way, usability issues tend to be viewed by engineering and marketing teams not as the essential processes that they are, but as just so many bureaucratic obstacles to be avoided on the way to the market. Worse, the mechanical application of cookbook processes to this class of problem (often in the form of so-called "voice of the customer" methodologies) tends to lead to what amounts to games of Twenty Questions between engineers and users. Such techniques may have had some efficacy in a simpler age, but given the complexities we now face, executing such methods effectively is generally prohibitively time consuming and expensive.

Not surprisingly, the free-thinking, agile world of the tech industries has not in general succumbed to this particular trap. Unfortunately, they have often erred in the opposite direction. The mantra in Silicon Valley has long been *ship early, ship often*. Agile manufacturing techniques, "extreme programming" methodologies, instant customer feedback via social networks, and free design advice from an army of bloggers conspire to make the temptation to use paying customers as beta testers nearly irresistible. This can be good, and it can be bad. If "ship early, ship often" is interpreted as the willingness to expose not-quite-feature-complete but well-tested products to the healthy pressures of real users, everybody wins. But if it is used as an excuse for shipping half-baked, flaky products; using your customers as unpaid quality-assurance staff—and counting on ever-lowering expectations of quality in a slipshod marketplace numbed by crashing TVs and bug-filled software—it is another matter entirely.

Even more dubious is the expectation that such run-it-up-the-flagpole techniques will lead to true innovation. We have already spoken about the conservative nature of the wisdom of crowds. For all its efficiencies, market forces always produce local hill climbing. They will very effectively determine the relative merits of BlackBerry versus Palm smartphones. But they will never lead us to the iPhone.

The Goldilocks Principle: Make Unbearable Products Just Right
By David Bishop

MAYA's Goldilocks Principle: Optimal product usability is achieved when the amount of complexity required for operation—neither too much nor too little—enhances rather than impedes the user's experience. I've seen products of all kinds, from software to sailboats, suffer from feature creep: the tendency of systems to have features added but never removed. Feature creep can get so bad that the overabundance of features, especially those that are rarely used, obstructs users as they try to perform routine tasks. How can the complexity of such products be tamed without reducing their utility? Antoine de Saint-Exupéry suggested this way: "A designer knows he has achieved perfection not when there is nothing left to add, but when there is nothing left to take away."

Excising features can sometimes help. It is not uncommon to pursue simplicity to the extreme, lopping off features to the point of impotence. But in mature products, complexity is often part of the value proposition, providing a high level of utility through the inclusion of many controls, adjustments, and functions. Consider the International 420 racing sailboat, with its many lines, blocks, and cleats necessary to control the shape of the sail. Now, for comparison, look at the sail configuration, called a transition rig, invented by Richard Dryden (Figure 6.1).

The transition rig has a designed-in variable geometry that adjusts to changing wind conditions. Of course, so does the rig of the 420, but it requires a lot of pulling on several control lines (a halyard, a vang, a cunningham, an outhaul, and a downhaul, at least) to achieve the same effect. Although sailing with the transition rig is a more straightforward experience, manufacturing it is not. It requires a rotating base and several joints constructed from carbon fiber and stainless steel.

What's happened here is that the complexity didn't disappear. It shifted. Larry Tesler's Law of Conservation of Complexity states, "You cannot reduce the complexity of a given task beyond a certain point. Once you've reached that point, you can only shift the burden around." With the transition rig, complexity has moved from the sailors using the product to the manufacturers making the product. In many cases, this is a desirable trade-off, especially for mature products, whether they are software interfaces, physical controls, or even web sites. As computers get more powerful, materials more advanced, and methods more sophisticated, it makes sense to move more of the complexity away from users. Shifting complexity puts the burden back on the product designers and developers, who have the difficult task of finding the just-right balance between complexity and usability. That's where a design partner with expertise in taming complexity provides value. By using testing and research to reveal what users are trying to accomplish, focusing on giving them control where needed, and designing the system to do the rest on their behalf, products can achieve their greatest effectiveness and power while more closely fulfilling the ideal to "do what I mean." Not too hot, not to cold, but just right.

David Bishop is a MAYA Fellow, Senior Practitioner, and Researcher at MAYA.

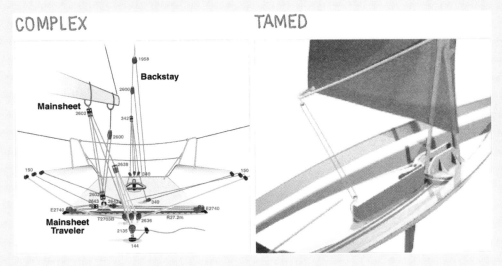

COMPLEX   TAMED

Figure 6.1 Shifting complexity: the International 420 and the Transition Rig

It is tempting to conclude that only someone like Steve Jobs will lead us to the iPhone, and there is no doubt that hiring this person is the most efficient path to that kind of innovation. Unfortunately, such people are a bit hard to find. The suite of participatory user-centered techniques that the design community has evolved in recent years is motivated precisely by the need to fill this gap.

All of science is based on cycles of HYPOTHESIS >> MODEL >> TEST >> NEW HYPOTHESIS, and design science is no exception. In designing on Trillions Mountain, the TEST part isn't the only place where user-focused work need apply. Instead, it must begin at the beginning of a design cycle and be carried through to the end, often bridging to the next, follow-on cycle.

During the HYPOTHESIS stage the designer has available a number of open-ended user-centered design techniques, going under such labels as *participatory design*, *cooperative design*, and *co-creation*.[2] These methods are the methodological descendants of techniques such as brainstorming and synectics that were developed throughout the 1950s and 1960s under the broad label of *design methods*. The difference is that these contemporary techniques place a far greater emphasis on active participation by end users out in the field.

During the early iterations of the process, user engagement may involve just a few tries on a really informal task—"here, put these things into separate piles; you decide how many piles"—to check out some first guesses about how a user will perceive her options. Later, during more formal activities, there may be more detailed video data gathering, with a larger sample, to settle disagreements that have arisen among the design team. Later still may come preference interviews regarding the more superficial aspects of the design, where preference *is* the issue.

When performed in this continual integrated way, something interesting happens to user research efforts. They lead to creative divergence as well as convergence. The traditional view of user studies is that they are a tool for convergence: to focus in on the one right answer to questions like "exactly how far apart should those screen buttons be?" But now they have become, especially at the early stages of a project, tools for divergence, a way to reveal the questions that we didn't even know we should ask; a way to reveal unmet or unvoiced needs.

The data so obtained are then passed through the MODEL stage of the process. This is a process of summarization, generalization, and abstraction from raw observation. Once again, the nature of the work product varies by iteration. The outcomes of the early stages may be captured in a form no more sophisticated than digital snapshots of whiteboard sketches, or stapled-together piles of sticky notes. Later on, we will see sketches evolve to foam models or interactive mock-ups of screen interactions. In all cases, care is taken that divergent paths be preserved so that the structure of the "space of possibilities"

---

[2]Each of these terms is associated with one or more communities of adherents who attach more or less precise definitions to each term. Such distinctions are not of the essence for our purposes.

is not lost. The reason for this is that the goal is not to converge on a single product. Rather, it is to evolve an *architecture* that defines an entire family of potential products. We will have more to say on this topic presently.

A Wide Area User Study

Progress in science is paced not just by advances in theory, but also by advances in methodology. Design science is no exception. Each generation of design professionals faces the need to develop new techniques for answering the unique questions posed by the design challenges of its era. In our age, this means developing techniques for understanding the needs of users in the context of an increasingly connected and instrumented world. Here is a story of a technique we developed in collaboration with Eaton Corporation.[3]

Early in this particular product cycle, we sent out packages to several volunteer families across the country. Imagine you are one of them. You are our user representative. You and your family are pretty typical people—couple of kids, a dog, a house with a garage, close enough to your parents to be helpful, yet you let them have their independence.

The package arrives in today's mail. It contains a packet of ten numbered yellow sticky notes, a month-long pocket-sized log book, a disposable camera, a cool-looking watch that can wirelessly receive and display text messages, a return mailer, and a set of instructions. The instructions say to think about places or things in your house that you'd like to be aware of, or keep track of, even when you're not at home. They ask you to place the sticky notes on or near those things and take a picture of where you've placed them.

Typically, the first few sticky notes go on the doors. One goes in the basement by the water heater, another in the garage. Perhaps one on the furnace will help you to lower heating costs by remembering to change filters when needed. One could even go to the neighbor next door—you take a picture of him holding it, bewildered expression and all. This leaves a couple of sticky notes left over. How about one on the TV and one above the dog's water bowl? And you might place one in the kids' room with "air quality" written on it. The camera and its pictures get sent back in the return mailer. You put on the watch, place the logbook in your pocket, and go on with your day.

Over the course of the next month, the texting watch gets occasional messages, as if they were coming from those magic sticky notes. Some of your fellow participants get messages that just say, "Alert—Sticky Note #1, two minutes ago!" But you get more specific messages like, "Water in the basement!" "Someone is looking at things in your garden." "Front Door open for 20 minutes." "Critter movement in the garage right now!"

(Continued)

---

[3]The research led to the development of five U.S. patents and the launch of a new product category that won an innovation award from the Consumer Electronics Association.

When a message comes in, you grab your logbook, flip to the date, and answer a few questions like "What do you think the alert means?" "Where are you right now?" "What did you do after getting the message?" From homeowners who receive alerts that are vague, the logbook answers often read something like this, "I don't remember what Sticky Note #6 is!" Just like the output from nearly all of the home security systems on the market at the time, this information, without much context, is timely but almost completely useless. From those like you, who got more detailed text messages, the logbook answers tell a different story. For instance, if you were at your parents' house when the message about water in your basement popped up, the answer to the question of "What did you do next?" might be, "I called my sister, who lives down the block, and asked her to get over there and save the box of wedding photos I left down there." The answers are personal and, in the aggregate, provide a good cross-section of the concerns that are on the minds of homeowners.

In most cases the participants in this experiment—in what we would now think of as "having your house send you tweets"[4]—used their social networks to resolve issues. They seldom, with the exception of fires, wanted a security system to dispatch emergency personnel. With the magical sticky note system, you seemed to just sense what was going on, much as you would if you were at home, and it provided a bit of awareness that fit into the context of your daily life.

Of course, in this early trial those sticky notes are completely dumb—just placeholders for not-yet-designed devices. The volunteers are part of an experiment in pervasive computing using a process called Wizard-of-Oz prototyping. Rather than having to create working wireless sensors and an entire system to coordinate messages, the design team simulated a month in the life of a collection of homeowners using sticky notes and text messaging. Much like the kindly old wizard who hides behind the curtain and pulls levers to make the mighty head speak, the designers sat at their desks, reviewed the pictures they had been sent, and sent out text messages as if they were coming from the magical notes. This simulation revealed important clues about what real people would really do with something like "house tweets" years before that terminology even existed.

Interaction Physics

Material objects follow the laws of physics. Always. If an item loses its support, the item falls. If two items rub together, they get hot. If the lights go out, the items disappear from view. The chains of cause and effect, action and reaction, work so consistently that we can act with precision and confidence. We have a pretty good idea how physical stuff will behave. We and our ancestors have been accumulating intuitions about such things for millions of years.

---

[4]When this research study was conducted, Twitter didn't exist yet and wouldn't come into existence for another three years.

When it comes to design in cyberspace things are different. The rules are not forced upon us. We have choices to make. In the case of a simulation, the task may be obvious—make the virtual thing behave just like a real thing would. We just copy the laws of nature. But design is not all simulation. We now have the opportunity to design things that were not possible before the information era. What happens to a number when you let go of it? When an idea becomes important, does it look any different? How does color overtake and inhabit space? In a virtual world, what happens to Wile E. Coyote when he runs off a cliff?

So we have to invent the physics, and it's not a task to be taken lightly. For starters, it isn't easy. An interaction physics is not the same things as the more familiar notion of user interface guidelines. The difference is this: Guidelines are suggestions, to be used when they seem appropriate and to be eschewed when they are inconvenient. That is not how a physics works. Physical laws admit no exceptions. Gravity may not always be convenient, but you can count on it. So, if we are going to devise an interaction physics, we need to be prepared to commit to living with every rule we make under every single circumstance. Moreover, just as in physical law, no rule must ever contradict any other rule. Anyone who has ever attempted this realizes that you can't make very many such rules without violating one or the other of these strictures. One quickly runs out of degrees of freedom. The bottom line is that finding a set of rules that qualify as an interaction physics and is also useful is no easy task. And so, it is rarely even attempted.

As a result, we have come to a point in the computer industry in which users have come to expect very little consistency in their interactions with devices. Everybody knows the drill: You download a new app, or you press MENU on yet another new remote control in your living room, and you immediately go into puzzle-solving mode—sorting through the dozen or so familiar patterns that the designer might have chosen—trying to get into her head so as to get some traction on the guessing game to follow. Worse, if it is not a device that you use every day, you will probably end up playing the game over and over—there are just too many permutations to remember them all. It is credit to human cleverness that we get by at all.

But it doesn't have to be this way, and in the world of Trillions, it can't be this way. Our collective goal must be convergence toward a unified user experience. A common interaction physics is the golden path to this goal. Consistency builds confidence, and confidence provides feelings of control, security, and comfort. A consistent physics provides the trust that "this thing I put down today will still be there tomorrow." Such trust is the foundation for our ability to build new things. You wouldn't put a book under your child to boost him up in his chair if you thought the book might suddenly slide through the seat and fall through the floor. You wouldn't attempt to build a hut, or a bridge, or a city if you couldn't trust in a few basic rules like gravity, and inertia, and friction. Our ability to build civilization itself would be called into question if everything were as plastic as most software products.

The opposite of physics is magic. Before we had the scientific method, some wise shaman believed that if he slaughtered a goat, it would bring rain—not because he was a fool, but because a few times the rains did really come just after a goat had been slaughtered. The correct name for such behavior is *superstition*, and superstitious behavior is extremely common in users of complex software. You ask people why they saved that word processing document, quit the program, and then reopened the same document. They say things like "I don't know, but for some reason I've found that I have to do that whenever I create new sections that have different formats." Other users believe that the same task requires that they use three or four consecutive drop down menu choices in a fast succession of moves that seem more like an incantation than a rational interaction. It's a vulnerability common to many life forms; research psychologists have induced superstitious behavior even in pigeons.

When users engage with a system, they naturally try to form mental models of how it operates. These models evolve with experience as each user plays a kind of guessing game with the system—trying to learn the rules of the game. The quality of the model at any given time is a major determinant of how well the user will get on with it. The existence of a physics (natural or artificial) provides a solid foundation for these models. But in the absence of a physics, there is often no self-consistent underlying model to be learned. Every tentative hypothesis by the user is eventually contradicted by some new behavior. Rather than systematically piecing together an increasingly accurate and detailed mental model of the system, the user thrashes from one crude model to another—each accounting for the most recent observations, but having very little of the predictive value that supports true fluency with the system. In these cases, users resort to keeping long lists of exceptions in their head or scribbled on sticky notes. Without a few stable, trusted, never-failing interaction "laws," users are left to carry the burden of all those exceptions. Eventually, they give up even trying to learn new features. The ultimate result is that the most powerful features of many programs and devices go unused by most users. Consumer satisfaction, the ability to build new things from a product's basic capabilities, the ability to perform critical but rarely encountered tasks—often the very features that differentiate a product from its competitors—are all put at risk.

It should be emphasized that although interaction physics implies strict self-consistency, it does not necessarily imply consistency with nature. There must be *a* physics, but not necessarily *the* physics. As game designers know well, users are capable of rapidly adjusting to novel—even bizarre—virtual environments and quickly becoming highly skilled in them; but only in the presence of consistency that they can count on. Gravity that works sideways? No problem. Eyes that see through disembodied floating cameras that follow your avatar? Got it!

This is fortunate. In the world of Trillions, we expect to be surrounded by embedded devices that do things that are far from natural. After all, if all we did was slavishly copy nature, what would we have gained? In such an environment, how far can we push the physics? Where will the Most Advanced become Unacceptable?

Thus, designing on Trillions Mountain won't involve just the application of rigid interface design rules. There's research to be done, new things to learn. As design scientists, we are left to our imagination and intelligence to propose a hypothesis that seems reasonable and testable, and then to put it through the wringer of experience. In complex systems, it is essential to get the physics straight before the designing can begin in earnest. For the people who will ulti-mately own, use, and live with the design, their comfort and quality of life is at stake.

Information-Centric Interaction Design

It is possible to identify four distinct stages in the evolution of human-computer interaction. The earliest of these was what might be called *command-centric*. When you logged into a timesharing computer in 1970, or turned on an early personal computer a decade later, your teletype machine (or its "glass" equivalent) presented you with a one-character prompt, indicating that it was time for you to type a command. You were expected to know the list of options, which generally consisted of such verbs as LIST, PRINT, DELETE, and COPY. You literally told the computer what to do, and it did it immediately and exactly. And that was the end of the story. The experience was much like using a very powerful typewriter, or perhaps running an extremely flexible slide projector. The information itself felt far away and abstract.

Stage 2 was *application-centric*. It first appeared in the form of an addition to the above list of commands. The newcomer was RUN, and it introduced an additional level of abstraction between the user and the computer in the form of applications—computer programs that were not part of the machine's operating system, but were devised by third parties to perform some specific task. There were applications to read e-mail, perform word processing, man-age spreadsheets, and do a thousand more tasks. At first, they had their own sets of commands, analogous to those used to control the operating system, but specialized for a specific task. The feeling here was a bit like using those remote manipulator arms in nuclear power plants. You could grab hold of your data, but only indirectly. You would say, "Please, e-mail program, show me my next unread message," and your e-mail app would fetch it on your behalf.

Although application-centric interaction is still common, it has in many cases been supplanted (or perhaps supplemented is a better term) by stage 3 interaction, which is commonly known as *document-centric* interaction. Here, the applications recede into the background, and the user is encouraged to focus on the document as the unit of interaction. Instead of thinking about commands or indirect manipulation, direct manipulation is the order of the day. One can grab an image from a PC web browser, drag it out of its win-dow and drop it into a word-processing document or onto the desktop. On an iPhone or iPad, one can flip through the albums of a music collection or scroll around on a map with the slide of a finger. The remote manipulator arms are gone, and if it weren't for that pesky piece of glass, it feels as though you could literally get your hands on the data.

Stage 4 takes the progression to its logical conclusion. First introduced by a collaboration between MAYA and Carnegie Mellon University, this stage is known as *information-centric* manipulation. Like stage 3, it makes aggressive use of such direct manipulation techniques as drag-and-drop and gesture-based interaction. What distinguishes it from the document centric approach is that, rather than limiting the "currency" of manipulation to the document, it is extended to every level of detail in a display. In the information-centric approach, a display is not so much drawn as it is *assembled* out of more primitive graphical elements, each of which is itself a representation of a more primitive information object and is itself directly manipulable.

If the user is given, say, a document containing a table containing a list of cities, not only can the document and the table be dragged and dropped into a different context, but so can the cities. Thus, for example, a subset of the cities could be selected, dragged out of the table, and dropped into a bar graph designed to show population. Instantly, the lines that list the cities will morph into bars whose height is proportional to the city's population. Then, perhaps, the user might use this display to select the cities with the tallest bars (and thus, the highest populations) and drag them in turn onto a map, which would automatically morph the bars into the appropriate icons and "snap" them to their proper location according to the cities' latitudes and longitudes (Figure 6.2). This concept is kinetically illustrated online at http://trillions.maya.com/ Visage_polymorphic.

To appreciate the power of this approach, it is important to fully understand the nature of the morph operations in the above story. This operation is easy and intuitive when experienced, but it has no direct analog in the real world, and so is a bit tricky to describe. The key to the technique involves the distinction between the identity of the information object and the form in which it is presented in a given display. Information as such is invisible. Humans have no sensory apparatus to perceive it directly. And so, we use displays—whether on paper or on computer screens—as concrete, physical surrogates for the data. What computers let us do that paper never could is to dynamically *change* the form while maintaining the underlying identity of an information object. Thus, in our example, the row of text in the table, the bar on the bar chart, and the symbol positioned on the map are all representations of one and the same abstract information object—namely an object containing various information about a city. Each representation lets us perceive a different facet of the information we have about the city. The table shows us the city's name, the bar shows the population, and the map icon shows us the location. Different representations are valuable for different tasks, but all ultimately refer to the same underlying object—our city object.

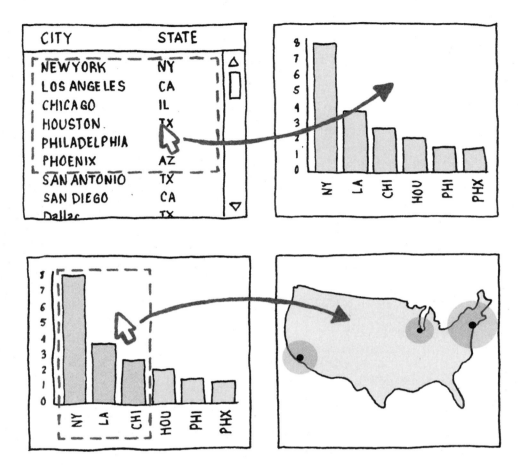

Figure 6.2 *Information-centric data manipulation*

As should be clear, information-centric interaction design is intimately related to the ideas of persistent object identity and of cyberspace that we have discussed previously. These are powerful and somewhat radical techniques, but they are, we believe, exactly the power we need to make significant progress toward a tractable future.

Computation in Context

As we begin to develop pervasive computing systems, issues related to *context awareness* will increasingly come to the fore. As a result, we will need to apply significantly more precision to the notion of *context* than is afforded by common usage of this term. Just as in previous sections we found it useful to distinguish among people, devices and information, we may usefully identify three distinct realms of context. First, the *physical context* allows us to make our devices responsive to their actual, real-world locations. Second, the *device context* concerns the relations among information-processing systems as such—machines talking to other machines. Finally, computing systems have an *information context*. The study of information contexts is the province of the discipline of information architecture, which the next chapter will explore in detail but in brief may be defined as the design of information entities abstracted from the machines that process them.

Perhaps the pinnacle of eighteenth- and nineteenth-century high technology was the commercial sailing ship. The design and operation of these craft represented a subtle and challenging enterprise. This challenge was rooted in the fact that these devices needed to operate simultaneously in three distinct but interacting realms. A merchant ship is at once in the ocean, in the atmosphere, and "in" a constantly flowing current of passengers and cargo (Figure 6.3).

It may seem peculiar to speak of the ships as being "in" the flow of cargo rather than the converse, but this is a perfectly sensible and useful description of the situation. The peculiarity comes from thinking only of the goods and passengers who are on a particular ship. Think instead about the continuous flow of all the people and things in the world that are on their way, right now, from one place to another. Ships are unquestionably "in" that flow. From the

Figure 6.3 The three environments of a sailing ship

point of view of a ship and its designers, this stream of commerce is as real and as important a context as wind or current: Its pressures shape the holds and staterooms and decks just as surely as the imperatives of hydro- and aero-dynamics determine the streamlines of the hull and the catenaries of the sails.

The need to balance the often-conflicting design constraints imposed by these three contexts, combined with the reality that sailing ships spent most of their lives operating without infrastructural support, raised naval architecture to a level of art unmatched in its day. The sense of appreciation—even awe—that many people feel in the presence of a gathering of tall ships reflects an intuitive recognition of the success of their designers in meeting the challenges of this multiply constrained design space.

As designers of information devices, we are embarking on a great enterprise whose challenges are, in certain ways, reminiscent of those of our seafaring past. No longer can computer designers make the simplifying assumption that their creations will spend their lifetimes moored safely to the desk of a single user or plying the familiar channels of a particular local network. Nor will most devices be tethered to some remote corporate cloud service. It seems clear that, before long, most computing will happen in situ and that most computing devices will find themselves operating in diverse and changing contexts. Context awareness will soon become a hallmark of effective information products and services.

Talk of context-aware computing has become common. Yet such discussions nearly always significantly understate the issue. Each of these realms—physical, device, and information—presents a unique set of challenges. But they are not independent, and we treat them so at our peril. Thus there is a compelling need for the development of a framework within which we can begin to reason about information systems in the large—dealing at once with context awareness in each of the three realms.

Physical Context

The physical context is the first and most obvious of our three contexts of computation. This is what is most commonly meant when the term *context aware* is encountered in the literature. It is about imbuing our devices with a *sense of place* by the most literal interpretation of that phrase. But even here the notion of context is not simple. We can mean many things by physical context. Most obvious, perhaps, is geographic location. Here we are heir to a rich and sophisticated body of work inherited from the disciplines of cartography and navigation. As the etymology of the word "geometry" demonstrates, we have been measuring the earth for a very long time. Consequently, we are not lacking for well-developed standards for denoting locations on the earth's surface.

Indeed, there is an embarrassment of riches in this regard: The novice soon discovers that referencing a spot on the earth is no simple matter of latitude and longitude. Various geographic, geodetic, and geocentric coordinate systems are in common use—each optimized for a different purpose. Although practice in this area can be extremely complex, it is for the most part well defined, with precise—if not always simple—mathematics defining the relations involved. The field of geographic information systems (GIS) is quite mature; we have comprehensive (if sometimes overly complex) standards for the machine representation and interchange of geographic information of all sorts.

However, as we move beyond mere geolocation to the more interesting problem of denoting geographic features (whether natural, man-made, or political), the situation rapidly becomes murky. Suppose, to pick one of the easier cases, we wish to refer in an unambiguous way to, say, Hanover, Pennsylvania. Should we simply use the place name? If so, we will have to devise a way to indicate whether we mean the Hanover near Wilkes-Barre, the one by Allentown, or the one at York (this is assuming we don't mean Hanover Green, Hanover Junction, Hanoverdale, or Hanoverville). We could use latitude/longitude, but what point on the earth, exactly, should we choose to represent Hanover?[5] If we do not choose *precisely* the same coordinates, comparing two references to the same location becomes an exercise in trigonometry.

If we look to other challenges, such as denoting street addresses, we discover similar issues. There is no shortage of schemes for encoding these kinds of data, and there exist many high-quality databases of such information. However, each such database is a referential island, defining a local namespace adequate to support a particular application, but nearly useless for enabling the kinds of large-scale, open information spaces implied by the pervasive computing agenda.

But there is more to place than mere geography. Human artifice has structured space in many complex ways, creating new challenges. Consider a large skyscraper. It may have 100 floors, each having 100 rooms. Already today, each room likely contains multiple networked processors—smoke detectors, door locks, building alarms, lighting controllers, thermostats. A single building may easily contain tens of thousands of embedded computers. To do its job, each of these processors must in some sense be "aware" of its location. But location means different things to different devices. To some it is room number; to others it is floor, distance from a fire exit, topological location on a local area network, or proximity to a window. The state of the art in such systems is such that each device is imbued with its requisite address by an installer on a ladder—often keeping paper records of his progress. Standardization efforts are underway within the relevant industry trade groups, but they are proceeding with little thought to how such standards might fit into a larger ecology.

---

[5]There is a U.S. Board on Geographic Names that sanctions official U.S. place names, but it treats U.S. and foreign names differently. For example, web-accessible resources from this source present unique numerical identifiers for foreign but not domestic places. The Getty Research Institute has compiled an extremely thorough thesaurus of geographic names that is both worldwide and hierarchical, and also includes unique identifiers. However, this work is not in the public domain and is not generally recognized as authoritative.

It will not be long before the tens of thousands of processors in each office building become tens of millions, and it will not end there. When light switches built into modular room dividers are expected to turn on neighboring lights, how will they determine what lights are neighboring? When sensors in office chairs are able to identify their occupants by weight, how will this information be made available to nearby devices, and how will *nearby* be defined and determined? When every manufactured thing, from soda cans to soap dispensers joins the network, what role will context play? There are soap dispensers, sold in grocery stores today, that have a small processor, a sensor to allow hands-free operation, and a power supply. With just the one small step of adding communications to the mix, we could easily have the means to enhance our parenting skills with respect to our kids' hand-washing habits. But how will we capture the dispenser's physical location, and how will we control how afar the resulting information should be allowed to roam?

Device Context

Just as various kinds of sensory apparatus—GPS receivers, proximity sensors, and so forth—are the means by which mobile devices will become geographically aware, another class of sensors makes it possible for devices to become aware of *each other*. The superficial similarity between such sensors and ordinary communications channels belies their significance. There is a fundamental difference between the mere ability to transfer data between two or more devices along preconfigured channels and the ability of a device to discover the presence of its peers and to autonomously establish such channels without the aid of some external designer. The first situation involves fixed infrastructure; the second doesn't. And we have precious little experience with computing in the absence of fixed infrastructure.

This, the so-called service discovery problem, forms the basis for a kind of context awareness that is different from that based on physical context. A cluster of vehicles driving in convoy across the country forms a persistent context that is quite distinct from that of the countryside rolling by. Peer-to-peer communication in such circumstances is largely uncharted territory. If we ignore such rudimentary communications channels as horns, turn signals, and CB radios (which in any event involve humans in the loop), no direct communication occurs among today's vehicles. This will certainly change soon. The question is whether the inter-vehicle systems now being developed will be isolated stunts, or whether they will be designed to evolve as part of a larger information ecology.

Even if we broaden our search to include all information-processing devices, the pickings are slim. It is surprisingly difficult to find significant instances of peer-to-peer communications that do not involve the mediation of fixed infrastructure. Anyone who has witnessed the often comic antics of two technically adept laptop users attempting to establish direct communications between their machines without the use of external media will appreciate just how primitive is the state of the art. Progress is being made, however. For example, a little-noted feature of recent versions of Apple's OSX operating system called Airdrop allows properly-equipped computers to automatically become aware of each other's presence, allowing painless drag-and-drop file transfers among such machines.[6] Modest progress for 20 years of effort, but it is a start.

Sooner or later, the practical ability to establish zero-infrastructure ad hoc networks will be achieved. But this in itself does not get us very far toward a true realm of mobile devices. Let's assume, for instance, that you and a friend are riding a New York subway along with 80 strangers. Let's further assume (this being the near future) that everyone on board has in his or her pocket a cell phone that is also physically able to communicate with each of the others, and each device has succeeded in discovering the presence of the other 81. So, what do we do now? Even ignoring engineering issues, how will your friend's device know to cooperate with yours while remaining wary of the 80 strangers? How will these devices even be identified? More basically, what exactly will constitute identity for purposes of such policy?

Before leaving this topic, we should note that device contexts are not necessarily defined by physical proximity. Devices employing a common radio channel may share a context even at great distances. In the case of wired networks, topological distances are typically (but not always) more relevant than topographic proximity.

Many other kinds of "distance" (e.g., how far am I from an Internet connection—and at what cost?) will have importance in specific situations. In general, what it means to define a "space" is precisely to define such distance measures. Building a true "cyberspace" will in large part be a process of coming to agreement on such matters.

Finally, there is the issue of mobile code. The vision of small bits of behavior moving freely from device to device raises many issues of device context awareness. Strictly speaking, code is not a device, but simply data (and therefore the subject of the following section). But the *running computer programs* to which such code gives rise *are* in effect devices. As such, they exist in contexts, raising many of the same issues of context awareness as do physical devices, as well as a few new ones: On what kind of machine am I executing? Whom am I sharing it with? What resources are available to me, and what restrictions must I observe? These are matters of context awareness no less than the more obvious ones of physical context.

Information Context

The third—and least discussed—of our three contexts is the information context in which computation takes place. The study of such contexts is the

---

[6] One of the reasons this feature is "little noted" is because it only works on the very latest hardware. Why? Because until recently, the designers of WiFi chips saw no reason to provide for simultaneous P2P and infrastructure connections.

province of the discipline of information architecture, which we define as the design of information entities abstracted from the machines that process them. This topic has not received the attention that it deserves, largely due to our long habit of thinking of data as residing "in" our computers. As we have already seen, in a pervasive computing world it is useful to take quite the opposite perspective—increasingly, data are not "in" our devices any more than a phone call is "in" a cell phone. In this regard, our earlier nautical analogy is particularly evocative, suggesting a future in which computing devices float freely in a vast sea of data objects—objects whose existence and identity are quite distinct from those of the devices that process them. In this world, the data have been liberated from the devices and have claimed center stage.

This provocative image is compatible with the often-stated ideal of the computer "disappearing" or receding into the background. From this view, computing devices are seen as merely "transducers"—a sort of perceptual prosthesis. We need them in order to see and manipulate data just as we need special goggles to see infrared light. In both cases, it is the perception that is of interest, not the mediating device.

People are beginning to talk about a *vapor of information* following us around as we move from place to place and from device to device. But what, exactly, *is* this vapor? What is it made of? What are its properties? How will it know to follow us? How can we make it usable? These are strange and difficult questions, but beginning to view computing from an information-centric perspective is a first step in dispelling the strangeness.

Already, users of mobile web browsers routinely carry around replicas of web pages that are automatically cached on their devices. As it becomes easier to pass such information objects from device to device, they will begin to take on an existence (and a persistence) that is quite independent of the server machines of their origin. Services exist that extend this concept to other kinds of data, allowing appointments, to-do lists, and even editable text documents to exist as coordinated replicates on any number of mobile devices and desktops simultaneously. Today, these capabilities are typically implemented via the kinds of centralized pseudo-cloud services discussed in Chapter 3. But we will soon begin to see true peer-to-peer implementations. This mode of operation is presently the exception rather than the rule, but we are clearly heading toward patterns of normal activity that will stretch and ultimately break our present conception of the "location" of information.

All modern smartphones and other mobile devices ship with multiple gigabytes of storage. (It is increasingly difficult for a manufacturer to even source memory chips any smaller.) All that storage represents yet another of the underutilized resources we have so often encountered in our story. In this context, what happens when we step beyond the relatively simple client-server model that dominates the web today? What happens when our pocket devices get good at communicating directly with each other? As such devices are released by the billions into the wild, it is inevitable that widespread data replication will rapidly become the norm. Popular web pages and other data objects will be replicated countless times as they flow from device to device. Explicit backup utilities will disappear—replaced by the inherent redundancy of cyberspace. Corrupted or momentarily unneeded data will be casually deleted from local devices by users confident in their ability to grab fresh copies out of the ether when needed. Damaged devices will be replaced with a shrug: The data stream will soon replenish each emptied vessel. Such a world will be characterized by the primacy of information itself, and no one will be tempted to think of data as being "in" machines.

This is not to suggest that all data will be available everywhere. Contrary to predictions that all computing devices will someday have continuous Internet access, we assume that connectivity will always be intermittent, and there will always be devices that are too small and cheap to support direct continuous access. Storage capacities, although huge, will always be finite and unevenly distributed. These and a variety of other factors, ranging from intellectual property issues to bandwidth and security policies, will guarantee that only a small subset of the aggregate data space will be immediately available to any given device at any given time. The sea of data will be far from homogenous. Natural patterns of human and machine interaction, as well as deliberate data replication, will create currents and eddies of data flow within the larger sea.

Thus, devices will find themselves at any given time in this context of the third kind, and awareness of that context will involve a whole new set of questions: What information "objects" are floating around in my immediate neighborhood? Which devices contain them? Are they in a form that I understand? What are the transactions going on among devices for which these information objects serve as currency? In the long run, this kind of context awareness may prove to be the most basic of all. Yet the current dominance of the client-server networking model found in most cloud implementations—with its assumptions of fixed infrastructure, centralized authorities, and walled-off repositories— means that this crucially important context, information-context, is not even part of the discussion today.

What About the User?

In our discussion of computing contexts, the role of the user has been conspicuously and intentionally absent—until now. Surely humans will represent an important, perhaps the ultimate, context for both devices and data. Where do people fit into our three-contexts scheme? In fact, they form a curious cut through the entire space. On the one hand, people are clearly part of the physical context. Awareness of who is present and of their needs, interests, and characteristics will surely be a hallmark of successful "smart spaces." On the other hand, it is often useful to think of the user as a "living information device"—an architectural peer to the computers, participating in the worldwide data flow as a source and sink of data like any other system component. Yet again, we must acknowledge the user as a teleological force—the source of purpose and meaning for the system, guiding it from the outside.

All of these points of view have validity. But most importantly, we must consider people from the perspective of system usability and usefulness. We are on the verge of building systems unprecedented both in their scale and in their very nature. It is one thing to design a usable computer program. It is quite another to design a usable environment when that environment comprises innumerable semiautonomous devices mediating an unbounded swirl of constantly flowing information. Usability, or the lack thereof, will be an emergent property of such a milieu. How does one design an emergent property? The answer is not at all clear. But it is a good guess that the place to start is in defining a basic ontology of existence in this strange new world, with an eye toward imbuing that existence with a consistency of behavior that in some measure approximates the consistency that we get for free in the physical world.

While we touched on the idea of Universally Unique Identity in earlier passages, it is important to raise it again here. No amount of clever hacking will achieve our goals unless it is layered on top of a common model of identity and reference. It is unambiguous identity that is the sine qua non of "objects" of all kinds, and until we start treating information as objects, we will be stuck in an ever-growing pool of informational quicksand.

CHAPTER 7

Architecture with a Capital "A"

Technologies get obsolete within 1 year, applications are replaced in 10 years, but the strong visions would survive more than 100 years.

—HIROSHI ISHII

Throughout this book we have invoked the notion of Architecture with a capital "A"; the idea being that, unlike *architecture,* which refers to the design and construction of buildings, *Architecture* refers to the organizational principles of a collection of objects, a concept or a system, which give it a basis for order, structure, change, or growth (Figure 7.1). Architecture, in this sense, is one of the essential qualities of design on Trillions Mountain. For a film on Architecture, see http://trillions.maya.com/Architecture.

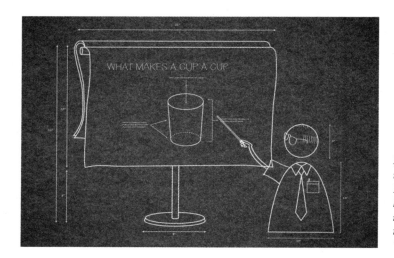

Figure 7.1 *"What makes a cup a cup?" Even a basic object like a cup has an underlying architecture that defines its "cupness."*

Architecture and Architects

We have occasionally been taken to task by a few of our colleagues in the architecture profession for what they perceive as our usurpation of the term *architecture.* From their point of view, an architect is a designer of buildings, and so *architecture* properly refers to the art and science of building design.

We understand their point. Their profession has a long and distinguished history, and we would be the first to say that it represents by far the most mature and methodologically sophisticated of all the design disciplines. They have long taken seriously their role as a community of practice tasked with attending to the big picture concerning the way we as a society build, and therefore, live. Earning the right to call one's self an architect is an arduous process, so it is a title worth defending. Indeed, we agree that the uninflected term *architect* is appropriately reserved for them.

But, the term *architecture* is another matter. It is true that the Greek root of the word can be interpreted as "master builder." But it also shares the Proto-Indo-European root *tek- with such words as texture, textile, and techno-. The Oxford English Dictionary associates the term "architectonic" with "the systemization of knowledge." Hence, we have computer architectures, organizational architectures, and information architectures.

In the broadest sense, *architecture* refers to what might be called metadesign —that is, the stepping back from mere design to consider the deeper patterns in entire families of designs. This kind of abstraction, as we have discussed, is at the heart of generativity. It is the golden path to coherence across large numbers of independently designed artifacts of any kind, be they buildings, cities, devices, computer programs, or information. This kind of abstraction is at the very core of the art of taming complexity.

By our thinking, architects should take pride in the generalization of the mode of thinking that their forebears pioneered. The only reason that the term is historically associated with buildings at all is because for most of human history, cities were essentially the only example of human artifice exhibiting enough aggregate complexity to require such techniques. Architects were the pioneers of the style of design that will reach its apex in the age of Trillions.

ARCHITECTURE AS ORGANIC PRINCIPLES

Frank Lloyd Wright labeled his philosophy "organic architecture," which has been described as an attempt to be "more natural than nature itself." What could such a boast possibly mean? Many people assume that Wright's choice of the term *organic* was meant to imply an imitation of, or at least compatibility with the natural world—hills, trees, animals. Such an interpretation misses the point. Wright believed that his work reflected not idiosyncratic genius, but a genius based on an understanding of deep principles—the very principles manifest in nature's patterns. Amplified by human reason, such principles, he hoped, could guide the creation of a rational, humane, and deeply beautiful built world.

When Wright used the term *organic architecture*, he meant the discipline of designing buildings with an intrinsic integrity that stems from Architecture with a capital "A." Buildings (or any other designed objects) that are informed by such a conception of Architecture will harmonize not only with nature but also with each other.

Implicit in this way of thinking is the supposition that these rules are discovered, not invented. They are "out there," existing a priori waiting to be found. This is to some extent a Platonic view of reality. It is a view that is out of fashion in many circles. But we have never been able to understand the alternative. It seems obvious to us that patterns of possibility exist implicitly in the laws of nature, whether we apprehend them or not. Can it really be said that the pattern representing, say, an overhand knot did not exist until some protohuman tied the first one?[1] We think not. And if not, can we really say that the overhand knot was "invented" rather than discovered? If knots are out

---

[1] Or until some windblown vine was tied into one by chance?

there waiting to be discovered, are there not larger, more complex, and more abstract patterns out there as well? We think so.

ARCHITECTURE AS MODEL

One of the less obvious uses of the process of abstraction implicit in the idea of Architecture is as a means of description. Specifically, Architectural thinking permits us to create abstract *models* of reality that are far more powerful than more literal descriptions. Consider the difference between traditional architectural drawings of a house and a computer-assisted design (CAD) model of the same house (Figure 7.2). In the old days, an architect would draw floor plans, reflected ceiling plans, various elevations and details. Each of these drawings was intended to represent the same house, of course, but each was executed as a separate drafting task. The idea was to produce a consistent set of pictures of the house in the designer's head, with the goal of communicating the specifics of that house to a builder. But because the pictures were all independent, their consistency was completely dependent upon the skill and attention of the draftsperson. There is nothing about such a system that guarantees that the various pictures will comprise a consistent description of a realizable object. In point of fact, no such set of drawings of any complexity are ever completely consistent. This is not fundamentally due to the hypothetical nature of the house-in-the-head; the same problem would exist if the drawings were the result of reverse-engineering an actual house. It is a fundamental problem with a view-based medium, not just with the process.

Now consider a representation of the same building made with a modern 3-D CAD system. This is an entirely different situation. Though one may use such a system to produce exactly the kinds of views that were formerly done by a draftsperson, those views do not themselves constitute the fundamental

DRAFTED PLAN

MODEL-BASED PLAN

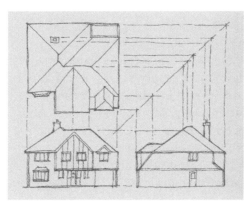 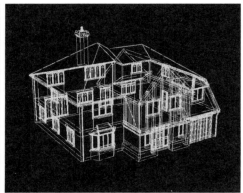

Figure 7.2 Plans as pictures versus plans as models

representation of the building. Instead they are simply renderings of something deeper: an intrinsically self-consistent model of the house completely separated from any particular view of it. The model itself is not a picture. It is abstract, and makes no assumptions about viewpoint or presentation. Each detail of the house is derivable from the model and brought into play as different views require it. No contradictions are possible, since there is only one model. And since the pictures generated by the CAD system are derived via a consistent process from a self-consistent model, they, too, are guaranteed to be consistent with each other.

But there is another difference as well: CAD models are (or at least they can be) parametric. A parametric model is factored into constants and variables. Together they form a scaffolding on which all information about the model hangs. The constants are its essence, its Architecture with a capital "A," the boundaries of its "design space." The parameters (variables) are adjustable. They are like knobs we can turn, and in turning them we can produce an infinite number of particular house-variations, all manifestations of the same underlying Architecture (compare this to our "snack food matrix" from Chapter 4). In doing so, we not only get lots of different houses (which may or may not be good houses), but we also achieve a much deeper understanding of our own Architectural efforts. In the end, we will have attained a much deeper and more profound thing, all the way around.

By now it should be clear that the application of this approach is not limited to the description of physical objects. We can create parameterized abstract models of computing devices, of network topologies, of user interfaces, of social networks. And most importantly, we can create such models of patterns of information. The metaphor of a parametric CAD-style model for cyberspace can help us crystallize the fog of information.

ARCHITECTURE AS "STYLE"

Yet another way to conceptualize Architecture with a capital "A" is as a matter of style—style in the sense of Gothic, or Art Deco, or Postmodern. As Walter Dorwin Teague put it, "at those historical moments when a dominant style exists . . . a single character of design gets itself expressed in whatever is made at the time, and not a chair, a teapot, a necklace or a summerhouse comes into existence except in a form which harmonizes with everything else being made at that time. . . . The scene has unity, harmony, repose, and at least one irritant is absent from the social organism." If one were to call a furniture store and—sight unseen—order a room full of, say, Mission Style furniture, the result might not merit coverage in *Architectural Digest*, but it would likely hang together pretty well.

Where do styles come from? Well, they don't come from committees, and (at least in general) they don't come from lone engineers. Rather, they emerge as rough shared consensus among communities of practice—more specifically among communities of designers.[2] This is unfamiliar territory to many technology-oriented designers, but it's a key point of this book. When designing at the scale demanded by pervasive computing, we will inevitably be forced to abandon our dreams of perfect rigor, and, when we do, the only remaining alternative to chaos is the loose but pervasive consensual shared agenda that we refer to as *deep Architecture*.

Style in this deep sense is not altogether absent from the computing scene. System architects have evolved a very definite style for the building of computers themselves. The packaging of logic in functionally specialized integrated circuits (ICs); putting main memory chips on little daughter boards; the use of application programming interfaces (APIs); object-orientation; and semi-standardized data types—all of these are elements of style within the engineering community. Similarly, within the human-computer interaction (HCI) community, the WIMP (windows, icons, menus, pointing device) paradigm represents a loose, evolving but near-universal style of user interface design for desktop PCs.

There is a danger: A dominant style can cause one to accept designs without examining their consequences. The modernist esthetic in architecture gave us countless sterile, windswept urban plazas built on a scale divorced from human experience and which militate against the possibility of social life in their spaces. At its best, however, style can bring unity, harmony, and a sense of familiarity to the new. In this way, style performs the legitimate—even vital—function of facilitating environmental coherence by admitting at least the possibility that an ensemble of products—designed, manufactured, and purchased independently in a competitive market—may be assembled into a collection that will look and operate together in an efficient and pleasing manner.

Architectural thinking should be particularly attractive to business leaders because it is the one true path to genuine and sustainable innovation. The infinite combinatorial possibilities that are implicit in a generative Architecture constitute the wellspring of design potential. To a design scientist, a specific innovation is never a one-off stunt, never the result of luck or hacking, but rather the tip of an architectural iceberg. The fast followers and knock-off artists may imitate the product you ship today, but they can copy only what they see. It didn't take long for Apple's competitors to produce shallow knock-offs of the iPod, but they couldn't anticipate Jobs's plans for the coming iPhone, much less the iPad. In a sense, Jobs couldn't see them, either. But what he could see was a path forward. He had a plan; a plan in the form of an Architecture. For practitioners of Architecture (and their clients), there's always more where that came from, and it doesn't require starting over from scratch; the next innovation follows naturally from adjusting the parameters of the principles already put into play.

But the trillion-node network will require the emergence of another distinct kind of style, namely a style of information architecture (IA). Lying just above systems architecture (which deals with how the computing devices themselves are built) and just below user interfaces (which is about how

---

[2] We're using this word broadly, to mean "creator of artificial structures," not in the narrow senses of "graphic designer" or "industrial designer."

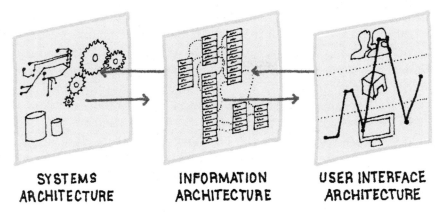

SYSTEMS ARCHITECTURE   **INFORMATION ARCHITECTURE**   **USER INTERFACE ARCHITECTURE**

Figure 7.3 An information architecture is everything you can define about a system without specifying the underlying technology or the particular user interface that will be employed. This involves thinking about the architecture of how information is interrelated, how it flows, and how it fits within the user's world.

systems communicate with users), IA deals with the design of the information itself (Figure 7.3). The trillion-node network implies a vast, heterogeneous worldwide dataflow of information. The only commonality across its vastness is information, and it is here that we must concentrate new design effort if we are to achieve a semblance of global integrity. For a film on information see http://trillions.maya.com/Information.

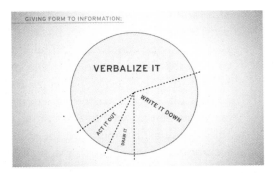

Figure 7.4 We often confuse information with the form it takes, but information itself has no form.

INFORMATION ARCHITECTURE

Don't confuse information architecture with the more basic concept of Architecture with a capital "A." IA is an *application* of "capital A" principles in a particular domain—the domain of information. Information architecture is the specification of abstract patterns governing the relationships among information objects. Of course, all information is itself abstract, so IA represents a second order of abstraction—patterns of patterns.

So, if the Industrial Revolution gave rise to industrial design, just so, information design is the natural outgrowth of the Information Revolution. That thought might prompt you to ask, "You can't *design* information, can you? It's immaterial; what is there to design about it?" True, information has no form. And if you think of design as only "look and feel," then the idea of designing information makes no sense. Information doesn't have a look and feel. You can't see information. So what exactly would you "design" about it?

To the casual observer, design is about the skin. The design of a hardcover book means the appearance of the dust jacket. And if you exclude the jacket, you might hear, "What do you mean, the design of it? It's a book." But books have a great deal of design—much of it having nothing to do with appearance. When an author organizes topics into an outline, that is an act of design. The choice of voice and expository tone are design issues. None of these things are "content," they are decisions that structure and organize the content.

But books don't just have design; they also have Architecture. The outline and expository structure of a book are specific to that particular book; hence we call them "design." But there are patterns that transcend the design of any single book. We structure books into chapters. We start them with prefaces and end them with epilogues. We put tables of contents in front and indexes in the back. These are decisions that float above not just the content, but also above the design. They are acts of information architecture.

These examples provide a concrete illustration of how the articulation of abstract patterns (like the idea of "chapters") can permit us to bring coherence and familiarity to an open-ended set of books—even books that have not been written yet. But books are relatively simple things. How much more important is it to provide coherence and familiarity to the vast and burgeoning universe of data that is the Internet? If that universe still consists largely of chaotic collections of disconnected, independent data silos and safe but sterile walled gardens, it is the absence of virtually anything worthy of the name information architecture that we have to blame. If we have managed to make the web useful without such sophistication, credit is due to amazingly clever and subtle techniques of search engine design combined with virtually unlimited amounts of brute force computing power and storage. But these are stopgap measures. We can do much better, and we will. The trends that we have been exploring throughout this book will require it.

Personal Universal Controller

In 2001, with many new handheld digital devices beginning to flood the market—PDAs, MP3 players, GPS devices, and so on—we embarked on a collaborative research project with Carnegie Mellon University. The project was partially funded by a consortium of leading tech companies that included the likes of Sony and Casio. Our project was aimed at developing a general architecture for mobile devices as they begin to interact with the connected environments around them. We called the project "PUC" for Personal Universal Controller. The PUC was envisioned as a universal mobile interface through which the owner of a house or a worker in an office could communicate with and control any product that was at hand in the built environment—a phone, a CD player, a thermostat, an alarm clock, a refrigerator, a house, a copy machine, whatever.

The concept differed from the familiar "universal remote control" in a fundamental way: Rather than applying a thin veneer over the diverse user interfaces that such independently designed devices inevitably possess, the PUC took a different approach. The device implemented a complete and general user interface paradigm, and it communicated with the diverse controlled devices via an abstract, high-level protocol. Thus, for example, instead of sending manufacturer-specific "volume up" and "volume down" commands to a television set, it would send an abstract "set percentage value of a quantitative range." Each controlled device would negotiate its requirements with the PUC when they first encounter each other, and these abstract parameters would be mapped onto the PUC's single, uniform UI. In turn, the user can choose from among a library of UI styles and "skins" (highly realistic knobs and displays; minimalist; even, in principle, command line or Braille), and the preferred style would be used consistently for all devices. The bottom line was that the user interface decisions would be associated with the user, not with each device. Users could literally carry their UI preferences in their pockets. The relevance of this pattern to taming the chaos of the pervasive computing future is obvious.

The goal was not actual commercialization, but to provide a concrete product context that would require us to do some deep work about the Architecture of user interfaces at the intersection of information and atoms—to understand and describe data types (continuous, discrete, binary, etc.), decision sequences (to save, or autosave?), kinesthetic principles (point, push, slide, twist, etc.)—all the actions and feedback elements of user interfaces that we commonly encounter in a multitude of combinations and permutations.

We built a prototype PUC system to test what we had learned. Each device in our test environment was equipped with a wireless adaptor that could send and receive XML-coded descriptions of every way that it could be controlled and every kind of information it could provide. (In a practical implementation, such adaptors would provide a transitional technology until "PUC native" devices started to appear.)

One test was to find out if users could walk up and use never-before-seen devices, and if so, whether they could learn how to use these devices in record time. For the test we configured a PUC controller device so that it requested the control description from any PUC-aware system within wireless range and dynamically assembled a user interface to control these devices. If it found a stereo system, it dynamically laid out an interface to control it, if it found a multifunction alarm clock, it did the same. By removing the whims of a given physical or UI design from the equation, and instead developing interfaces that dynamically optimized the whole environment, we found dramatic improvements in both the time to learn a task as well as the number of errors made. In our tests, users completed tasks with many fewer errors, and in half the time.

The test consisted of timing users—who were not familiar with any of the systems in the environment—as they learned to perform tasks directly on the

(Continued)

actual products versus doing so via the PUC. The improvement in performance with the PUC may be due in part to just good interface design. But the improvement *across* product types demonstrates the extra benefit an Architectural approach brings to an experience.

The concept was simple. If you always used that volume dial on the side of the PUC to turn things up or down, all devices in your environment could be turned up or down with that dial. If you always had the on/off button in the upper left corner, all systems in the physical world could be turned on or off by looking at the upper left corner of the display.

It is noteworthy that even nonvisual interfaces benefited from this approach. The CMU researchers were working on natural language processing, so they built a wireless microphone and speaker system that could query the devices within the environment using a consistent language and grammar. The potential of this technology for the improvement of interfaces for the visually impaired is clear.

Consider what happens when a user is given the ability to learn one interface paradigm and employ it across different products or applications, even if built by different manufacturers during different design eras. This approach naturally brings a measure of future proofing and customer satisfaction to diverse product lines—including future products that have not yet been conceived. But more importantly, the evolution of the interface can benefit from the community of users and evolve in the wild into something that could never have been conceived by a single manufacturer.

The power of this approach is clear, and we believe that something very much like it will prove to be in the critical path of our climb up Trillions Mountain.

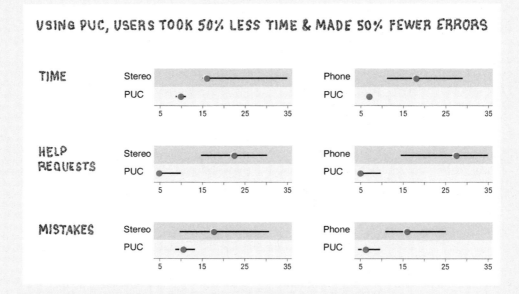

PUC Testing Results: PUC usability exceeded that of the actual appliances in time to completion, help requests and missteps.

We should caution the reader that although we are prepared to defend our usage of the term *information architecture* in the specific sense that we have defined, such usage is not universal. People talk about the IA of a website or of a visualization. But such usages often refer, not to an architecture at all, but to relatively superficial (or at least case-specific) decisions concerning the stylistic features and look-and-feel characteristics of ensembles of coordinated designs. We have no quibble with this kind of design; it is productive and important. It is just that it isn't Architecture. To be worthy of that term, a pattern must transcend a single project and a single designer. Designs belong to individual designers; Architecture belongs to communities of practice.

We earlier posed the question "How does one design an emergent property?" We are now prepared to offer an answer. It involves two steps: First, develop and perfect an architecture. Second, subject your architecture to market forces. This recipe, of course, is flippant. But it captures an essential point. Architecture and evolutionary processes are the Yin and the Yang of complexity design. We believe that this is how Nature works, and that it is the only tractable approach to designing any system whose aggregate complexity vastly exceeds the bounds of human cognition.

Information architecture transcends almost every other issue in the field. By its use, one can give information an essential structure that permits it to flow and recombine freely, much as the structure of the genetic code provides a corresponding liquidity for the information of life. Getting it right is vitally important because the result will be an incalculable increase in the value of all the world's information as we move onto Trillions Mountain.

Architecture on TV

Many of your favorite television programs, whether serious drama or situation comedy, have a written document associated with them that illustrates the importance of Architecture. The document is called "the bible" of the show. It's not the script of any specific episode. Rather, it's a detailed description of the show's DNA, so to speak—the set of premises upon which episodes of the show are built. The bible contains, for example, a comprehensive description of each character: his or her physical appearance, key biographical points, salient personality traits, major behavioral quirks.[3] It also delineates the basic dramatic premises of the show and the relationships of the characters to each other.

If you know the show's bible you know, perhaps, that two of the characters have had a love affair in the past and that some of the other characters know

(Continued)

---

[3]The resemblance of these character sketches to the user "personas" frequently developed by interaction designers is not coincidental.

about it and some don't (these facts may or may not ever be made known to the viewers). You know that in a certain kind of situation, character A would likely do X, might occasionally surprise us by doing Y, but would never do Z. You know that certain situations will arise all the time and certain other situations will rarely or never arise. And you know that the show's drama has a clearly defined tonal range. That range might occasionally be extended to accommodate P, but Q would be a fatal violation of the show's tone.

The bible is the show's architecture. It is not a script. You can't watch it. But it provides coherence and continuity across episodes. And if the bible is not carefully produced and logically consistent, its failings will sooner or later play havoc with the show. Significant gaps or contradictions will eventually surface as episodes that "do not compute," in which characters behave without proper motivation, striking wrong notes and doing things that are unbelievable or just plain wrong.

ARCHITECTURE AND DESIGN SCIENCE

Before we leave the topic of Architecture, we would like to make one final point. It concerns the relationship between Architecture and the idea of design science. All true sciences have two facets: the observational and the theoretical. What distinguishes science from its "natural philosophy" antecedents is less in the observational than in theoretical. Prescientific data collection was often both comprehensive and thorough. Its practitioners were prodigious producers and collectors of data. What was lacking were the techniques of abstraction and mathematical generalization that permit us to make simple statements about vast swatches of information. Isaac Newton is rightly known as the father of modern science precisely because he showed the world how a few lines of equations can capture fundamental truths with more precision and to far greater useful effect than any mere list of observational facts, no matter how voluminous or carefully collected.

If design science is going to be more than mere pretension, it must develop work products that exhibit the same powers of abstraction and generalization as do the differential equations of the physicist and the periodic table of the chemist. As we hope we have made clear, capital "A" Architecture is the medium for such generalization. It is by definition transcendent of particular instances and thus intrinsically abstractive. And generalization goes hand in hand with generativity. As we face the task of sculpting a future of unprecedented complexity, Architectural principle will sketch the outlines and market forces will fill in the innumerable details.

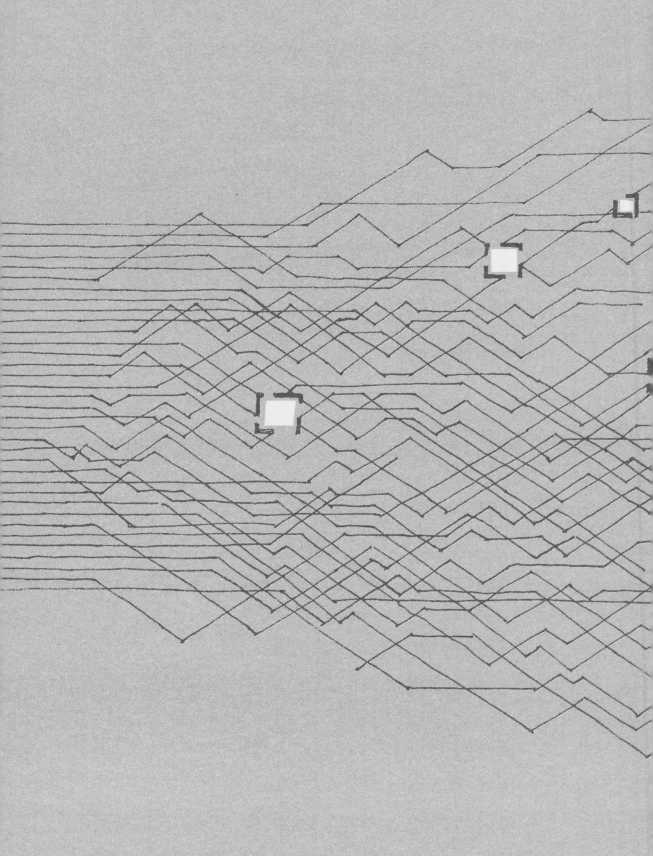

CHAPTER 8

Life in an Information Ecology

If you wish to make an apple pie from scratch, you must first invent the Universe.

—CARL SAGAN

A humane and vibrant trillion-node world will result only from principled design, but not design in the sense that most people understand that term. Like the global financial economy, the trillion-node world will be a deeply complex *ecology*, not simply a collection or even a "patterned arrangement" of devices, information, power, and so on. An ecology carries with it a lot of embedded—often implicit—information about how things are related—not just what the things are. The ecology reveals who lives with whom, who eats whom, what happens to waste, how things are born and die, where the energy comes from, how things become aware of the other things around them, how new needs are recognized, opportunities to colonize, threats about being colonized . . . and much more.

An ecology has no "authority" serving as a central control. It is self-regulating in much the sense that a market economy is self-regulating. Yes, outside forces can tinker with it, resulting in a shift in the ecology's equilibrium position. But too much tinkering results in its actually becoming a new or different ecology or, at the extreme, a catastrophic failure.

Small World
By Joe

The simplest example of an ecology in my personal experience is the fishpond in my backyard. It was there when we bought the house about ten years ago. At first it seemed like a big responsibility to keep it clean, feed the fish, fertilize and prune the water plants, and make sure the water chemistry was right. Then I had a heart-to-heart with a guy from the local "water garden" shop who knew much more about these things than I do. It turns out that by trying to "be in control" I was making my life harder than necessary and doing the pond no good. My oversight of this little world was much easier than I had imagined. It's true, we still have to filter the water (automatically) and clean the pond (just once a year) because a fishpond is a somewhat artificial ecosystem. It is bounded (by the edge of the pond) and the water supply is artificial (city water), so it doesn't have the full resources of a natural fishpond, and we have to do a bit of tweaking to make up for those differences—and we do have a great blue heron that lives at the lake of a nearby park and sometimes visits us for easy fishing. But life in the pond goes on. And if the life is balanced—the right number and kind of fish, and the right number and kinds of plants, not too many visits from the heron—they pretty much take care of each other, and you almost never have to feed the fish. The plants live off the chemicals in fish poop, and the fish nibble at the plants and small critters that grow on them, and the water never gets cloudy.

The important thing is that unlike a simple "arrangement" of things, you can't add, subtract, or change one thing in an ecology without causing ripples in the existence of other things. In order to live in the ecology of the next computing paradigm, the designers, users, sellers, and consumers must behave in an ecological way or risk extinction. It's not necessary that everyone have a deep understanding of this, but the design scientist must. And even the surface understandings that most people rely on to get through their daily lives have to be built on top of a deep understanding on the part of the environment's architects.

COMPONENTS

Any person or firm that desires to be an active participant in creating, influencing, or making money from the information ecology will have to become familiar with ecological principles and the properties of ecologies. It will be necessary to know how to recognize an ecology when you run into one—and to understand what's missing when a claimed ecology is not working (too much fish food clouding the water?). It may be rightly claimed that the ordinary user in the ecology need not have such a level of understanding. We don't want the technology to become a barrier to those who will enjoy its benefits, and the working of an ecology does not depend on conscious meta-thinking by all of its participants. But the players who will make money in such a world will be precisely those who *do* get good at such top-down awareness. What we should expect to see from such a vantage point are four main components of an ecology:

1. The life forms
2. The currency
3. The architectures
4. The environment

The Life Forms: Devices

In an information ecology, information devices are the equivalents of life forms. They are animate, and they consume energy and other resources. There will be simple life forms that perhaps do no more than announce their presence by the exchange of information. There will also be complex life forms that process information, transducers that convert energy into information or vice versa, and devices that represent information in such a way that humans can interact with it or simply be informed by it.

Devices don't exactly eat each other, but they certainly do compete in the marketplace. Moreover, one lives off another by consuming or otherwise processing the information that the other produces or leaves behind. Over time more organizations will recognize that even their waste data can be aggregated, recycled, and turned into value for other life forms. For instance, a manufacturer of home appliances may have a sensor built into its washer and dryer to detect if someone has entered the laundry room. This small bit of information may be used to help conserve energy and turn on the appliances' displays when a user is present. After this bit of data about presence is used, it may be thrown away. Imagine, however, an organization that provides eldercare services to homes. The waste data about movement in the laundry room may be highly valued information to them. Knowing whether an elderly parent has moved around in the last few hours could be the difference between life and death. The cost of exposing that information may be minimal to you, yet it could turn out to be a valuable asset to other members of the information ecology. Devices form an ecology when they all share, trade in, consume, and transform some common element, generically categorized as the currency.

The Currency: Information

Complex interconnected systems require a currency. In Joe's fishpond, the currency comprises the carbon-based molecules that constitute the cells of plants, fish, and all the other critters. Those living devices process the molecules for energy, to grow new cells, and to discard waste.

A currency is something that embodies value, can be exchanged on the basis of its value, and can be transferred from place to place. In the world economy, the currency is money, not a thing of value in itself but a carrier of value, a surrogate of value.[1] Finally, the currency must be fluid—easily flowing from place to place or situation to situation—in order to bind the ecology together. It is what makes the ecology a single system rather than a mere aggregation. If currency is hoarded, it is unproductive and does nothing to increase the overall value of the ecology. In a balanced ecology, nothing is wasted. Each actor has an essential freedom of action, and so is free to discover and exploit locally available resources that would have been overlooked and thus wasted by a system that relied upon centralized control. If you're not fast, you become food. And there's no begrudging the discarded waste that somebody else finds useful.

Information Architecture and Device Architecture

The architecture of an ecology sets the rules of the game by which the life forms or devices exchange and process the currency. If the currency of the ecology is thought of as a sort of a language for communicating among the life forms, then the architecture is the syntax of that language. In biology, the architecture has two facets: On one hand there is an architecture based upon DNA,

---

[1] Indeed, in the final analysis, money is a carrier of *information*.

chromosomes, and genes (among many other structures). This is basically an information architecture (IA), in that it comprises a structure for the storage, replication, and interpretation of the patterns necessary for the creation of new organisms. On the other hand is what we might call an organism architecture, comprising the patterns of physical structure—cells, organs, bilateral symmetry, and all the other usual techniques used by biology to build the machinery of the living world.

A true ecology of information devices will inevitably exhibit the same two-faceted structure. It starts, as we have seen, with an IA based upon a well-defined notion of information objects, mediated by universally unique identifiers (UUIDs). Out of these primitives, it is quite possible—even relatively easy—to rebuild all of the standard data structures that have evolved over 50 years of writing code for stand-alone computers. This involves not so much invention as reinterpretation of standard patterns, but liberated from the computers into the larger ecology. The equivalent of organism architecture is what we call device architecture (DA). Made up of things like application program interfaces (APIs), modular packaging standards, and the like, the DA guides the evolution of the ever larger and more complex systems that will evolve within this new ecology.

These architectures are not laws or any other kind of coercive mechanism. They work with carrots, not with sticks. They operate like the lines painted in a parking lot. Their mere presence tends to result in drivers doing the right thing all on their own. You don't need traffic cops or physical barriers. You just need to establish the proper patterns. People then (mostly) follow them in their own self-interest. In the case of the parking lot, the evidence of the architecture is boldly there for all to see. Such is not always the case. Sometimes the architecture is hidden or subtle. Such architectures depend upon professional training and the existence of healthy communities of practice for their effectiveness. The evolution of such communities is an indispensable component of our expedition up Trillions Mountain.

Rock, Paper, Scissors
By Mickey

A friend of mine seems to be obsessed with using the game of Rock, Paper, Scissors to settle just about any dispute that arises in our team meetings. Many people think Rock, Paper, Scissors is a simple game of chance. Everyone knows the rules: rock breaks scissors, paper covers rock, scissors cut paper. Since it seems random, most of us just decide to play a favorite; I usually play rock, as an opening gambit. Sure enough, every once in awhile I get lucky. I've noticed

(Continued)

that most of the time though, my friend wins.

I decided to find out why he wins far more often than he loses. I discovered that the game of Rock, Paper, Scissors isn't entirely a game of chance. Nor, to my surprise, is it just a one-off idea for a game. I always assumed that some kids just thought the game up back during the Depression or something, when they couldn't afford fancy games like Go Fish.

Before I get to the part about chance, though, I'd like to delve into the second discovery. Rock, Paper, Scissors actually has a hidden architectural richness.[2] It is an example of a category of patterns that are called strange loops. Douglas Hofstadter explained the underlying architecture of these sequences in his book *Gödel, Escher, Bach*.

A Strange Loop

In a strange loop, each part of the sequence is linked to another but there is no highest or lowest level as there is in a hierarchy. Unlike a deck of cards, where

there are clearly high-value and low-value cards, when you play Rock, Paper, Scissors there is no single element that sits at the top of the stack. Think of Escher's illustration of a hand emerging out of the paper to draw a hand, emerging out of the paper to draw a hand. Bach's musical composition "Canon a 2, per tonos" is another. Bach used an auditory illusion, similar to a phenomenon called Shepard Tones that convinces our ears that the tones of the music are climbing ever upward in pitch and yet never actually get any higher. A strange loop is a sort of feedback loop that shifts paradoxically across levels. You can experience Shepard Tones—the auditory illusion of escalating pitch online at http://trillion .maya.com/Shepard_tones.

Other cultures have Rock, Paper, Scissors games of their own. An Indonesian game called Earwig, Man, Elephant follows the same rules. Even Nature gets into the game: Analogous rules are in play with three variations of bacteria within the digestive system of mice. In Nature the rules of the game modulate survival among each bacterial colony.

When I realized that Rock, Paper, Scissors had an underlying architecture, and that many other systems reflect the same pattern, it was exhilarating. Not only did it help me to recognize related patterns, but also to predict new applications of the architecture. This realization made me understand that a good architecture is generative. It is like fertile soil in a vibrant ecology. It permits the growth of new organisms and constrains

---

[2] Note by Pete: I first learned this game during my juvenile infatuation with James Bond novels. Ian Fleming used it as a high-drama plot device in the opening pages of *You Only Live Twice*. The effectiveness of the game for this purpose in Fleming's capable hands relies upon the psychological subtleties to which Mick alludes.

and suggests what might grow in the future.

In our work we often find that an existing information system has been built as a monolithic solution that jumbles the raw plumbing of the system with the business process and the way customers interact. This leads to opaque, brittle solutions that usually expose the complexity of the underlying implementation directly to the user. It also makes it difficult for the system to be generative and often nearly impossible for it to evolve with new delivery platforms, new underlying systems, or new business realities.

The category of architecture that we term information architecture, or IA, has the potential to frame those underlying business activities in a more fruitful way. It gives us predictive power over what might be and supports far more agility to react to changing needs in the marketplace. It also acts to mediate between the raw complexity of the underlying machinery and the way the user interacts with the system.

As we have said, we characterize information architecture as "everything you can define about a system without knowing the underlying machinery that will make it work, or the interface you will use to communicate with the system." Looking at a system in this way frees you to think about what you really care about, and what you deliver to your customers—no matter the underlying machinery

or current vogue in user interface. The IA becomes an island of stability for your system as well as your users' experiences.

Back to my discoveries about Rock, Paper, Scissors: If you play the game over and over again you begin to see that people often reveal nonrandom preferences that masters like my friend can exploit. For instance, it is said that casual male players often lead by choosing rock (something is usually mumbled here about how it is more masculine and shows power). It is also claimed that scissors are thrown less often than rock or paper (maybe it has to do with human dexterity). When you combine these two insights, you conclude that leading with paper is a winning strategy. No doubt other subtle patterns of strategic value are hidden in the nuances of when to "hold" and when to "change."

The game of innovation has similarities to Rock, Paper, Scissors in this regard as well. Many businesses treat innovation as if it were a game of chance alone and wind up missing the resilient underlying patterns their inventions imply. Others learn to read the signals coming from the markets (and more importantly their customers). The best of them explore the underlying architecture of the problem and discover its hidden depths, ultimately giving them the agility and strategic reserves needed not only to play, but also to change, the game.

The Environment: Human Culture

All of this interplay among life forms, currency, and architecture takes place in the context of an environment. In a bio-ecology, the environment is a multivariate aggregation of natural elements, temperature, acidity, radiation, an abundance or scarcity of chemical resources, and so on. In the information ecology, the environment is rather different: It is nothing less than all of human culture. For all of its similarities with Nature, this ecology was created (or at least initiated) by human artifice, and it exists to serve human needs.

But just as the environment affects the ecology that it hosts, so does the ecology affect its environment. Life has been molded by conditions on Earth, but it has also transformed the Earth beyond reckoning. Just so, the emerging information ecology will transform human culture profoundly. The ultimate nature of that transformation is a story not yet written. But, if the shifts in human social intercourse wrought by the relatively trivial social networking technologies deployed to date are any indication, the story of life in the age of Trillions will prove to be a profound and exciting narrative.

Much of the good news of this book proceeds from the ecological nature of the trillion-node world. Learning to describe, understand, and participate in a global information ecology represents a tremendous opportunity. The new research, experimentation, and education implicit in this next stage of our technological development will spark a second knowledge revolution in which many of our readers and their children will participate.

CHALLENGES IN THE INFORMATION ECOLOGY

This book has two themes that are somewhat in tension. On one hand, we claim that the information ecology is upon us whatever we do or don't do. On the other hand, we say that it is critical to apply the principles of design science to guide its emergence. This may strike some readers as contradictory. But it is really just an example of the familiar tension between trusting our fate to self-determining, natural forces and centralized, rational efforts to bend such forces to our will. This is the tension underlying the conservative/liberal axis in politics; the subtle balance between free-market economics and government regulation intended to reign in the excesses of unbridled capitalism. The skills involved are those of the surfer who sizes up patterns in a wave's unalterable energy and rides them toward her own goals. They are the skills of the entrepreneur with the insight to foresee a high-leverage branch-point in the chaotic but nonrandom processes of the marketplace and to capitalize upon it for self-profit and social progress.

Moving a River

In *Life on the Mississippi*, Mark Twain provides practical instruction on how significant sections of the great river might be (and, he claims, have been) relocated by a single individual in a single night:

The water cuts the alluvial banks of the "lower" river into deep horseshoe curves; so deep, indeed, that in some places if you were to get ashore at one extremity of the horseshoe and walk across the neck, half or three-quarters of a mile, you could sit down and rest a couple of hours while your steamer was coming around the long elbow at a speed of ten miles an hour to take you on board again. When the river is rising fast, some scoundrel whose plantation is back in the country, and therefore of inferior value, has only to watch his chance, cut a little gutter across the narrow neck of land some dark night, and turn the water into it, and in a wonderfully short time a miracle has happened: To wit, the whole Mississippi has taken possession of that little ditch, and placed the countryman's plantation on its bank (quadrupling its value), and that other party's formerly valuable plantation finds itself away out yonder on a big island . . . , and down goes its value to a fourth of its former worth.

Twain's yarn provides a metaphor for how one must approach the design of an ecology—information or otherwise. Like the river, an ecology must be thought of as a dynamic system of vast aggregate power and operating according to its own patterns and rules. At first glance, such systems give the impression of inevitability and imperviousness to external influence. Standing on the riverbank, even at the very neck of Twain's horseshoe, would reveal no hint that one was located at a point of unique leverage and potential control. Discovering this requires knowledge of the river's rules, but also the topsight gained either from a thorough familiarity with the landscape or else a well-prepared and properly scaled map.

The designer who aspires to build on the scale of an ecology must abandon the conceit of absolute control of her medium and instead seek the abstract understanding of the scientist, and then apply this understanding to natural processes with the force-subverting skill of the jujitsu master. We cannot specify an ecology, but nor are we powerless to affect its evolution.

We have spoken much about the opportunities appertaining to these evolutionary processes, but the risks and challenges are always there, too. Some of these challenges will arrive unanticipated, but others are readily discernible or already upon us. It is worth discussing a few of the most obvious of the latter. Of these, three goals stand out: resiliency, trust, and what we might call human rightness or perhaps felicitousness.

Resiliency

Every psychology student learns the story of the celebrated Phineas Gage, the nineteenth century railroad gandy dancer who, having had a 13-pound iron bar propelled directly through his brain by an ill-timed blast of powder, was able to speak and walk within a few minutes, and led a reasonably normal life for 12

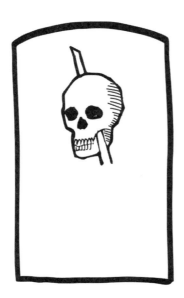

Figure 8.1 Phineas Gage and his iron bar

more years (Figure 8.1). Gage did not escape wholly unscathed, but given the magnitude of his injuries, his recovery was striking.

Now, imagine an analogous amount of damage to a modern PC or smartphone. No. Imagine a vastly smaller amount of damage—say, some kind of microscopic lesion through the device's circuitry involving only a few hundred transistors. How would the device survive such damage? The chances are that it would not survive at all. In all probability, the device would be junk. It is a credit to modern engineering that we have learned how to make such fragile devices reliable. But they are not very *resilient*, which is a different thing entirely. The reliability of modern electronic devices depends upon *ultra*reliability of the devices' components. The failure of any one of the billions of transistors in a modern CPU chip has a good chance of rendering the chip useless, so reliability of that CPU depends on the assumption that every transistor will work perfectly every time. An animal brain, on the other hand, has an architecture that makes no such assumption. Quite the opposite. Individual neurons are slow, noisy, and unreliable devices. And yet, a human brain is capable of functioning nonstop for a century or more, while sustaining serious abuse along the way. This is resiliency at work.

We see from these examples that there are two different approaches to achieving robust systems: bottom-up ultrareliability, and top-down resiliency. The computer industry has so far mostly relied on the former.[3] But in the coming information ecology, the former will not work. None of the techniques that have allowed manufacturers to make it work—centrally controlled choices of

---

[3] The original architecture of the Internet being a notable exception.

components; uniform manufacturing environments; mass-replication of nearly identical vertically integrated systems; factory-level unit testing—will characterize the age of Trillions. Creating large, complex systems will be less like factory manufacturing and more like growing a garden. One will plant, cultivate and prune—not expecting every sprout to blossom.

So, the cultivation of resilient systems will be a major thrust as we learn how to build in the new technological landscape. Where does resiliency come from? There are many answers to this question, but three characteristics have particular importance. These are redundancy, diversity, and stochastic processes.

Redundancy

In Nature, there are no singletons—there is never just one of anything. Everything is massively replicated. Andrew Carnegie advised that one should "put all your eggs into one basket—and watch that basket." This may have been good advice for a nineteenth-century robber baron, but it is not Nature's way, and it is not good advice for a twenty-first-century information ecologist.

Component redundancy can effectively protect against some failure modes, but it is powerless against certain others. In particular, if a design flaw or systematic manufacturing defect introduces a vulnerability into a component, the redundant deployment of that component will just make matters worse. As an obvious example of this, the extreme amount of standardization within the PC world on the Windows operating system—for all its advantages—is largely responsible for the sorry state of security on today's Internet.

Diversity

Protecting against this class of threat requires not just redundancy, but also diversity. Actually, diversity is itself a kind of redundancy—a redundancy not just of deployed components, but also of the design of those components. It is redundancy up a level of metaness. No ecology—natural or technological—can thrive for long without genetic diversity. Relying on a single vendor's solution—whether it be a particular integrated circuit or an entire operating system—as a de facto standard is the "cheap" and dangerous path toward standardization—we follow it at our peril. A trillion nodes with a high incidence of common defects would be setting us up for a disaster of unprecedented proportions. We must learn how to preserve and encourage diversity as we build toward the pervasive future. But here too, ham-handed attempts to follow this advice are likely to lead to new problems. The challenge is to preserve diversity while simultaneously achieving the uniformity of experience—both for end users and for those who deploy and maintain systems on their behalf—that will become a practical and economic necessity in the age of Trillions.

It is here, once again, that architecture becomes important. A properly layered architectural approach to systems design tends to focus attention not merely upon making something work, but upon functionally specified subcomponents with well-defined requirements and interfaces. Such specifications are, as we have seen, essential to device fungibility; and fungibility among independently developed equivalent implementations in the context of a free market of components is the royal path to diversity.

Stochastic Processes

Mainstream computing can trace its ancestry directly back to the giant calculator era of computers. As a result, numerical accuracy is an integral part of the DNA of the industry. If anything can be said about computers of virtually all stripes it is that they don't make errors in arithmetic. Getting the same answer every time is axiomatic. This may seem like a strange constraint to relax, but trading off precision and determinacy for resiliency will become an increasingly important part of the systems designer's repertoire of techniques as ecological computing takes hold. Stochastic processes—those that have some random component and thus are nondeterministic—are forced upon us by the tyranny of large numbers and by certain computational operations that are unavoidably expensive. A prime example of the latter involves what is known as "transactional consistency." To make a long story short, this refers to the operation of making sure that some piece of replicated information has consistent values in all of the places it is stored. This turns out to be a very expensive guarantee to make, computationally speaking. As a result, it needs to be avoided when possible, and that usually means compromising moment-to-moment consistency.

Transactions
By Pete

When computer scientists use the term *transaction*, they are referring to a very specific and mathematically precise operation between two spatially separated computing devices. Such transactions are the minimum operation necessary to guarantee that a piece of "'state" (think "item of information") in one machine is consistent with a similar piece of state in a second machine. For example, before an ATM machine agrees to dispense some cash from your banking account, it (obviously) phones home via a computer network to a master computer back at the bank's data center to make sure that your balance is sufficient to cover the withdrawal. It then gives up the cash and debits your account by the appropriate amount.

But it is a little more complicated than that. What if your husband—somewhere across town—were to attempt a similar withdrawal at *exactly the same time*? Couldn't you get lucky and have the "sufficient funds" check succeed for both of you if the steps of the withdrawal happened at just the right times? The answer, of course, is "no," and making sure of this is what transactions are all about. Between the time that the first machine makes its request and when the account is debited, the bank's system puts a lock on your account, so that your husband would be forced to wait for his money. When the first transaction is complete, an all-clear message goes out to release the lock.

As it turns out, that lock operation is expensive, and it is expensive in a way that no amount of additional computing power or cheap disk space will ever fix. A moment's thought will show that any possible approach to implementing this lock will require at least one round trip exchange of messages between the two machines. But Albert Einstein taught us that no message can travel faster than the speed of light. That may not sound like much of a constraint, but it turns out to be a huge bottleneck, and one determined not by how fast we manage to make our computers run, but by the laws of physics. Computers will get faster, memory will get cheaper and more abundant, but transactions will never get easier.

If this seems counterintuitive to you, you are not alone. I have spoken about this many times, including to gatherings of highly sophisticated engineers. Whenever I do, I always give the audience the following challenge: "Without doing a calculation—just using your intuition—estimate the maximum number of round-trip messages per second that could possibly be exchanged between New York and Los Angeles, assuming that the speed of light is the only constraint." In audience after audience, I get estimates ranging from a few thousand to a few million. The correct answer is 38.[4] This number represents an absolute upper limit on the sequential transaction rate at this distance. By the standards of computing this is extraordinarily slow. Transactions are a scarce resource indeed, and this is not going to change.

Any designer whose intuitions are that divergent from reality is in trouble. The fact that the engineers designing our future have such consistently bad intuitions about a process so basic to computing in the age of Trillions speaks volumes about how uncharted is the territory into which we are marching. Climbing Trillions Mountain is going to require some different thinking.

An example of this can be found in the massive server farms that lie behind giant, high-volume websites. If you watch carefully the behavior of a large, rapidly changing site—cnn.com, for example—you might notice that if you access the site using two identical web browsers at roughly the same time, you will occasionally see different information. This, as you probably know, is because such websites are not served from a single giant server, but rather from farms of thousands of independent machines. Updating all those machines takes time, and exactly what you get at any given instant depends upon the luck of the draw. These machines *could* be explicitly synchronized every time a change is

---

[4] 186,282 miles/second divided by 4,900 miles (round trip).

made, but this would be at the expense of bringing everything to a screech-ing halt during every change. We would find ourselves back to the days of the World-Wide-Wait. The designers of these server farms chose to sacrifice a bit of consistency (a kind of accuracy) for a lot of performance. Similar tradeoffs will become an inevitable part of a successful information ecology.

Trust

Our willingness to embrace a technology or a source of information (and there-fore their market viability) is completely dependent on our willingness to trust them. We fly in airliners because we trust that they will not fall out of the sky. We rely upon physical reference books found in the library because we trust that they are not elaborate forgeries and that their publishers have properly vetted their authors. But trust is a relative thing. We trust—more or less—well-known websites when we are shopping for appliances or gadgets. But we are more careful about things we read on the Internet when the consequences are high. We consider web-based sources of medical information, but we do so with caution. We tend to discount random political rants found on personal blogs. We trust not at all e-mail from widows of former Nigerian ministers of finance. Wikipedia has earned our trust for many routine purposes, but would we be willing to have our taxes calculated based upon numbers found there? Similarly, we trust consumer computing devices[5] for surfing the web, for TiVo-ing our television programs, and perhaps for turning on our porch light every evening, but we do not trust them to drive our cars or to control our cities.

As these examples illustrate, our requirements for trust vary proportion-ately with the criticality of the applications. The average level of trust of the Internet or of consumer computing devices is fairly low, but this is acceptable since we do not yet use them for the things that really matter. As we have seen, this is about to change, and so the stakes with respect to trust are going up.

Where does trust in a technology come from? This is yet another question with many answers, but some obvious ones involve reputation, provenance, and security. These three are intimately related. *Reputation* is practically syn-onymous with trust itself. Other than personal experiences, which are inevita-bly limited, what basis do we have for forming trust besides reputation? But, there can be no reputation without provenance. An anonymous note scribbled on a wall can almost never be trusted, simply because we know so little about its origin. Similarly, material obtained from today's peer-to-peer file sharing services is inherently untrustworthy. There is, in general, no way of knowing whether a file is what it claims to be, or whether it has been subtly altered from its original. Which brings us, inevitably, to security. Our confidence in the prov-enance of an item in the real world depends critically on one of two things:

---

[5] By this we mean computers not tightly controlled by IT professionals, as opposed, say, to those located in a bank's data center.

We believe that an object is what it seems to be either because it is technically difficult to duplicate, or because its history is accounted for. Dollar bills are an example of the former, and a fork once owned by George Washington might be an example of the latter.

As these examples suggest, most traditional approaches to security are tied to physical attributes such as complex structures of various kinds or brute-force barriers to entry. These familiar approaches have also formed the basis for the security of information systems in the great majority of cases. It is true that "private places" in cyberspace such as web-based services are "protected" by passwords, but as a practical matter, most private data are protected via physical security. We protect the contents of our PCs by keeping strangers away from them. We keep our cell phones and our credit cards securely in our pockets and purses. Large corporations keep their data crown jewels locked away in data center fortresses.

But there's a new sheriff in town. His name is "encryption." Of course, there is nothing really new about encryption. It has been around for millennia. But modern computing, combined with modern mathematics and modern networking, has raised the art of code making to both critical importance and—if properly deployed—near perfect trustworthiness.[6] This is fortunate, because on Trillions Mountain nothing else will work. In a world moving irrevocably into cyberspace, and in which cyberspace itself will be implemented in a radically distributed manner, how could it be otherwise?

Encryption is already indispensable to the functioning of the Internet. The channels along which our data flow are and should be considered intrinsically insecure. Any attempt to "fix" this situation would involve throwing out the baby with the bathwater. A safe Internet would be a sterile Internet—innovation would cease. Fortunately, this is unnecessary. End-to-end encryption is fully capable of providing secure communication over insecure channels. The same technologies are also capable of meeting the needs of data provenance. Techniques going under the name of cryptographic signatures allow even plaintext data to be reliably identified as to its source in a way such that any tampering can be reliably detected. These techniques are mature, and they are reliable. The problem is that they are at present only deployed in very limited settings and for very narrow purposes. A successful information ecology will require the use of these techniques to become universal and routine. They will be the only practical means of security in the future.

---

[6] It is true that the development of a practical quantum computer would compromise this trustworthiness, but such a breakthrough is not imminent; and, if and when it does happen, the same technology will no doubt provide new tools for the code makers as well as the code breakers. Moreover, the significantly more mature techniques of quantum key distribution, which rely on the process of quantum entanglement, are believed to be fundamentally impervious to any possible attack.

Let us be clear about this point: The time will soon come in which it will be necessary to almost completely abandon physical security as a component of our system of trust. In a world of immaterial, promiscuously replicated data objects, all secrets must be encrypted and most nonsecrets must be digitally signed. In this world, if you would not be willing to hand copies of your most important data to your mortal enemies (properly encrypted, of course), then any sense of security you may have will be illusory. For all practical purposes, this is already true. If you are a user of any of the so-called cloud computing services, or any other network service for that matter, your precious data pass through many hands on the way to that service, and not all of them are necessarily friendly. The world we describe simply takes the next small steps of using encryption routinely during storage as well as during transport, and then giving up the illusion of physical security.

These issues of trust, provenance, reputation, and security don't apply only to information. In the age of Trillions, they will be equally important when dealing with physical devices. This is a relatively minor issue today. If you go to your local Apple Store and buy something that looks and acts like an iPhone, you have reason to believe that it is indeed an iPhone, exactly as Apple designed it. And so your level of trust in the device should pretty much equal your level of trust in the Apple brand (whatever that level may be). On the other end of the spectrum, if you buy a four-banger pocket calculator at the dollar store, it may well have no brand at all—certainly no brand that you will have heard of. You don't know or care who designed or built it. As long as it does correct arithmetic (which in all likelihood it will), what harm can it do?

But, in the age of Trillions, things won't be so cut and dried. When every piece of bric-a-brac will have enough computing power to do real mischief, the provenance of trivial things will come to be of concern. Even today, how would you know if deep inside the CPU chip of your new Internet-connected TV there was some tiny bit of unnoticed logic—the result of some secret mandate of some unscrupulous foreign government—implementing a latent back-door Trojan horse, waiting for an innocent-looking automatic firmware update to begin doing god-knows-what? Has such a thing ever been done? We have no idea. Is it implausible? Obviously, not in the least. The odds may be small in any given case. But, as we may have mentioned before, a trillion is a large number. There will soon be a great many places to hide, and malicious functionality hiding in insignificant hardware is going to be a whole lot more insidious than malicious code hiding in information objects. In the future, the provenance of mundane objects is going to become of real interest.

This is a serious issue that has not received nearly as much attention as the protection of information via encryption. Short of X-raying a chip and accounting for every transistor, it is really not clear how the authenticity of a chip that has ever been out in the wild can really be established. The seriousness of this issue has recently been brought into focus by a series of incidents involving the discovery of "counterfeit" (actually recycled) chips in

U.S. military electronics. Although it is not clear that these incidents involved anything beyond an attempt to make extra profit, the potential consequences of the appearance of enemy Trojan horses embedded deep into military hardware needs no elaboration. How these risks can be addressed is an open question. Fortunately, the very problem may prove to contain the seeds to its own solution. There already exist electronic shipping tags that, when attached to crates containing high-value cargo, monitor them for rough handling and other physical abuse, and in some cases even track exactly where the items have been and when. It seems plausible that the kind of supply-chain transparency that such technologies make possible may become a routine and essential part of establishing and maintaining the provenance of even commodity products.

Felicitousness: Designing for People

I recently came across a short story I wrote back in high school. It was an apocalyptic tale of a nuclear war fought in some vague future epoch. The twist was that the war was fought by automated systems centuries after humanity was wiped out by a viral epidemic. Evidently my adolescent taste for irony blossomed earlier than any sense of literary merit. In any event, the story serves admirably as the antithesis of the story we are trying to tell in this book.

—Pete

The information ecology that we have been sketching involves a kind of automation, but it is not the automation of a lights-out robotically controlled factory, or of the missile system in Pete's story. Far from being a system apart from humanity, it will be a seamless symbiosis between human and machine systems.[7] In this respect, it is more like a home or a city than it is like a factory. This is a crucial point, because it gets to the heart of why pulling off the next 50 years is going to be a challenge. In a nutshell, the challenge is this: We are facing an engineering project as big as any that humanity has ever faced, but the system being engineered will be as much human as it is machine. The trick will be to insure that it is also *humane*.

At the time we are writing, the current next big thing (that is to say, the thing for which it is currently easiest to obtain venture capital) is any Internet

---

[7] If you doubt this, walk down a busy street in any city in the world and estimate the percentage of young people who are visibly attached to some piece of information technology. Then, make a similar estimate for the percentage with some kind of body modification. Can there be any doubt that when the day comes that implantable iPhones become feasible (and that day is not distant), a nontrivial number of people will opt-in?

business plan containing the words *social networking*. This is just the latest in what will prove to be a very long row of profit-making dominos that the industry will knock down more or less one at a time, but at an ever-increasing rate. But it is a fortunate one at the present juncture, since it focuses the industry on the basic issues of human interaction, which is where the important developments are going to lie from now on.

Networks of Trust

Before we leave the topic of trust, we should explore the increasingly important notion of networks of trust. People have always participated in multiple, overlapping communities of various kinds. But prior to the mass Internet, the number of such communities available to any individual was as a practical matter very limited, and usually very local. There was family, and neighborhood, and work, and perhaps church or fraternal lodge or knitting club or Boy Scout troop. All of these were community based, which basically means that everybody pretty much knew everybody else—at least well enough to size them up for trust purposes. If your interests spilled out beyond your local community, then you were more or less reduced to magazine subscriptions or mail-order society memberships, both of which were largely one-way read-only relationships.

But, from its earliest days, the Net has been changing all of that. Arguably, the very first practical use to which the early ARPAnet was put was to support a dozen or so "mailing lists," which were in fact topically grouped networks of people who used mass-emailings to form something new in the world: persistent, intimate, real-time discussion groups made up of total strangers.[8] In other words, the very first computer networking was social networking. And, suddenly, the number of social networks that one could belong to was no longer limited by geography, but only by one's enthusiasms, energy, and willingness to stay up late.

What was striking about these early online communities, and all that have followed, is that they quickly lead to new kinds of interpersonal relationships. Instead of gaining a broad understanding of other people, one gains a very deep understanding about very narrow slices of other lives. You may have one circle of friends whom you would trust intimately if you were repairing your antique motorcycle, and another whose advice about New York City nightlife is beyond reproach. On all other topics, you wouldn't know these people from Adam and would trust them even less. And yet, for the matters for which you *do* trust them, the level of trust is often far higher than would be the case with generic friends. And, it must be remembered that these kinds of microcommunities-of-interest exist in vast numbers and on just about every conceivable topic. This democratization of access to specialized knowledge is

---

[8] Google Groups has indexed many messages from these days—going back as far as 1981. It is disorienting and sometimes embarrassing to come across one's own footprints in that lost world.

where the real significance of social networking lies. Just as mobile access to Google has destroyed the bar bet by giving everyone instant access to any fact, the emerging vast web of trust networks has given everyone access to expert opinion and judgment.

The notion of networks of trust is also important in the implementation of systems of data provenance. As we have already seen, the ability to judge the trustworthiness of a document is dependent on the ability to have trustworthy knowledge of who wrote it. But, most documents are written by strangers, so the problem reduces to deciding whether you can trust a stranger. How do you do this? Basically, you need to find a path through a network of trust. If the document is written by a friend of a friend whom you trust, that is often enough. But theories of "six degrees of separation" notwithstanding, finding such a path on the interpersonal level is often not practical. What is needed is connectors—aggregators of trust. There is a name for such aggregators. They are called publishers. If you strip out incidental (and increasingly irrelevant) functions like printing and warehousing physical books, the essential residue of what commercial publishers do has everything to do with vouching for authors. Given two books by equally obscure authors, are you more likely to trust the one that was self-published, or the one that was published by a major publishing house? This function of vouching for authors will be at least as important in the new information ecology as it has been historically.

Privacy

This is a tough one. On one hand, there is the position epitomized by Sun Microsystems' CEO Scott McNealey's infamous 1999 pronouncement that "You have zero privacy anyway. Get over it." When video cameras are the size of pinheads and cost approximately nothing, it is sometimes difficult not to conclude that the jig is up. And, it can't be denied that everyone from subway riders to FedEx delivery men are thinking twice these days before misbehaving. On the other hand, we have all read *1984*, and it is hard to get that one out of your head. Maybe the path we are on is just not acceptable. We just don't know. But, what we do know is that whether or not we choose to treat a modicum of privacy as a basic human right, we have to acknowledge it as a basic human need. And even if not, it still seems obvious that simple prudence dictates that we cede control of much personal information to the individual to whom it appertains. Sooner or later, we think, there is going to be pushback from consumers, and purveyors of information products and services will ignore privacy issues at their peril.

For all the wonders that pervasive computing will bring, it must be admitted that it will not in the natural course of things be very good for privacy. These negative side effects of a generally positive technological trend are analogous to the air and water pollution that inevitably accompanied industrialization. They can't be entirely avoided, but they can and must be mitigated.

Amid the circus of the O.J. Simpson murder trial, a lot of people were more than a bit startled to discover that every swipe of those hotel room key-cards is recorded and subject to subpoena. Similarly, if you lose your ticket when parking in an airport parking lot, you might be surprised to learn that the management will know how many days you have been parked, courtesy of the automatic OCR (Optical Character Recognition) performed on your license plate. Both of these examples are old news. The new situational awareness technologies that are becoming practical every year are beginning to boggle the mind. And, of course, we have been focusing only on the physical world. The ability to surreptitiously collect data in cyberspace is too obvious and too well known to require comment here.

As in every other technological revolution, some kind of middle ground will have to be carved out over time, and doing so will very likely require the force of law in at least some cases. But once the consequences of these new capabilities begins to sink in, we suspect that there will be enough consumer objections with enough negative effect on the corporate bottom line that, even without government action, being privacy friendly will soon acquire as much cash value as being environmentally friendly already has.

Empowering Power Users

The early days of the PC were a classic case of a solution in search of a prob-lem. It was pretty obvious that a computer-on-your-desk was an exciting prospect and had to be good for something. But what? Storing recipes per-haps? We were in a hunt for a killer app. When we finally found one in the late 1970s, it was at first a bit surprising. It turned out to be something called VisiCalc. VisiCalc was basically a glorified financial calculator, but it had two features that are critical to our story: First, it had an architecture. Better yet, it had an architecture tied to a good metaphor. The metaphor was that of a financial spreadsheet—a grid of rows and columns forming cells. These cells were (literally) little boxes into which one could put numbers and text. If this sounds familiar, it is not coincidental. Spreadsheets are a microcosm of the data container idea that we have been discussing throughout this book. By label-ing columns with letters and rows with numbers, each cell was given a unique identity (albeit only unique within a given spreadsheet) that permitted it to be referred to independently of its contents. It was a simple, powerful concept that made sense to business users. Second—and critically—VisiCalc was *scriptable*. It wasn't so much an application as a box of Lego blocks. It did almost nothing out of the box, but it was relatively easy to build highly specific *appliances* that fit like a glove into the workflows of particular offices and did a far better job of meeting the myriad needs of those offices than could any canned accounting package.

This is a good story, but it may strike you as being out of place in a sec-tion about social processes in pervasive computing. But the story is *essentially* social. To see why, we need to point out one more fact about spreadsheet programs: Many users who routinely employ spreadsheets really don't understand them very well. Although developing new spreadsheet appliances is *relatively* easy when compared with writing a computer program from scratch, it is still a somewhat arcane process requiring certain specialized skills and a certain temperament. Most people prefer to just get on with their jobs. The true breakthrough of the spreadsheet program was that it empowered the former to support the latter (Figure 8.2). Many people would rather have a root canal than create an elaborate spreadsheet. But everybody knows the wizard down the hall who is great at it and loves the challenge. These aren't programmers, they are *scriptors*—paraprogrammers.

This story of Architecture empowering people to help each other in intimate local settings is of crucial importance in envisioning how the coming information ecology will operate. Both the sheer scale of the systems we will be deploying and their vast diversity and sensitivity to local conditions simply precludes any deployment and support system that does not have the essential characteristics of locality and interpersonal communications that is epitomized by the end-user/power-user axis. No Geek Squad is going to

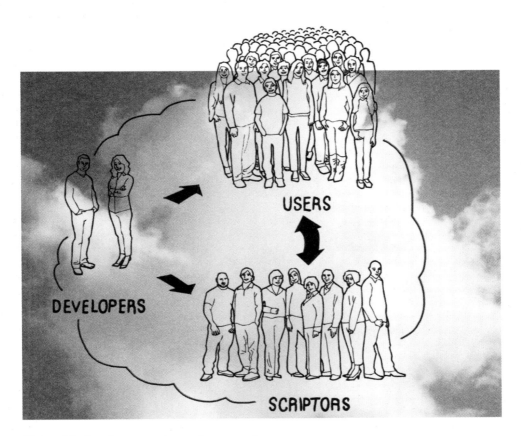

Figure 8.2 Developers serving scriptors serving users

suffice to come into your house every time you want to rearrange your furniture (which, being information devices like everything else, will be part of
the fabric of your local information environment). A lot of that kind of thing
will have to take care of itself. For most of the rest, it is your geek nephew,
or your friendly next-door neighbor that will be your go-to person. This is a
fundamentally social process, but one that is enabled by subtle and deliberate
design decisions by the device and information architects who conceive and
cultivate the DNA of these new life-forms.

CHAPTER 9

Aspects of Tomorrow

The only simplicity for which I would give a straw is that which is on the other side of the complex—not that which never has divined it.

—OLIVER WENDELL HOLMES, JR.

Figure 9.1 *YESTERDAY'S TOMORROWS*

Source: Used with the acknowledgment of the
Frank R. Paul Estate.

There is a framed poster that has been around MAYA's offices from almost the beginning. Its title is YESTERDAY'S TOMORROWS, and it advertised some long-past art exhibit featuring old visions of the future—skyscrapers shaped like art deco spaceships and so forth. The image (Figure 9.1) is a useful reminder that detailed predictions about the future are a fool's errand and that one's efforts in this direction are doomed to pathos. History is fraught with chaotic and idiosyncratic processes that determine its salient details, and we are no better than anybody else at reading those kinds of tea leaves. We know enough to steer clear. Nonetheless, we can see no way to make our exit without painting some sort of picture to provide coherence to the story we have been telling. So, we will attempt an impressionist painting—endeavoring to emphasize the essential patterns that we can see clearly, while avoiding dubious detail. When we drift too far into specificity, we trust the reader to smile at our naïveté and just squint.

BEYOND THE INTERNET

The Internet will be with us for the foreseeable future. At its core, it is just too simple and too correct to change much. Indeed, the Internet in the age of Trillions is likely to be even more like the Internet as it was originally conceived than it is today. At present, the vast majority of the Net's traffic is aggregated into a few very large "pipes" that are operated and controlled by a small handful of commercial entities. Moreover, these systems are highly managed, using semi-manual processes and a great deal of human tweaking. Much of the self-configuring and self-healing nature of the original, far flatter Internet, while still latent in the architecture has little relevance in its present mode of operation.

We do not predict that the big pipes will go away. Indeed, they will grow in number and size, but not in importance. As bandwidth requirements continue to grow without bound, these trunks will evolve into specialized services, moving vast amounts of audio, video, and other very large and/or time-critical data objects in highly optimized ways. Such optimization will worry advocates of Net neutrality (a community of which we consider ourselves members), but it will hardly matter. By the time this happens there will be so many alternative paths for data to flow that effective neutrality of payload will have long since been assured. Billions upon billions of cooperative, Internet-enabled, peer-to-peer devices will have grown together in an incomprehensible but very effective tangle of self-configuring arteries and veins such that the very concept of an Internet connection will recede from consciousness.

A much larger percentage of data flow will be strictly local. No longer will e-mail messages travel across continents on their way between two cell phones in the same room. Suburban neighborhoods and urban apartment buildings will enjoy immense intramural bandwidth simply by virtue of the devices—wired and wireless—owned by their residents. Such short-haul data will flow as the Internet's founders imagined—through ever-changing, self-healing, dynamically determined paths, whose robustness to hardware failure, changes in demand, and censorship will go unquestioned.

Returning to the analogy of a circulatory system, the commercial trunk lines will serve as the major arterial pathways, feeding a vastly larger web of peripheral veins and arteries formed by individually owned, locally communicating peer-to-peer devices. All of these devices will speak today's Internet protocols, with only evolutionary improvements. But vast as this network will be, it will pale in size to a third, even more local tier—the capillaries of our metaphorical circulatory system. Comprising trillions of single-purpose data paths, many of them trivial in capacity, this layer of the network will lack the generality (and so, the complexity) of the Internet protocols. Installed and configured by blue-collar technicians and consumers, such links will support data flows in very local settings, more often than not between an unchanging pair of devices. Not only is it not necessary for light switches to have the ability to connect directly to any other device in the world (the sine qua non of the Internet), it is harmful. Harmful in two ways: First, as we have seen repeatedly, complexity of any kind has a cost, and so should be avoided when possible. More importantly, it is *dangerous*. The Internet—like all public places—is potentially dangerous, and always will be. Yes, we can build firewalls, but they will never be perfect and will very often themselves contain more complexity than the devices they are intended to protect.[1]

We will eschew the complexity of the Internet at the lowest levels of our infrastructure with good riddance. But something will be lost. The Internet

---

[1] At the time of this writing, the U.S. Post Office is running an ad campaign listing all the things (refrigerators, cork boards, snail mail) that have never been hacked. The effort is kind of pathetic, but they do have a point: The best way to protect a device from being hacked is to make it too simple to be hackable. In a sufficiently simple system, there is just no place to hide. This, it seems to us, is a desirable trait for the light switches in hospital operating rooms.

brings with it ready-made answers to many difficult questions concerning communications protocols and standards. In its place will emerge a free market of best practices for dealing with the myriad of special-case requirements that such a scenario implies. We see this in today's building trades, where a relatively small number of standard component specifications and design patterns have emerged from years of accumulated experience in a marketplace of both products and ideas. There are lots of different plumbing components in the hardware store—more than are strictly necessary. But they represent time-proven, cost-effective designs that emerged from a process that works better than any process involving central planning or attempts at grand unification.

SIMPLIFICATION

That last point extends far beyond network protocols. Throughout this book we have been careful to use phrases like *taming complexity* rather than *simplification*. This was no mere affectation. Computers are all about complexity, and we wanted to make clear that our goal is to manage it—to harness its power—not eliminate it. Here, however, we will use the "S word" and mean it. Although the aggregate complexity of the systems we will build on Trillions Mountain will make today's systems look like toys, this will only be possible by the vast simplification of the building blocks of those systems. Not only is today's PC the most complex integrated artifact that humanity has ever produced, we suspect that it will prove to be the most complex single artifact it will *ever* produce. It is on the edge of what is worth building in this way. As we learn how to orchestrate vast numbers of tiny devices, we will come to realize that many of the tasks for which we use PCs[2] today can be done with vastly simpler devices.

Here are two examples: Almost every urban parking garage contains one or more machines that dispense gate tickets, compute parking charges, and read credit cards. If you ever get a chance to peek over the shoulder of the service guy when this machine is opened up, you may get a glimpse of how it is built. Very likely, you will see some kind of a PC. Similarly, if you go to your local library branch, the librarian will have an electronic system for scanning barcodes on books and library cards, and a simple database to keep track of who has borrowed what books. It is overwhelmingly likely that this system is built using a PC. In other words, we are using a device that in many ways is more complex than a space shuttle to perform tasks that require less computing power than is found in a typical pocket calculator. Why? Because, unless you are prepared to commit to huge unit volumes, the only economically viable way to deliver a quantum of computing power is to buy and program a PC.

---

[2] And in this we include the only marginally less-complex post-PC devices such as tablets and smartphones.

There just aren't enough libraries or parking garages to justify purpose-built hardware. These examples typify why gratuitous complexity proliferates.

How will we get out of this box? The answer, as we have seen, lies in fungible components. Component architectures and open APIs will finally lead us to the packaging of much smaller units of computation in a form that is practical for developers to use without engaging in a science project. The simplification implicit in this agenda will come in three stages: Stage 1 will involve the exposure of the internal capabilities of otherwise conventional products. As the clock-radio example of Chapter 2 illustrates, this will be driven by the needs of interoperability. We will probably never witness the absurdity of ticket dispensers with clock radios inside them (not that this would be much more absurd than using a computer running Windows). But once we get in the habit of exposing the internal power of the devices we sell, we will discover that there are a lot of MacGyvers out there who will find creative uses (and thus create new markets) for the strangest combinations of components.[3] Slowly, the market will sort out which of the exposed capabilities of existing products are in high demand, thus leading to Stage 2, which will involve the engineering of components that directly implement those capabilities in more rational packages.

The outsides of these transitional components will tend to be simple (the market will by now value simplicity and reward those who deliver it). But the insides will still be complex. The reason is that, for a while, this will be the only practical way to engineer such modules. The accumulated crud of unavoidable complexity has poisoned the market for simple, low-functionality components, and so designers have little choice but to use overly powerful, overly complex microprocessors and absurdly large memory chips, whether they are needed or not. So, at this stage, we will not so much be reducing complexity as sequestering it. Designers will compete in the open-component marketplace to deliver the most general, stable, and inexpensive implementations of the simplest possible standardized APIs. Market pressures will quickly shape these APIs into simple elegance, but the insides of the boxes will still be needlessly complex.

But this will not last long. Once we get this far, the absurdity of the situation will finally become apparent to all. Because a successful component will find uses in many vertical markets, its volumes will rise. This, in turn, will revive markets for less powerful and simpler components. Old chip designs will be dusted off and brought back into production, and new manufacturing techniques (such as organic semiconductors) that have been kept out of the market due to performance limitations will start to become economically viable. And so, in Stage 3 the insides of the boxes will finally shed their complexity. We emphasize yet again that the complexity won't go away, but it will

---

[3] One sees this kind of thing today in the hobbyist "maker" community. Unfortunately, it usually involves voiding warranties, skirting safety certifications, and other practices that are unacceptable to professionals. Engineered component architectures will solve these problems.

migrate from the low levels of our systems, where it is malignant, up to the higher layers where it can be shaped and effectively managed by exposure to market forces. Prices will drop, tractability, volumes, and profits will soar. By this three-step process we will have pulled off a slick trick. The menacing tide of undesigned complexity will be stemmed, and we will finally be able to return to the normal pattern of "complex things built out of simpler things" that characterizes all competent engineering design.

DEVICES

It is interesting to imagine what the hardware store of the future will be like. On a given day, its customers may include a DIY homeowner repairing a "smart room" that can no longer accurately detect its occupants; a contractor preparing a bid on an air-conditioning system that has to play well with a specific building energy management system; and a one-person repair shop sorting out a botched home theater installation that never did work properly. How will all these folks cope with the kinds of complexity we have been talking about? We can assume that the aisles will still be organized by physical function (plumbing, lighting, structural . . .). But then what? Universal standards will be too much to hope for, so by no means will everything be able to communicate with everything else. What we *can* hope for is the incremental evolution of well-defined groups of loosely interoperable devices. In MAYA's architectural work, we call such groups *realms*. A realm is defined as a set of devices, all of which are capable of directly passing at least one kind of message to each other. In practice, this means that they have a common means of communication, and they speak a common language (or at least a common subset of a language). Thus, if I can connect a light switch to a light fixture and have the switch successfully send "on" and "off" messages to the fixture, then the switch and the fixture are in the same realm. Note that objects in different realms might still be used together, it is just that some kind of an adaptor would have to be used to bridge the realms. (As mentioned in Chapter 2, MAYA calls such adaptors *transducers*.)

We have long since reached this stage with more mature technologies, such as plumbing. While there are many realms of plumbing, consider just three: water pipes, gas tubing, and a garden hose. Most of the pipe and tubing that constitutes these realms falls in approximately the same range of scale—a fraction of an inch to a couple of inches in diameter. And, while all three do roughly the same thing—conduct a fluid along a controlled path—they are intentionally incompatible. This is accomplished by specifying slightly different diameters and incompatible screw threads at the connections (device interfaces)—a means for facilitating the adherence to various building codes. Of course, some interrealm connections are possible—you can connect a garden hose to a water pipe—but it takes an adapter.

The notion of realm is deceptively simple. It in no way restricts, or even informs, the development of new communications technologies or protocols, so you might think we were right back where we started. But merely recognizing the existence of such an architectural principle gives designers and manufacturers something to aim for, and purchasers in our hardware store something to shop for. In other words, it helps to *organize a marketplace*. The notion does not imply any kind of heavy-handed standards process—an approach that we view with considerable skepticism. Rather, it looks to market forces to sort out the wheat from the chaff. Popular realms will attract many products, since they represent a proven market. On the other hand, flawed realms, even if popular, will beg for competition by those who think they can do better. If this works like other markets, we will first see chaos, followed by plateaus of stability punctuated by occasional paradigm shifts.

The payoff happens in the hardware store. Assuming some trade organization emerges to assign unambiguous identifiers to popular realms (a relatively easy task) and perhaps do some compliance testing (a harder but still tractable process), we can envision a world in which every product on the shelves is labeled as to its realm membership. This is not all that different from what happens in today's hardware stores. In the electrical department, you will find two or three incompatible styles of circuit breaker boxes— with perhaps several different brands of each. If you go in to purchase a replacement circuit breaker, you had best know beforehand which style of box is in your basement. The same is

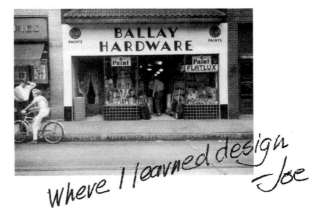

Where I learned design —Joe

true of basic styles of plumbing pipe, backyard irrigation systems, and so on. The realm idea simply extends this pattern to pervasive computing devices— adding just a little bit more structure, as demanded by the greater complexity of computing devices. Just as there are often adaptors that permit the intermixing of otherwise incompatible products, the aforementioned transducers will be offered by various manufacturers when the market demands them.

Healthy markets always live on the edge of chaos, and our future hardware store will be no exception. But if manufacturers can resist the urge to hide behind closed, proprietary standards and protocols (and those who cannot will in the long run simply fail), and if the design community does its ordained job of defining open, forward-looking architectures to provide a modicum of organization, that store will be the hangout of a vibrant, creative, and generative community.

And, of course, we must not forget that, as always, disruptive new technologies will come onto the stage from time to time. This is a particularly dicey place to attempt predictions, so we will for the most part forbear. But one important area to which we have already alluded involves new circuit and display fabrication technologies. We do not refer to exotic, high-end, ever-faster and denser chip technologies. These are always with us, and so are not particularly disruptive. We mean the opposite: low-end, slower, lower-density, but much cheaper circuits and displays. Our poster child for such technologies is circuits literally printed on paper using something like ink-jet printers and semiconductor inks. Whether this particular technology works out is not of the essence. Throw-away, cheap electronics in one form or another will not be long in coming. This, combined with device fungibility will be the last nail in the coffin of computing feeling like something we "do" rather than being just part of the milieu. When one can pick up a discarded newspaper on the subway and use it to check your e-mail, any sense of distance between space and cyberspace will have vanished.

THE INFORMATION COMMONS

The next step toward the emergence of the kind of "real cyberspace" that we have already discussed will be the gradual unfolding of an Information Commons. The Commons will be a true public resource—dedicated to the commonweal. We are not describing something like Wikipedia. In fact, the Commons in some ways is the exact opposite. Wikipedia, although free, philanthropic, and dedicated to the public interest, is in fact a single collection of information under the ultimate control of a single organization (some would say a single individual). Users of the service must ultimately trust the reliability and integrity of that organization for its continued availability. In contrast, the Commons will be controlled by no one (although it probably *will* require some kind of nongovernmental organization to coordinate it). Its purpose will be less the accumulation of information than its organization. It will serve as a kind of a trellis upon which others may hang information (both free and proprietary).

The essence of this trellis will be what amounts to an enumeration of the basic facts of the world, starting with simple assertions of existence. Thus, to start with the most obvious and compelling example, it will maintain a definitive gazetteer of geopolitical and geophysical features. It is a remarkable fact that no single, universally-recognized worldwide list exists (recall our discussion of the Hanover problem in Chapter 6). The consolidation of such a list from readily available sources, and the assignment of each entry a single universally-unique identifier will alone have an immeasurable impact on our ability to coordinate disparate, independent datasets. No longer will search engines need to employ exotic text-processing algorithms just to figure out whether the string "Jersey" is meant to refer to a state, an island, a breed of cow, or an article of clothing. Now, imagine if we also had such definitive lists of corporations and other businesses and of not-for-profit organizations; of cars and appliances and all other manufactured products; of all known chemical compounds; of all known species of plants and animals; and on and on. It is not that we don't already have such lists. The problem is that we have too many. They are compiled over and over for special purposes, they are often proprietary, rather than freely available, and they come in diverse formats and organizations, with idiosyncratic and mutually incompatible identifier schemes. All of these things conspire to make them ineffective as the foundation for a true Commons, although their existence makes the creation of one very feasible.

One thing to note about these basically ontological assertions is that they are for the most part, noncontroversial. People argue about the age of the Earth, but rarely about its existence. A few basic organizational facts about geopolitics are in dispute (e.g., the status of Taiwan as an independent state), but such disputes are infrequent enough so as to not challenge the basic utility of the agenda. As long as the Commons sticks to basic facts, its wide acceptance as the definitive source of universal identifiers will remain within reach.

It is hard to overstate the improvement that such a regime will make to the information architecture of the Internet. When widespread consistency is attained on the simple matter of reference to real-world entities, search will become vastly more efficient, "data fusion" across independently maintained datasets will move from being a black art to a trivial science, whole new industries of higher-level data organization and visualization will be enabled. In a sense, the web will be turned inside out. Today, virtually all content is organized by the owner of the information, and we depend on the miracle of the search engines to sort it all out. The existence of the trellis of the Commons will support the evolution of a web organized by *topic*. This will not eliminate the need for search engines, but it will make their task much easier, and accelerate their evolution toward truly intelligent agents, sharing a common referential framework with the humans they exist to serve.[4]

THE WORLD WIDE DATAFLOW

Getting past the client-server model will be a long, slow slog. Technological inertia and backward-looking economic interests will conspire to ensure this. But slowly the barriers to progress will yield. The pressure will come from several sources. The already-common disasters associated with too-big-to-fail centralized services will become ever more common and serious. As a result, it will begin to dawn on the public that the vulnerabilities that these events expose are not

---

[4]MAYA has worked for many years toward the development of an architecture for the Commons in the context of its "Civium" initiative. Read about it here: http://www.civium.org.

growing pains but are inherent in the model. Moreover, the potential for political and criminal manipulation of vital information infrastructure will become an increasing concern.[5]

A second source of pressure will be the growing need for a more nuanced model of data ownership and control. It is an inherent characteristic of today's database technologies (and the client/server model is simply a thin veneer over these technologies) that whoever controls the database also controls all of its contents. For practical purposes, the database and the entries it contains are one entity. But it doesn't have to be this way. The kinds of information architectures explored in Chapter 7 are quite capable of separating the ownership and control of an aggregation of data from that of the individual data items themselves. Thus, for example, an aggregator of urban travel information could maintain geographically organized collections of, say, restaurant menus, while the restaurants themselves could maintain ownership and control of their respective menus. (The web accomplishes this today only via the use of lists of links, which assume constant connectivity and cannot achieve uniformity of information presentation.) More importantly, since the restaurateurs own and can edit the "truth copy" of their menus, they need make their updates only once, without having to worry about dozens of obsolete copies floating around in other people's databases, as is common practice today.

But the most important motivation to abandon client-server lies in the requirement for data liquidity. As we climb toward Trillions, it will become increasingly obvious that the number of mobile devices for which the average consumer will be willing to pay a $29.95/month Internet connectivity fee will be extremely limited. And, as we have seen, for a great many information devices, direct Internet connectivity of any kind is simply not appropriate. Yet, these devices will need to be able to acquire and hold information objects of various and, in general, unpredictable kinds. We cannot build such a world if all access to information is predicated upon real-time connectivity with remote, centralized servers.

Two major changes will have to happen before there is much progress here: Peer-to-peer networking has to cease being thought of as synonymous with music stealing, and end-to-end encryption of consistently identified data objects must become routine. Once both of these milestones are reached, things will start to move quickly. First of all, various kinds of *storage cooperatives*, some planned and others completely accidental, will start to appear. All users will be in possession of more data storage capacity than they could possibly know what to do with (they won't be able to help it). Therefore, the cost of backing up your

---

[5] On the very day that we write these words (January 18, 2012), many web sites, including Wikipedia have "gone dark" in a 24-hour protest against pending legislation—the Stop Online Piracy Act (SOPA) and the PROTECT IP Act (PIPA). We happen to agree with their sentiment, but the fact that a single organization (or in some cases, a single individual) can unilaterally flip a switch and disable what has become a vital bit of worldwide infrastructure deserves even more attention than a piece of ill-advised legislation.

friends' data objects will be negligible. But, the same will be true of strangers' data. The data will flow where they will, being cached repeatedly on the way. People will just stop thinking about it. It will be realized that the best way to protect data will be to scatter copies to the wind, trusting to encryption to protect sensitive data. If you lose your last copy, Google or some descendent of it will find a copy somewhere using its UUID as its definitive identity.

The resulting information space will eventually begin to feel less like a network and more like an ocean, with data everywhere, flowing both in waves of our making and also in natural currents. It is not that everything will be everywhere all the time, but what data objects are available, and where, will be a complex function of deliberate actions on our part and the natural results of vast numbers of uncoordinated incidental actions. Increasingly intelligent caching algorithms will speculatively "pre-position" data where they are likely to be needed. For example, the act of using the Net to research a summer vacation road trip from the comfort of your living room will automatically cause all relevant information about points of interest along all of the candidate routes to be pushed to your car down in the garage, where it will be available on the trip, even if you are in the middle of nowhere out of Internet range. If your plans change, your car will be able to fill in missing information along your new route—picking it up from cooperative passing vehicles.

Kids too young to have real cell phones will have toy facsimiles for use on the playground—talking and texting to each other, and their parents, via short-hop no-cost P2P data links. The range will be very short, but messages will hop from toy to toy bucket-brigade style, such that they will tend to work just fine over useful distances. Their parents, having *real* cell phones, will carry around a good slice of all human knowledge in their pockets. Certainly a recent snapshot of whatever Wikipedia evolves into will be routinely cached for off-line browsing, as will a large library of public-domain reference books, supplemented, as today, by purchased copyrighted materials. Also available for purchase will be tiny bits of very fresh data—reviews of today's specials in nearby restaurants and so forth—produced on a for-profit basis by bored diners with a few minutes on their hands and paid for via tiny microtransactions, rendered profitable by the lack of any middleman—not even the cell company.

But this is not to say that amateurism will reign. Even if we achieve the exceptionally high standard of usability design such that average users would be able to work such magic—a dubious premise amid such vast complexity—self-reliance will be limited by individual motivation. Put another way, most people have better things to do than to futz with their technological environs, no matter how fascinating and powerful. Entire new industries will be born around managing and visualizing people's personal information spaces. It will be taken for granted that—one way or another—any bit of data can be coaxed to flow to any desired place. But that doesn't mean that it won't sometimes be tedious. As today's technical challenges become routine and trivial, new ones will pop up.

PUBLISHING

In Chapter 8 we explored the idea of publisher as aggregator of trust. As we said, this is the one aspect of the role that publishers play today that is least likely to be supplanted by new technologies. This assumption interacts with the emergence of the Information Commons and the World Wide Dataflow in interesting ways. We are going to need a scheme that allows this important role to survive in the absence of ink and paper and physical bookstores and big central servers. In the case of traditional "large" documents like books and magazines, this is a problem that is nearly solved. Despite appearances, the publishing industry is actually a bit ahead of the curve in several respects, including content delivery in the form of locally-stored data objects, the use of per-item encryption, (mostly) multiformat off-line ebook readers (both hardware and software), and a fairly seamless cross-device reading experience.[6]

The industry was forced to embrace these forward-looking techniques by the market reality that readers were not about to accept electronic books until they were as portable and untethered as their traditional paper competitors. As a result, the rapidly emerging ebook industry provides a case study of the future of these techniques.

What has not yet happened is the extension of these ideas to smaller and more intimate acts of publication. Blogging is still almost exclusively client-server based and under the administrative thumb of large, dedicated service providers. The same is true of the many Internet discussion groups, which mostly depend on (and are bound to the policies of) services such as Yahoo! Groups. Wikipedia's success is dependent in part on its (and its users') willingness to eschew attribution and stable, well-defined releases. The latter example is particularly provocative. How might we evolve the Wikipedia model to support features requiring clear object identity and provenance (and thus make it acceptable for use in mission-critical situations, such as legislation and regulation) without killing the goose that laid the golden egg? We suspect that most members of the Wikipedia community would say that this is impossible—that we just don't get it. We respectfully disagree. The Wikipedia model as it now exists stands as a spectacular monument to the potential of distributed, community sourced authorship. But we believe taking it to the next level will require an equally bold experiment in distributed *publication*.

The key to making this work lies in the Information Commons. Wikipedia already contains much of the same information that will form the core of the Commons. It is probably the world's best source of "lists" of various sorts:

---

[6] We refer here to such features as the ability to read a single licensed copy of an ebook on multiple platforms; to have bookmarks and "what page am I on" information shared across devices; and such collaborative features as group annotation.

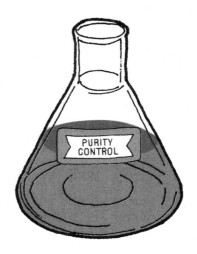

Countries and their administrative subdivisions, feature films over the decades, episodes of *The X-Files*—they are all there. But they are just lists, useful to humans but awkward and unreliable as organizers. Once they are moved into the Commons and given unique identifiers they will become much more. They will be part of the trellis against which third parties can publish their own information, outside of Wikipedia's (or anybody else's) administrative or policy framework. It will work something like this: If I wanted to post, say, a literary analysis of the important *X-Files* episode "The Erlenmeyer Flask," I would compose my paper in the form of an information object.

It (and all other objects in this story) would have a unique identifier and would identify me as the author. I would sign this document with a cryptographic signature. Although this would not prevent others from editing my document after I send it out into the wild, it would make it possible for any such modification to be detected by any reader, thus flagging it as unreliable. By signing the document myself, I am essentially self-publishing—nobody is vouching for the veracity of the information except me. On the other hand, if I wanted to publish the review under the auspices (and policies) of some third-party publisher, such as a future Yahoo! Groups, or even Wikipedia, I would instead submit the item to them for editorial review. After approval, *they* would sign the object on my behalf. I would still be author, but they would be publisher, thus presumably adding a modicum of credibility to my work. Note that in neither case do Yahoo! or Wikipedia assume physical control of my information. It remains a mobile data object, free to flow through the World Wide Dataflow without anybody's permission. But it can do so without losing provenance. Readers can count on the answer to the question "who says?" Publishers can count on being able to enforce their standards and practices; and authors always retain the ultimate ability to self-publish without anybody's permission.

As always, whether anyone will read the author's work is another matter. For starters, how will anyone *find* my review? The answer is largely the same as it is today: Indexing and search services will point to it. But the index will be slightly different. Note that in this story, my review has three basic attributes: It is *about* something ("The Erlenmeyer Flask"); it is a *type* of document (a literary review); and it has a *publisher* (myself, Yahoo!, Wikipedia, etc.). Courtesy of the Information Commons, each of these items has a unique identifier. So, the indexing task reduces to associating each information object with three numbers. This is technically trivial and can be easily done using existing search engine technology, although completely decentralized implementations are also possible. So, if one of my readers wishes to follow my literary "blog", they can subscribe to "Everything published by xxx about any topic of type 'Literary Review.'"[7]

Conversely, if I am an aficionado of the *X-Files*, I can subscribe to "everything published by anybody about 'The Erlenmeyer Flask'" of any type. Of course, I might then find myself drinking from a pretty indiscriminate firehose. A good compromise might be to subscribe to "everything published by Yahoo! or Wikipedia (or whatever publishers I prefer as my gatekeepers) about 'The Erlenmeyer Flask.'"

It can be seen from this rough sketch that it is quite possible to have our cake and eat it too with respect to distributed but trusted publication. It can also be seen that far from putting online publishers such as Yahoo! out of business, such a scheme defines a new and important role for them. Monetizing that role is a different matter, but it is a challenge not fundamentally different from the one faced in today's client-server world.

SAFETY, SECURITY, AND PRIVACY

Anyone who has ever received an electric shock at a home power outlet knows that we live our lives surrounded by potentially lethal power potentials. Every outlet is like a powerful and incredibly taut spring, waiting for a chance to release its destructive power. Yet, we never give it a thought. This is a testament to more than a century of accumulated engineering, design, and administrative wisdom in the management of our electrical infrastructure. As should by now be clear, the new infrastructure of pervasive computing, although embodying power of a different kind, will be no less potent and therefore potentially no less dangerous. For all the wonders of today's consumer computing milieu, most of us still think of it as a thing apart from the rest of our lives, not a critical part of our environment. As this changes, so must our attitudes concerning safety and security. Belatedly, references to the computational environment will begin to creep into the building codes. Whether they will be new standards, or an extension to the electrical codes, we cannot say. Just as the electrical code requires a minimum number of outlets in each room and a minimum amount of current for each house, so too, certain minimum data services will eventually come to be part of our definition of "suitable for human habitation." We are not referring to something like "minimum bandwidth Internet connection" (although, like "lifeline" telephone service, something like that may happen, too). Rather, we are talking about the basic infrastructure built into a house that will have to be there in order for everyday objects to operate properly.

---

[7]The skeptical reader might well ask, who assigned the ID to the document type "Literary Review?" This is an example of the so-called ontology problem. Creating generalized type systems of this sort is a known hard problem. Our answer is "don't worry about it." What is important is the framework, not the particulars. Once the information architecture is in place to make this an important problem, the creative pressures of the marketplace will soon carve out a good enough solution to this problem. Markets are better than designers at this kind of thing.

The time will come when such capabilities will be seen as basic necessities, like heat and light, and they will be subject to similar safety rules.

There is no point in speculating about the details of such rules, beyond getting a feel for their general nature. But, here are a few guesses: We have already said that many devices will have no need to be on the Internet. But, perhaps certain devices won't be *allowed* to be on the Internet. Just as today's electrical codes require a strict separation between 120 volt power circuits and low-voltage wiring such as doorbell circuits, it may be that strict rules about sequestering certain basic functions from the public information space will prove to be the ultimate protection against malicious remote tampering. Similarly, certain combinations of computational and physical power in the same device might be proscribed.

One of the most interesting potential safety rules involves *aggregate complexity*. We have already seen that the best single way to thwart the bad guys is to give them no place to hide. Microwave ovens have computers, but they do not at present get hacked. The reason they don't get hacked is that they *can't* get hacked. Their computational systems are simple enough that the ability to make this determination is within our cognitive capacity. Of all the bad things that happen when things get too complex, perhaps the worst is that *they become too complex to audit*. One could *never* prove that the last bug has been removed from a modern operating system, no matter how important it might be to do so. For this reason, anything that is too complex to understand is inherently dangerous. So, it is reasonable to predict that when we start taking the safety of our computing infrastructure seriously, part of our arsenal of danger-fighting weapons will be restrictions on the presence of unneeded complexity. We can't wait.

We have already discussed at length the issues around security, both of data and of devices. The only thing to add here is the observation that in a world as distributed as the one that we are describing, security must be everywhere. Just as every outside door of pretty much every building in the industrial world has a lock, so too will every venue of computation have to take appropriate security measures. Most data will flow in the form of digitally signed data objects. It is likely that the descendants of today's "firewalls" will, as a first order of business, check the validity of those signatures. Any objects that show signs of tampering will simply be turned away at the door. The next step up from this (and it is a big step) will be to discard (or sequester) any object that is signed by an unknown publisher. Such a policy, although very powerful, would be untenable today for most purposes. It would be like refusing all e-mail from anyone but your close friends. It would effectively limit spam, but you would be giving up much of the value of e-mail access. However, once an infrastructure for adequate networks-of-trust are in place, such tactics will begin to become viable. Traffic limited to "*n* degrees of separation," with an appropriately small value of "n," may well prove to be an efficacious approach to the security problem.

Which brings us to privacy. We have already admitted that we don't have a whole lot of new ideas in this space. As mentioned, we find the analogy with environmental pollution to be useful. In both cases, technologies that we find too valuable to forgo have very serious negative side effects that can be mitigated but not entirely avoided. As in the case of environmental issues, we suspect that we as a society will deal with the destructive effects of information technology on privacy with a pragmatic combination of government regulation, individual activism, public education, better technologies, and a certain amount of toleration. But, if we go into the future with our eyes open, we can perhaps avoid the analogs to the worst consequences of our blindness to the environmental impacts of the industrial revolution. In *The Lord of the Rings,* Tolkien had his Elves say, "We put the thought of all that we love into all that we make." If we love privacy, we need to keep its thought in mind during every step of our climb up Trillions Mountain.

Thriving in the Spacious Foothills

There are three kinds of companies: companies that try to lead customers where they don't want to go (these find the idea of being customer-led an insight); companies that listen to customers and then respond to their articulated needs (needs that are probably already being satisfied by more foresightful competitors); and companies that lead customers where they want to go but don't know it yet. Companies that create the future do more than satisfy customers; they constantly amaze them.

—GARY HAMEL AND COIMBATORE KRISHNARAO PRAHALAD

So, who's going to pay for all of this? It is instructive to compare the situation with that of who paid for the Internet. Economically, the Internet evolved in three distinct stages: Stage 1 was an invitation-only party, with the U.S. government picking up the tab. It was a fun time, while it lasted. Stage 2—the age of irrational exuberance—was paid for by investors who counted themselves among the smart money gang. They knew that fortunes were going to be made, and they weren't about to miss the boat. It wasn't exactly clear how the fortunes would be made, but it would sort itself out. It did sort itself out, but the process was a bit painful. Stage 3—after the bubble—was just business—the long mundane process of separating the wheat from the chaff with respect to the monetization of all those clever ideas.

Will the climb up Trillions Mountain exhibit this same pattern? Well, Stage 1, at least, is different. As we have seen, the laying of the foundations has basically had the characteristic of being self-funding. Unlike the early Internet, the proliferation of microprocessors has made economic sense from the beginning. The technology is cheap and useful, always a winning combination. So things have taken care of themselves—no government bootstrap was necessary. Nonetheless, we suspect, Stages 2 and 3 are likely to play out in pretty much the same way as they did last time. This closing section of our story takes a look at where things stand from a business perspective.

We have repeatedly employed a metaphor of climbing mountains to represent the familiar cycles of progress. Inevitably, we see long periods of local-hill-climbing within an established orthodoxy, punctuated by the occasional fundamental paradigm shift. The metaphor is rich, highlighting both the fact that each mountain is only so high, and also that higher mountains are very often clearly visible in the distance long before anyone other than adventurers is willing to journey to them.

But with the reader's tolerance, we would like to push the metaphor one step further: The base of a mountain is very large, with much room for exploration and many diverse resources to discover and exploit. But as we climb higher, this becomes less and less true. Diversity wanes, as does the available real estate. Climbers soon find themselves crowded together and queued up—jostling for access to a diminishing number of viable routes upward.

So it is in the technology business. In the early days of the Internet, the possibilities were boundless. The hegemony of the client-server pattern was far from a done deal. Nobody knew how to make money—but only the naive believed that it couldn't be done. Experimentation was the order of the day. We at MAYA—and the best of our colleagues—were very busy.

Slowly but inexorably, though, the horizons shrunk. Some footpaths became superhighways, while others—including some very worthy ones— were all but forgotten. A generation of technologists and marketers grew up among the crowds at the summit, never knowing the diversity that was once enjoyed down in the foothills. All they have ever known is cutthroat competition for a smaller and smaller range of alternative business models. Websites, smartphones, tablets, search engines—all are tethered to immense pseudo-cloud data centers. Facebook can succeed only by eating MySpace's lunch. Twitter wins at AIM's expense. Blogs and their formless commentaries supplant structured discussion groups. Often, superficial novelty trumps enduring quality. Everybody who wants to build a new fire tower up on the crowded mountaintop must displace somebody else's tower.

This is starting to not be fun anymore.

Not only that, it's unsafe. We know from the natural world that lack of diversity means loss of resiliency, and this is always a bad thing. In the increasingly monocultural world of centralized computing, a single mistake can set up global shockwaves—as we are starting to see in the recurring waves of virus attacks. On our current path, we are skirting genuine catastrophe. Centralized repositories, like the Library at Alexandria, tempt disaster.

It is time to return to the diversity and myriad possibilities of the spacious foothills. And trust us: Trillions Mountain has them, and they are even more expansive than the last ones were. We will move beyond PC Peak and on to the land of pervasive computing. The PC will soon be gone and along with it the very idea of an operating system. (There will always, perhaps, be something that engineers will call an "OS." What will vanish is the idea that users need to know anything about it, or even perceive it.) Powerful cell phones and tablets will still be there, but they will no longer be where the action is. The thought that all end-user computing would be stuffed into a "browser" (or any other single application framework) will soon seem absurd (the current apps craze is transitional in this regard). And, most importantly of all, the zeppelins will crash, and the skies will be cleared for The Real Cloud. Information will flow freely at last—often with no middleman.

How will money be made in this world? This question is understandably uppermost in the minds of many readers. Among the skeptical, the implication of the question is something like "We don't want to go there unless you can tell us precisely how we're going to prosper once we arrive." Unfortunately, understandable or not, life doesn't work that way. A lot of people didn't want to "go" to the World Wide Web, either. They quickly discovered that they had no choice. Life is an adventure. Going there is not an option; it's a done deal. We're going there because "there" is the future.

Again, it is useful to reason by analogy from the last turn of the screw. Memory is rapidly fading of the genuine terror with which the computing orthodoxy viewed the web in 1995. And, for those who tried to break the wave, that terror proved well founded. But not for those who learned to ride it. Of the two dominant players in today's computing industry, one (Google) didn't even exist in 1995, and the other (Apple) was a laughingstock. Both firms achieved their subsequent miracles because they had a reality-based, rather than a faith-based, view of the future. They were by no means the only ones to understand the logic of that future. But they were among the few who had the wherewithal to act consistently according to the logic of that understanding.

How will money be made on Trillions Mountain? To be honest, we have no idea. Not if you mean, "Which specific firms and products and services will emerge as the dominant ones?" No one knows that. We wish we could give you some stock tips, but the companies likely don't even exist yet. But, just like last time around, only the most naive will believe that the question "How will money be made?" has no answer. And they will be the ultimate losers. We have years of experimentation before us. But it will be profitable experimentation—even in the short run. What we *can* do is to attempt some reality-based reasoning about the question. If we focus on the aspects of tomorrow that *must* be true, and those that *should* be true, we can afford not to worry too much about the unpredictable details, at least for a little while. The following are a few big-picture considerations that we believe will inform the financial winners.

SEIZE THE LOW GROUND

If one accepts the mere premise of one trillion devices, then at least one additional conclusion follows inexorably: Unit costs will be very low. If we are to stay within the bounds of the gross national product, this is a matter of simple arithmetic. This is behind what is perhaps the single most important change in thinking that the winners on Trillions Mountain will have to achieve. Apple made it to the top of the heap by identifying (or, perhaps, creating) high-value, high-cost product categories and making them objects of desire. Such opportunities will always exist, but the action will increasingly move on to market segments in which the big dollars will be generated from selling low-cost devices and services in huge volumes.

This is good news, for it will be a democratizing force. Mounting a serious challenge to Apple in its core markets is a daunting challenge—it is a game for the big boys, and a new-start entrant is extremely implausible. But, the new market will be different, and not just because it is immature. Because we are talking about an ecology of devices, there will for a long time be opportunities for new ideas and new firms to get a foothold.

Can there be any doubt that if we can figure out how to build useful devices that don't come with monthly subscription fees, then volumes will rise? To pick just one example, can't we imagine filling in the gap between children's "toys" and adult "devices?" Aren't there educational and recreational possibilities that could not support monthly charges, but would be quite viable in a P2P environment? We believe that not only do such possibilities exist, but that they exist in vast numbers. And this is without mentioning similar green-fields to be found in other sectors, such as travel, home automation, health care, automotive, and a thousand others.

What will such a market reward? First on our list of answers to this question is *simplicity*. There are two reasons for this. The first one is that simplicity is cheaper. There are those who doubt this. They argue that the fixed overhead of, say, manufacturing an integrated circuit is so high that it will always pay to pack as much capability as possible into each one—that the complexity is free. But, if we have succeeded at making any single point in this book, we hope it is that complexity is never free. The calculations of the cram-in-everything-that-will-fit school of design ignore four critical points: (1) complex things are hard to get right. Simple things can be proven to be correct; complex things cannot; (2) simple things are inherently easier to use than complex things, and so will tend to sell better; (3) because they make fewer assumptions about how they will be used, simple things tend to have longer useful lifetimes than complex things, and so have more time to amortize their development costs; and (4) simple, less powerful devices can take advantage of emerging manufacturing techniques (which typically start their lives as technical underperformers) sooner and more expressively than can more complex, more demanding devices.

If these claims are correct, then the future will reward those who can resist the siren call of Moore's Law and produce products and components that are designed to find their place in the evolving ecology, rather than attempting to dominate. Or, put differently, the very nature of dominance will be fundamentally different in the future.

MICROTRANSACTIONS AND THE RISE OF T-COMMERCE

A corollary to "seize the low ground" is "don't disparage the pennies." Trillions of devices implies quadrillions of transactions. In such a world, one does not have to make very much per transaction in order to make it up in volume. Even in today's world of mere billions, we are rapidly learning how to monetize modest units of capability such as mini-applications for smart phones, and extra levels in online games. We saw this begin to emerge when simple bits of customization—like custom ring tones for cellular phones—became economically feasible to distribute electronically. In 2010 Zynga, a popular gaming platform made revenues of almost $600 million using a combination of advertising and the sale of in-game purchases. It has 58 million daily active users in 175 countries. In July 2011, Apple reported that over 15 billion apps had been downloaded by more than 200 million iPhones, iPads, and Ipod Touches. To date Apple has noted that they have paid out over $2.5 billion to application developers. When you have hundreds of millions of smartphones with the ability to complete monetary transactions at the touch of a button, impulse purchases costing a few cents at a time add up.

Imagine what happens when we move from e-commerce on the scale of billions of desktop computers and mobile devices, to commerce based on trillions of devices living in a rich sea of information. Think of this as *t-commerce*. The trick here, of course, is to figure out how to monetize transactions that are fundamentally out of our reach, because they are occurring, peer-to-peer style down in the capillaries of our information circulatory system. From where we sit today, this seems like an impossible challenge. But this is just an analogue of the challenge that our immediate predecessors faced in trying to figure out how anyone could possibly monetize the web. *That* seemed impossible, too, until Google showed us the way. We don't have the answers here, but we think we understand the question.

STRANGE BEDFELLOWS

In Chapter 8 we noted that a connected washer and dryer might usefully come to know about movement in the laundry room. While that movement isn't of particular value to the workings of the washing machine beyond triggering the illumination of the display, it may be very valuable to someone building an independent living product for eldercare. This is just one modest example from a nearly boundless space of possibilities. A water sensor in the basement of a house, manufactured by a home automation company to automatically turn off the water main in the event of a leak may have significant value to insurance companies looking to lower the cost of damage across their portfolio of homeowners.[1] Will casually-networked motion sensors and security cameras prove to be disruptive to the home security industry as neighbors begin to form electronic neighborhood watch programs in which they volunteer to keep an eye on each other's houses? When iPods suddenly became mandatory equipment for commuters and road-trippers, the automakers were caught with their pants down as consumers discovered how difficult it was to pipe external audio into their fancy, expensive car audio systems. When, a few years later, the most agile of the car companies started to offer iPod docks, the joke was that $40,000 cars had become accessories to $200 iPods. It wasn't long before at least an audio-in jack was as essential a feature as a power jack (they used to be called cigarette lighters, but no more). Of course, this small example is just random, but it is portentous. The general point is that in the future, *everything is going to be an accessory to everything else.* Sometimes you'll be the product, other times you'll be the accessory. The liquidity that comes from a truly connected world will allow for any number of monetization schemes that today seem implausible.

BIG DATA AND INFORMATION VISUALIZATION

Much has been made in recent years about the business benefit of strategic information. What used to be called data mining has moved into the mainstream and is driving significant business decisions. It goes by various names

---

[1] It is worth noting here that the Underwriters Laboratories,—the premiere appliance safety organization in the United States—is a child of the self-interests of the insurance industry.

but the *au courant* term is "big data." The focus of the field is how all the information we capture across countless transactions can be converted into value. The volume of raw data readily available as input to such processes is growing at an astounding rate. In the age of Trillions, we will have at our disposal a nearly boundless data feed from the physical world's ground truth to the liquid realm of cyberspace.

In such a context, no skill will be more valuable than the creation of lucid, unbiased visualizations of complex information spaces. Indeed, at its core, the very notion of cyberspace is inseparably bound to that of visualization. Visualization is one of the key enablers by which people harness the power of information in business, in health care, in personal growth and security.

This is all fairly obvious. What is less obvious is that visualizations do not have to be mere pictures—one-way displays that we simply look at. The kinds of interactive, information-centric, two-way displays that we described in Chapter 2 have the potential to form the basis of a new kind of collaborative environment. The ability to collaborate with others "over" information in a facile way has been one of our most fruitful areas of research.[2] When groups of people can comprehend information rendered in different forms, and watch each other manipulate it as they experiment with hypotheses and "what-if" tests, the quality of insight increases significantly.[3] High performing teams—when given collaborative visualization tools—build information literacy and collaborative interplay as they tune their tools—and their teams—to fit their business process.

Such collaborators won't all be humans either. Fostering a mixed dialogue between human and machine collaborators through a shared collaborative space will become critical to agile decision making. The simple fact is that people are good at some things, and machines are good at others. An architectural model of information will provide a common framework for such mixed dialogue and decision making.

THE TRILLIONS BUBBLE

Yes, there will be a bubble. There is always a bubble. Whether it is tulips or Internets, our enthusiasms and imagination (and greed) will always, for a while, get ahead of us. The story will be familiar. Millionaires will be minted

---

[2] One of MAYA's most significant projects involved its contribution to a situational awareness and collaboration solution for the U.S. military called Command Post of the Future, which has won numerous government awards, including the Defense Advanced Research Projects Agency (DARPA) 2004 award for Significant Technical Achievement and the 2009 award for "Outstanding Government Program."

[3] A DARPA-sponsored study of a four-day exercise conducted October 22–25, 2002, found that the radically different capabilities of Command Post of the Future increased decision making and mission planning effectiveness by 400 percent over the previous system. It also improved "Situational Awareness" by 300 percent.

overnight. Some of them will be just lucky—the beneficiaries of fortuitous timing. They will be the ones who get rich first, and good for them. But, there isn't much to say about them. They are like the winners at a roulette table. Assuming that the game is honest, there is little to distinguish them from the losers.

What we find more interesting is the blackjack card-counters. They take the time to deeply understand the game, and thus can win consistently. What annoys the casinos about card counters is that they aren't really cheaters. They are just smart, and it is hard to write rules against smart. Unlike in the casinos, in the marketplace being smart doesn't get you thrown out of the game.

On Trillions Mountain, "smart" means understanding the architecture of a true cyberspace and the potential of a world where every manufactured thing is connected. Those that have, or acquire, that understanding—those who place their faith in Architecture—will take the bubble in stride. Many other players will rush in at exactly the wrong time, trying to be rapid followers. Money will flow from the pockets of the latter to the pockets of the former. Our hope is that this book will have helped you find yourself in the right group. After the Trillions bubble, just like the dot-com one, we will get down to the serious business of harvesting the true potential of what will be.

So, how will we make money? How will the era of pervasive computing play out commercially? Concretely and specifically, we don't know, and neither does anyone else. What we do know, however, is that it *will* play out. In the next era of human life lived *inside the information*, old industries will perish, new industries will be born, and money will be made in ways presently unimaginable. When information truly flows freely, prosperity will flow freely, too. How exactly? That remains to be found out.

Let's find out together.

Top Ten Business Take-Aways for Trillions

1. **Pervasive computing is the next information technology paradigm.** It is ramping up right now and doing so exponentially. Connectivity is the seed of this change. When it hits its inflection point, the lift-off will be almost straight up. Major high-tech players will disappear, and new ones will be born overnight. The winners will win big, the losers will lose big, and it will all happen fast.

2. **Your current business risk in information technology may be much higher than you think.** The dominant IT technologies and practices—including client-server computing (whose latest guise is cloud computing), relational database technology, and the World Wide Web—are inadequate for the coming pervasive computing paradigm. They will not scale gracefully into a trillion-node network and beyond. Talk to your technical staff about malignant complexity and how resilient your systems really are. You may not be able to change in midstream to the new paradigm but there are considerations you can make today in your strategic planning that will give you the agility you need when the time comes.

3. **We need to move beyond open source and move toward open component ecologies.** On Trillions Mountain, simple stable components that are sometimes hardware and sometimes software will be layered together and will create new forms of value that will compete in market-driven feedback loops. While many players will continue to assemble systems out in the field, they will be building with professionally engineered raw materials that are stable, predictable, and auditable, just as physical materials are today. When combined with trusted physics, public APIs, and a liquid currency, creativity will flourish, and customers will help you build the future.

4. **The good news is that trillions is a very big number.** New revenue streams in the form of high-volume microtransactions will become viable. New business models based on little bits of information collected over vast networks will rule the day. Understand the value in your information and plan for an economy built on t-commerce.

5. **Complexity is inevitable, but bad complexity will kill you.** The only way to build good complexity is by combining simple, stable components in carefully designed layers. That's the meaning of *architectural thinking*. Consider how you can foster beautiful complexity in the form of hierarchy, modularity, redundancy, and generativity. Nature and evolution are the best teachers. To foster innovation, you must provide the most fertile soil possible; plant simple, robust seeds; and then let them grow.

6. **Design for generativity and emergence.** Complexity leads to emergent properties. Untamed complexity can have wildly unintended consequences. Factoring out malignant complexity is step 1. Use architectural thinking as the foundation for your work. Then get in the practice

(Continued)

of building dynamic simulations—even if made with sticky notes and disposable cameras at first—of your entire business ecology early and often. Interdisciplinary designing, protoyping, testing, and simulating can help you predict emergent properties so you can remain agile in the face of change.

7. **Design is not a paint job or product styling or user-interface "look and feel."** Properly understood, design is the whole shooting match. If your organization isn't design literate, you risk becoming a dinosaur lumbering among agile predators running around at your feet.

8. **Make your products and services human literate.** Human beings are vastly more complex, subtle, and important than machines. But we're often too impressed with our own creations to remember that. We've spent a half-century believing that people should become computer literate. That's precisely backward. Computing should become human literate. On Trillions Mountain people will no longer have the attention or patience to tolerate untamed complexity.

9. **Computing needs to fade into the woodwork so that humans living their lives can come to the foreground.**

If you want to understand how pervasive computing will fit into human life, think of the antilock brakes in your car. They represent deeply complex computing that you use everyday—that you depend upon to save your life—yet you don't even know it's there. Think of ways you can use connectivity and computing to hide and tame complexity for your customers. They don't really want to think about computers; they want to think about doing their jobs and living their lives.

10. **Explore ways that you can simulate and foster strange bedfellow relationships now.** When trillions of computing devices all become connected you need to make sure that you are a part of the information flow. Consider how your product could be an accessory to some other product or service or a foundation for others to accessorize. Consider what could happen if you harvested and shared all the information your current products could capture or "know" about their surroundings and use over time. The value of the information you collect, the needs you discover, the patterns that emerge, and the behaviors that you can foster is inestimable.

Notes

Although this is not a scholarly text, we have attempted to provide sources for all factual claims. We have gone to significant lengths to provide citations of persistent (that is to say, "paper") sources whenever possible. However, given our subject matter, a disturbing number of citations are necessarily in the form of web URLs. We are painfully aware that most of these links will soon "go dead." We can only offer our apologies and our assurances that we have done our best to characterize such information fairly and accurately in the text.

Preface

page xiv   *trends are widely recognized*: The literature on these trends is huge and dates back at least until the 1980s. In addition to the terms *pervasive computing* and *ubiquitous computing*, web searches for the terms *Internet of things, ambient intelligence, machine to machine*, and *smart environments* will produce useful results. A good general introduction can be found in M. Weiser, "The Computer of the 21st Century," *Scientific American* 265 (September 1991): 104.

page xiv   *"smart dust"*: Mohammad Ilyas and Imad Mahgoub, *Smart Dust: Sensor Network Applications, Architecture, and Design* (Boca Raton, FL: CRC Press, 2006), 1–3.

page xiv   *nuts-and-bolts issues*: A typical example of the genre is Stefan Poslad, *Ubiquitous Computing: Smart Devices, Environments and Interactions* (West Sussex, UK: John Wiley & Sons, 2009).

page xv   *"Most Advanced Yet Acceptable"*: Raymond Loewy, *Never Leave Well Enough Alone* (New York: Simon & Schuster, 1951), 278.

Chapter 1 The Future, So Far

page 1   *Behind all the great material inventions*: Lewis Mumford, *Technics and Civilization* (New York: Harcourt, Brace & Company, 1934), 3.

page 2   *more transistors than grains of rice*: R. Goodall, D. Fandel, A. Allan, P. Landler, and H. Huff, "Long-Term Productivity Mechanisms of the Semiconductor Industry," *American Electrochemical Society Semiconductor Silicon 2002 Proceedings*, 9th ed., May 2002, 125–143.

page 2   *ten billion processors per year*: Michael Barr, "Real Men Program in C," *Embedded Systems Design*. TechInsights (United Business Media), July/August 2009, 10.

page 4   *Sneakers that send*: Nigel K. Pope, Kerri-Ann L. Kuhn, and John J. H. Forster, *Digital Sport for Performance Enhancement and Competitive Evolution: Intelligent Gaming Technologies* (Hershey, PA: IGI Global, 2009), 152–153; see also J. D. Biersdorfer, *iPod: The Missing Manual*, 10th ed. (Sebastopol, CA: O'Reilly Media, 2011), 222–223.

page 4   *tags sewn into hotel towels*: Bruce Schneier, *Liars and Outliers: Enabling the Trust that Society Needs to Thrive By* (Indianapolis: John Wiley & Sons, 2012), 123–125; see also Terence Craig and Mary E. Ludloff, *Privacy and Big Data* (Sebastopol, CA: O'Reilly Media, 2011), 49; Roger Yu, "Hotels Use RFID Chips to Keep Linens from Checking Out," *USA Today*, July 28, 2011, http://travel.usatoday.com/hotels.

page 4   *bolts holding the seats*: Jean J. Labrosse et al., *Embedded Software: Know It All* (Burlington, MA: Newnes Publishing, 2008), 548–551; see also Aini Hussain et al., "Decision Algorithm for Smart Airbag Deployment Safety Issues," *International Journal of Electrical and Computer Engineering* 1, no. 5 (2006): 333–339; David S. Breed, "A Smart Airbag System," Automotive Technologies International, Paper Number: 98-S5-O-13, 1080–1091.

page 5   *types of computer music*: O. B. Hardison, Jr., *Disappearing Through the Skylight: Culture and Technology in the Twentieth Century* (New York: Penguin Books, 1989), 236–237.

page 6   *human beings spending their time*: For a discussion of humans in the loop as a block to progress, see Michael L. Dertouzos, *What Will Be: How the New World of Information Will Change Our Lives* (New York: HarperCollins, 1997), 85–88.

page 6   *"HotSync" capabilities*: Andrea Butter and David Pogue, *Piloting Palm: The Inside Story of Palm, Handspring, and the Birth of the Billion-Dollar Handheld Industry* (New York: John Wiley & Sons, 2002), 73–74, 138; see also Eric Bergman and Rob Haitani, "Designing the PalmPilot: A Conversation with Rob Haitani, in *Information Appliances and Beyond: Interaction Design for Consumer Products*, ed. Eric Bergman (San Francisco: Morgan Kaufmann Publishers, 2000), 87–88.

page 8   *one billion computers in use*: George Shiffler III, *Forecast: PC Installed Base, Worldwide, 2004–2012* (Stamford, CT: Gartner Inc., 2008).

page 8   *600 million automobiles in use*: "How many cars are there in the world currently?" Worldometers, http://www.worldometers.info/cars/. Accessed November 29, 2011.

page 9   *taken Digital Equipment Corp. from nothing to $7.6 billion*: Peter Petre and Alan Farnham, "America's Most Successful Entrepreneur," *Fortune*, October 27, 1986, 24.

page 10   *PC revenues peaked*: Steven Buehler et al., *Worldwide Personal Computing and Mobile Connected Devices 2012 Top 10 Predictions* (Framingham, MA: IDC, 2012).

page 11   *dark 1976 critique*: Joseph Weizenbaum, *Computer Power and Human Reason: From Judgment to Calculation* (San Francisco: W.H. Freeman and Company, 1976), 25–26.

page 12   *appropriation by Steve Jobs*: The tale of the early days of the PC industry has been told many times, but never more entertainingly than in *Pirates of Silicon Valley*, directed by Martyn Burke. Performed by Noah Wyle, Anthony Michael Hall, and Joey Slotnick. Turner Home Entertainment, 1999. Film.

page 13   *HyperCard*: Mark Levene, *An Introduction to Search Engines and Web Navigation,* 2nd ed. (Hoboken, NJ: John Wiley & Sons, 2010), 223–225; see also D. Kothari and Anshu Saxena, *Hypermedia: From Multimedia to Virtual Reality: A Managerial Perspective* (New Delhi: Prentice-Hall, 2004), 110–113.

Chapter 2 The Next Mountain

page 15   *the vision precedes the proof*: Walter Dorwin Teague, *Design This Day: The Technique of Order in the Machine Age* (New York: Harcourt, Brace and Company, 1940), 222–223.

page 20   *"virtual PC"*: Diane Barrett and Greg Kipper, *Virtualization and Forensics: A Digital Forensic Investigator's Guide to Virtual Environments* (Burlington, MA: Syngress, 2010), 12–15.

page 20   *Internet virus situation*: See, for example, Peter Szor, *The Art of Computer Virus Research and Defense* (Boston: Addison-Wesley Professional, 2005); Jeffrey Carr, *Inside Cyber Warfare*, 2nd ed. (Sebastopol, CA: O'Reilly Media, 2012); see also David Kim and Michael Solomon, *Fundamentals of Information Systems Security* (Burlington, MA: Jones & Bartlett Learning, 2010); Jatinder N. D. Gupta and Sushil K. Sharma, eds., *Handbook of Research on Information Security and Assurance* (Hershey, PA: IGI Global, 2009).

page 20   *A PC plugged into the Internet*: Byron Acohido and Jon Swartz, "Unprotected PCs Can Be Hijacked in Minutes," *USA Today*, November 30, 2004, B.3.

page 20   *Apple even retains the ability*: Berin Szoka and Adam Marcus, eds., *The Next Digital Decade: Essays on the Future of the Internet* (Washington, DC: TechFreedom, 2010), 154–155.

page 25   *five billion or more devices*: "Internet Connected Devices About to Pass the 5 Billion Milestone," IMS Research, Press Release, August 16, 2010, http://imsresearch.com/news-events/press-template.php?pr_id = 1532. Accessed March 2, 2012.

page 27   *The Box That Flattened the World*: 2006 was the fiftieth anniversary of the voyage of *Ideal-X*. The occasion prompted three excellent tellings of this fascinating story: Marc Levinson, *The Box: How the Shipping Container Made the World Smaller and the Economy Bigger* (Princeton, NJ: Princeton University Press, 2006); Brian J. Cudahy, *Box Boats: How Container Ships Changed the World* (New York: Fordham University Press, 2006); Arthur Donovan and Joseph Bonney, *The Box That Changed the World: Fifty Years of Container Shipping: An Illustrated History* (East Windsor, NJ: Commonwealth Business Media, 2006).

page 28   *Achieving some basic degree of understanding*: Michael L. Dertouzos, *What Will Be: How the World of Information Will Change Our Lives* (New York: HarperOne, 1998), 85.

page 29   *Wikipedia list*: "Application Layer," Wikipedia, https://en.wikipedia.org/wiki/Application_layer. Accessed February 25, 2012.

page 30   *coined by science-fiction writer William Gibson*: William Gibson, *Neuromancer* (New York: Ace Books, 1984); William Gibson, "Burning Chrome," *Omni*, July 1982.

page 30   *Cyberspace is the "place"*: Bruce Sterling, "Introduction" in *The Hacker Crackdown: Law and Disorder on the Electronic Frontier* (New York: Bantam Books, 1992), xi–xii.

page 31   *Steve Roth*: Corilyn Shropshire, "Obituary: Steven Roth/Maya Viz founder," *Pittsburgh Post-Gazette*, June 14, 2005; Nahun Gershon and Jake Kolojejchick, "From the Lab to the Field: Steve Roth—A Memoriam," *IEEE Transactions on Visualizations and Computer Graphics* 11, no. 6 (November/December 2006): 609–610.

page 31   *Xanadu*: Nelson published his ideas in a somewhat chaotic series of self-published books under the titles *Computer Lib/Dream Machine* and *Literary Machines*, appearing in many editions between ca. 1974 and 1993. These books are fascinating but difficult to find. A much more accessible telling of the Xanadu story may be found in Gary Wolf, "The Curse of Xanadu," *Wired* 3, no. 6 (June 1995): 137–202.

page 32   *ADVENT*: A thoughtful analysis of the significance of Adventure may be found in O.B. Hardison, Jr., *Disappearing through the Skylight: Culture and Technology in the Twentieth Century* (New York: Penguin Books, 1989): 265–267.

page 33   *Colossal Cave is a real place*: Dennis G. Jerz, "Somewhere Nearby Is Colossal Cave: Examining Will Crowther's Original 'Adventure' in Code and in Kentucky," *Digital Humanities Quarterly* 1, no. 2 (Summer 2007).

page 35   *Pioneer in the Reputation Business*: D&B, The History, http://www.dnb.com/about-dnb/history/14909191-1.html. Accessed November 16, 2011.

Interlude Yesterday, Today, Tomorrow: Platforms and User Interfaces

page 41   *not organized around applications* J. Johnson, T. L. Roberts et al., "The Xerox Star: A Retrospective," *IEEE Computer* 22, no. 9 (September 1989): 11–29.

page 42   *several attempts at reform*: George V. Popescu, "Distributed Indexing Networks for Efficient Large-Scale Group Communication," in *Handbook of Research on P2P and Grid Systems for Service-Oriented Computing: Models, Methodologies and Applications*, ed. Nick Antonopoulos et al., 360–381 (Hershey, PA: Information Science Reference/IGI Global, 2010).

page 42   *"Workscape"*: J. M. Ballay, "Designing Workscape: An Interdisciplinary Experience," in *Proceedings CHI'94 Human Factors in Computer Systems* (Boston: ACM, 1994), 10–15.

page 43   *Ajax*: Concerning Ajax, see Andre Lewis, Michael Purvis, Jeffrey Sambells, and Cameron Turner, *Google Maps: Applications with Rails and Ajax* (New York: Apress, 2007); see also Paul J. Deitel and Harvey M. Deitel, *AJAX, Rich Internet Applications, and Web Development for Programmers* (Upper Saddle River, NJ: Prentice Hall, 2008). The term "HTML5" is used in so many different ways and has been written about in such volume, we will not attempt to summarize here.

page 43   *created at a Swiss physics lab*: Tim Berners-Lee and Mark Fischetti, *Weaving the Web: The Original Design and Ultimate Destiny of the World Wide Web by Its Inventor* (New York: HarperCollins, 1999), 4.

page 44   *Semantic Web*: Tim Berners-Lee, James Hendler, and Ora Lassila, "The Semantic Web," *Scientific American* 284, no. 5 (May 2001): 34–43; Karin K. Breitman, Marco Antonio Casanova, and Walt Truszkowski, *Semantic Web: Concepts, Technologies and Applications* (London: Springer-Verlag, 2007).

page 44   *"Moore's Law.":* Discussions of Moore's Law are countless. A version of his original claim may be found in Gordon E. Moore, "Cramming More Components Onto Integrated Circuits," *Electronics* 38, no. 8 (April 19, 1965): 114–117. Moore's Law as a self-fulfilling prophecy is discussed in National Research Council (U.S.), Committee on Measuring and Sustaining the New Economy, *Enhancing Productivity Growth in the Information Age*, ed. Dale W. Jorgenson and Charles W. Wessner, 64–69 (Washington, DC: National Academies Press, 2007); see also Jennifer Gabrys, *Digital Rubbish: A Natural History of Electronics* (Ann Arbor: University of Michigan Press, 2011), 116–117.

Chapter 3 The Tyranny of the Orthodoxy

page 51   *At any given moment there is an orthodoxy*: George Orwell, Appendix I, "Orwell's Proposed Preface to *Animal Farm*," in *Animal Farm* (London: Martin Secker and Warburg Ltd., 1987), 207–208.

page 52   *"People Connection"*: http://www.peopleconnectionblog.com/2008/11/06/hometown-has-been -shutdown. Accessed March 30, 2009. As noted in the text, this and most of the other URLs concerning this incident are no longer operational. At this writing, they are still available via the Internet Archive's Wayback Machine (http://www.archive.org/web/web.php).

page 52   *11 million web pages*: Donald Munro, "The Net's Anonymity Gives License to Write and Post Freely," *Fresno Bee*, June 24, 2001, quoted in Hope Jensen Schau and Mary C. Gilly, "We Are What We Post? Self-Presentation in Personal Web Space," *Journal of Consumer Research* 30, no. 3 (2003): 385.

page 52   *The first official notice*: Posted by Minnie Apolis, "R.I.P. – AOL to disband Blogging 'Journals,'" *Newsvine*, September 30, 2008, http://minnieapolis.newsvine.com/ _news/2008/09/30/1937764-rip-aol-to-disband-blogging-journals. Accessed May 12, 2012.

page 54   *permalink that AOL thoughtfully included*: http://www.peopleconnectionblog.com/2008/11/ 06/hometown-has-been-shutdown/.

page 54   *"Ficlets Will Be Shut Down Permanently,"*: http://www.peopleconnectionblog.com/2008/ 12/02/ficlets-will-be-shut-down-permanently/. Accessed March 30, 2009.

page 54   *"I'm disappointed"*: Kevin Lawver, "Ficlets Est Mort" (2008), http://lawver.net/2008/12/ ficlets_est_mor/. Accessed November 30, 2011.

page 55   *"Forever is a long time.":* http://www.fictionwise.com/help/Expiring-Download-Replacement -FAQ.htm. Accessed April 10, 2009. Not surprisingly, as of this writing, this link no longer works.

page 55   *Google Research Datasets*: Alexis Madrigal, "Google Shutters Its Science Data Service," *Wired Science*, December 18, 2008. http://blog.wired.com/wiredscience/2008/12/ googlescienceda.html. Accessed December 28, 2011.

page 55   *Google Video*: Posted by Michael Cohen, "Turning Down Uploads at Google Video," http:// googlevideo.blogspot.com/2009/01/turning-down-uploads-at-google-video.html. Accessed December 28, 2011. See also Claudine Beaumont, "Google Announces End of Google Video, Jaiku and Other Projects in 'Cost-Cutting' Exercise," *Telegraph*, January 15, 2009, http://www.telegraph.co.uk/technology/google/4248045/Google-announces-end-of-Google-Video-Jaiku-and-other-projects-in-cost-cutting-exercise.html. Accessed May 15, 2009.

page 55   *Google Catalog Search*: Punit Soni, "Farewell Google Catalog Search," January 14, 2009, http://booksearch.blogspot.com/2009/01/farewell-google-catalog-search.html. Accessed February 19, 2012.

page 55   *Google Notebook*: "A Fall Spring-Clean," Google Official Blog, September 2, 2011, http:// googleblog.blogspot.com/2011/09/fall-spring-clean.html. Accessed February 19, 2012.

page 55   *Google Mashup Editor*: Eric Tholomé, "Farewell to Mashup Editor," Google Mashup Editor Blog, July 15, 2009, http://googlemashupeditor.blogspot.com/. Accessed February 19, 2012.

page 55   *Jaiku*: The "launch early, launch often" quotation may be found at: "A Fall Sweep," Google
           Official Blog, October 14, 2011, http://googleblog.blogspot.com/2011/10/fall-sweep.html.
           Accessed February 19, 2012.

page 55   *Zune music player*: Charles Pfleeger and Shari Lawrence Pfleeger, *Analyzing Computer
           Security: A Threat/Vulnerability/Countermeasure Approach* (Upper Saddle River, NJ:
           Pearson Education, 2012), 106.

page 56   *it wasn't the first time*: See Stephen Shankland and Tom Krazit, "Widespread Google Out-
           ages Rattle Users," May 14, 2009, http://news.cnet.com/widespread-google-outages-rattle
           -users/. Accessed December 29, 2011.

page 58   *I don't (yet) believe*: Lawrence Lessig, *The Future of Ideas: The Fate of the Commons in a
           Connected World* (New York: Random House, 2001), 7.

page 58   *catastrophic failure*: James Quinn, "AOL Officially Splits from Time Warner after 10 Years,"
           Telegraph, December 9, 2009, http://www.telegraph.co.uk/finance/newsbysector/
           mediatechnologyandtelecoms/6774324/AOL-officially-splits-from-Time-warner-after-
           10-years.html. Accessed December 16, 2011.

page 60   *Every day brings another story*: Eric Cole, *Network Security Bible*, 2nd ed. (Hoboken, NJ:
           John Wiley & Sons, 2009), chap. 14.

page 61   *mathematician and the chessboard*: Ray Kurzweil uses this parable prominently in *The
           Age of Spiritual Machines* (New York: Penguin Books, 2000), 36–37, which is an excellent
           source on the nature of exponential growth and the tendency of humans to misperceive it.

page 64   *efforts toward data preservation*: Elisabeth Eaves, "Publish and Perish," *Forbes*, December
           1, 2006, http://www.forbes.com/2006/11/30/books-information-preservation-tech-media_
           cx_ee_books06_1201acid.html. Accessed February 24, 2012.

page 65   *interesting thing about cloud computing*: Ellison's infamous statement quoted by *Wall Street
           Journal* technology blogger Ben Worthen, "Larry Ellison's Brilliant Anti-Cloud Computing
           Rant," *Wall Street Journal Business Technology Blog*, September 25, 2008, http://blogs.wsj
           .com/biztech/2008/09/25/larry-ellisons-brilliant-anti-cloud-computing-rant/. Worthen states that
           the statement was made at the Oracle Analysts Day held on Thursday, September 25, 2008,
           and that it was "slightly edited." As is typical, the original WSJ link is no longer operational, nor
           is the provided "permalink." However, the blog entry was widely reproduced around the web,
           and Worthen's original article is also available in the Internet Archives. See also "Oracle's Ellison
           Nails Cloud Computing," http://news.cnet.com/8301-13953_3-10052188-80.html. Accessed
           March 3, 2012.

page 67   *excited about things like "thin client"*: See, for example, Peter Burrows, "The Next Cheap
           Thing," *Bloomberg Businessweek*, July 3, 2006, 63–64; and Tineke M. Egyedi, Copyright
           2001 IEEE, "Why Java™ Was-Not-Standardized Twice," *Proceedings of the Hawai'i Inter-
           national Conference On System Sciences*, Maui, Hawaii, January 3–6, 2001.

page 67   *absurdly large and cheap*: During this time period, the rate of growth of disk-drive capacity
           actually exceeded Moore's law by a significant margin. See Andrew J. Herbert and Karen
           Spärck Jones, eds., *Computer Systems: Theory, Technology, and Applications* (New York:
           Springer-Verlag, 2004), 298; Dan Gillmor, *We the Media: Grassroots Journalism by the
           People, for the People* (Sebastopol, CA: O'Reilly Media, 2006), 159–160.

page 68   *Via Repository*: Peter Lucas and Jeff Senn, "Toward the Universal Database: U-forms and
           the VIA Repository," MAYA Technical Report #MAYA-02001 (2002), http://www.maya
           .com/file_download/35/maya_universal_database.pdf.

page 68   *Visage*: Peter Lucas, Steve Roth, and Christina Gomberg, "Visage: Dynamic Informa-
           tion Exploration," Association of Computing Machinery, CHI96 Conference, Vancouver,
           Canada, 1996.

page 68   *OceanStore project*: John Kubiatowicz et al., "OceanStore: An Architecture for Global-Scale
           Persistent Storage," *Proceedings of the Ninth International Conference on Architectural
           Support for Programming Languages and Operating Systems* (ASPLOS), November 2000),
           http://oceanstore.cs.berkeley.edu/publications/papers/pdf/asplos00.pdf.

page 70   *average life expectancy*: Arie de Geus, *The Living Company: Habits for Survival in a
           Turbulent Business Environment* (Boston: Harvard Business School Press, 2002), 1.

page 71   *a lot of the problems*: Stuart Feldman, "A Conversation with Alan Kay," Queue 2, no. 9
           (December/January 2004–2005): 25, 26.

page 72   *A plumber will never install*: 2006 National Standard Plumbing Code, Plumbing-Heating-Cooling Contractors National Association (2006). Sec 10.5.2: 114–115.

page 72   *An electrician will never install*: National Electric Code, 2005 ed. National Fire Protection Association, Inc. (2004), Sec 110.26: 70–36.

page 72   *A building contractor will never build*: International Building Code 2006. International Code Council, Inc. (2006). Sec 1008.1.2: 208.

page 72   *nonconformant wires are wrapped*: Ray C. Mullin and Phil Simmons, *Electrical Wiring Residential*, 17th ed. (Clifton Park, NY: Delmar Cengage Learning, 2012): 158–161.

page 73   *first National Electric Code*: *National Electric Code: An American Standard* (Quincy, MA: National Fire Protection Association, 1897).

page 73   *Edison's Pearl Street Station*: George S. Bryan, *Edison: The Man and His Work* (New York: Alfred A. Knopf, 1926), 160–161, 169.

page 73   *Software Engineering Institute*: Peter Middleton and James Sutton, *Lean Software Strategies: Proven Techniques for Managers and Developers* (New York: Productivity Press, 2005), 61–62.

page 74   *"Most software today,"*: Feldman, "A Conversation with Alan Kay." op. cit., 23.

page 74   *minicomputers that booted in seconds*: Andy Hertzfeld, *Revolution in the Valley: The Insanely Great Story of How the Mac Was Made* (Sebastopol, CA: O'Reilly Media, 2005). See also Alan Cooper, *The Inmates Are Running the Asylum: Why High-Tech Products Drive Us Crazy and How to Restore the Sanity* (Indianapolis: SAMS Publishing, 2004).

page 74   *"Nobody knows anything."*: William Goldman, *Adventures in the Screen Trade: A Personal View of Hollywood and Screenwriting* (New York: Grand Central Publishing, 1989), 39.

page 75   *sensations of power and control*: Joseph Weizenbaum, *Computer Power and Human Reason: From Judgment to Calculation* (San Francisco: W. H. Freeman, 1976); Nathan L. Ensmenger, *The Computer Boys Take Over: Computers, Programmers, and the Politics of Technical Expertise* (Cambridge, MA: MIT Press, 2010); Stefan Helmreich, *Silicon Second Nature: Culturing Artificial Life in a Digital World* (Berkeley: University of California Press, 1998), 69, 84, 85, 95; Robert X. Cringely, *Accidental Empires: How the Boys of Silicon Valley Make Their Millions, Battle Foreign Competition, and Still Can't Get a Date* (New York: HarperCollins, 1992), 59.

page 76   *how much a new ship weighed*: R. Buckminster Fuller, *Your Private Sky: Discourse*, ed. Joachim Krausse and Claude Lichtenstein (Baden, CH: Lars Muller, 2001), 264.

page 77   *"The Cathedral and the Bazaar"*: Eric S. Raymond, *The Cathedral & the Bazaar: Musings on Linux and Open Source by an Accidental Revolutionary* (Sebastopol, CA: O'Reilly Media, 2001), 19–64.

page 78   *though he was master of the world*: Arthur C. Clarke, *2001: A Space Odyssey* (New York: New American Library Corporation/Penguin Group, 1968), 222.

page 78   *by geeks for geeks*: Walt Mossberg, "An Interview with Walt Mossberg," *Bisnow on Business*, October 17, 2005, http://www.bisnow.com/archives_ew/index_mossberg_original.html.

page 30   *Python programming language*: Guido van Rossum, *An Introduction to Python* (Bristol, UK: Network Theory Ltd., 2003).

page 79   *half of his time on Python*: Richard Dooling, *Rapture for the Geeks: When AI Outsmarts IQ* (New York: Three Rivers Press, 2008), 194.

page 80   *World Wide Web as it was originally conceived*: Tim Berners-Lee with Mark Fischetti, *Weaving the Web: The Original Design and Ultimate Destiny of the World Wide Web by Its Inventor* (New York: HarperBusiness, 2000); Ian J. Taylor and Andrew B. Harrison, *From P2P and Grids to Services on the Web: Evolving Distributed Communities*, 2nd ed. (London: Springer-Verlag, 2009), 108.

page 80   *Books quite a bit thicker*: Adrian Johns, *Piracy: The Intellectual Property Wars from Gutenberg to Gates* (Chicago: University of Chicago Press, 2009); William Patry, *Moral Panics and the Copyright Wars* (New York: Oxford University Press, 2009); Lawrence Lessig, *Free Culture: The Nature and Future of Creativity* (New York: Penguin Books, 2004); James Boyle, *The Public Domain: Enclosing the Commons of the Mind* (New Haven, CT: Yale University Press, 2008).

page 81   *Diana was presenting*: Diana Dee-Lucas and Jill H. Larkin, "Content Map Design and Knowledge Structures with Hypertext and Traditional Text," *Proceedings of ACM Hypertext'91*—Posters 1991-12-15, 7.

page 81   *official W3C history*: http://www.w3.org/History.html. Accessed March 1, 2012.

Chapter 4 How Nature Does It

page 83   *proliferation of microprocessors*: George B. Dyson, Darwin Among the Machines: The Evolution of Global Intelligence (New York: Perseus Books, 1997), 13.

page 84   *Pando*: Michael C. Grant, "The Trembling Giant," *Discover Magazine* 14, no. 10 (October 1993): 82–89, http://discovermagazine.com/1993/oct/thetremblinggian285. Accessed November 14, 2011.

page 84   *Experiments that employed a rototiller*: "Quaking Aspen," National Park Service, U.S. Department of the Interior, http://www.nps.gov/brca/naturescience/quakingaspen.htm. Accessed November 14, 2011.

page 84   *mycorrhizal network*: B. Wang and Y. L. Qiu. "Phylogenetic Distribution and Evolution of Mycorrhizas in Land Plants," *Mycorrhiza* 16, no. 5 (July 2006): 299–363.

page 84   *Mycorrhizal networks have been shown*: David J. Read, Ecology and Biogeography of Pinus, ed. David M. Richardson (Cambridge: Cambridge University Press, 1998), 336.

page 84   *interplant communication*: Y. Y. Song, R. S. Zeng, J. F. Xu, J. Li, X. Shen, et al., "Interplant Communication of Tomato Plants through Underground Common Mycorrhizal Networks," *PLoS ONE* 5, no. 10 (2010): e13324, doi:10.1371/journal.pone.0013324.

page 84   *fungi often benefit*: Li Huiying, Sally E. Smith, et al., "Arbuscular Mycorrhizal Fungi Contribute to Phosphorus Uptake by Wheat Grown in a Phosphorus-Fixing Soil Even in the Absence of Positive Growth Responses," *New Phytologist* 172, no. 3 (November 2006): 536–543.

page 84   *Carbon has been shown to migrate*: Suzanne W. Simard et al., "Net Transfer of Carbon Between Ectomycorrhizal Tree Species in the Field," *Nature* 388, no. 6642 (August 7, 1997): 579–582.

page 85   *inoculating degraded soil*: D. Southworth, X. H. He, W. Swenson, C. S. Bledsoe, and W. R. Horwath, "Application of Network Theory to Potential Mycorrhizal Networks," *Mycorrhiza* 15, no. 8 (December 2005): 589–595. doi: 10.1007/s00572-005-0368-z.

page 85   *hubs interconnecting various species*: D. Southworth, "Application of Network Theory to Potential Mycorrhizal Networks."

page 85   *rigorous definition of the term information*: Claude E. Shannon, "A Mathematical Theory of Communication," *Bell System Technical Journal* 27 (1948): 379 –423, 623–656.

page 85   *fossil record*: David Wacey, Matt R. Kilburn, et al., "Microfossils of Sulphur-Metabolizing Cells in 3.4-Billion-Year-Old Rocks of Western Australia, *Nature Geoscience* 4, no. 10 (October 2011): 698–702.

page 86   *no two fermions*: Wolfgang Pauli, "On the Connexion Between the Completion of Electron Groups in an Atom with the Complex Structure of Spectra," *Zeit. Physik* 31 (1925): 765–783.

page 89   *then-unknown element*: Dmitri Mendeleef, "The Periodic Law of the Chemical Elements," *Chemical News* XLI, no. 1056: 83, as seen in *Classic Scientific Papers: Chemistry, Second Series* (American Elsevier, 1970), 299.

page 89   *now called Germanium*: Nils Wiberg et al., eds., *Holleman-Wiberg's Inorganic Chemistry* (San Diego, CA: Academic Press, 2001): 893–895.

page 90   *Cambrian Explosion*: Mark Denny and Alan McFadzean, *Engineering Animals: How Life Works* (Cambridge, MA: Harvard University Press, 2011): 38.

page 91   *Life's idea of liquid currency*: Chris S. Smillie et al., "Ecology Drives a Global Network of Gene Exchange Connecting the Human Microbiome," *Nature* 480, no. 7376 (December 8, 2011): 241–244.

page 91   *human drugs in their milk*: L. Rudenko, J. Jones, and E. Evdokimov, "The Future: Modern Animal Biotechnology," in *Animals, Diseases, and Human Health: Shaping Our Lives Now and in the Future*, ed. Radford G. Davis (Santa Barbara, CA: Praeger, 2011), 253.

page 91   *students at MIT*: Shetty, Reshma P., "Applying Engineering Principles to the Design and Construction of Transcriptional Devices" (PhD diss., MIT, 2008); see also "Bacterial Odor Generators," Eric Sawyer, *Scitable* (March 21, 2011), 1, http://www.nature.com/scitable/blog/bio2.0/bacterial_odor_generators. Accessed May 2, 2012.

page 91   *Vaccines for hepatitis B*: Y. Thanavala and A. A. Lugade, "Oral Transgenic Plant-Based Vaccine for Hepatitis B," *Immunologic Research* 46, no. 1–3 (March 2010): 4–11.

page 92   *Manhattan-sized phone book*: Janet Caldow, "The On Demand World: Mapping the Government Genome," in *The Agile Enterprise: Reinventing Your Organization for Success in an On-Demand World,* ed. Nirmal Pal and Daniel C. Pantaleo (New York: Springer Science+Business Media, Inc., 2005), 88.

page 92   *cut on your skin*: K.S. Midwood, L.V. Williams, and J. E. Schwarzbauer, "Tissue Repair and the Dynamics of the Extracellular Matrix," *International Journal of Biochemistry & Cell Biology* 36, no. 6 (2004): 1031–1037. See also Ruth Memmler et al., *Memmler's the Human Body in Health and Disease,* 8th ed. (New York: Lippincott Williams & Wilkins, 1996), 44.

page 93   *layered semantics*: Clifford Neuman, "The Prospero File System: A Global File System Based on the Virtual System Model," *Computing Systems 5,* no. 4 (Fall 1992): 407–432.

page 95   *Tale of Two Watchmakers*: Herbert A. Simon, "The Architecture of Complexity," *Proceedings of the American Philosophical Society* 106, no. 6 (December 1962): 470.

page 97   *Lego Technics*: Gwendolyn D. Galsworth, *Smart, Simple Design: Using Variety Effectiveness to Reduce Total Cost and Maximize Customer Selection* (Essex Junction, VT: Omneo, 1994), 195–196.

           The trick doesn't work: Margo Berman, *Street-Smart Advertising: How to Win the Battle of the Buzz* (Lanham, MD: Rowman & Littlefield Publishers, 2007), 34–35.

page 98   *Figure 4.5 A Studio Exercise* Visual design educational materials created by Professor J. M. Ballay at the School of Design, Carnegie Mellon University.

page 99   *Generative grammar*: Noam Chomsky, "Aspects of the Theory of Syntax," *Special Technical Report,* Number 11, Massachusetts Institute of Technology, Research Laboratory of Electronics (Cambridge, MA: MIT Press, 1965).

page 101   *Figure 4.7 Generative Sketching*: Visual design educational materials created by Professor J. M. Ballay at the School of Design, Carnegie Mellon University.

Chapter 5 How Design Does It

page 105   *role of the designer*: Arthur Pulos, *The American Design Adventure* (Cambridge, MA: MIT Press, 1988), vii.

page 106   *support of all human lives*: R. Buckminster Fuller (Kiyoshi Kuromiya, Adjuvant), *Critical Path* (New York: St. Martins Press, 1981), 124.

page 106   *"Call me Trimtab."*: Barry Farrell, "Playboy Interview: R. Buckminster Fuller," *Playboy* 19, no. 2 (February 1972), 59.

page 106   *discovery of buckyballs*: Nobelprize.org, the Official Web Site of the Nobel Prize, http://www.nobelprize.org/nobel_prizes/chemistry/laureates/1996/illpres/discovery.html. Accessed December 1, 2011.

page 107   *I seem to be a verb*: R. Buckminster Fuller, Jerome Agel, and Quentin Fiore, *I Seem to be a Verb,* 1st ed. (New York: Bantam Books, 1970).

page 108   *design its factory*: Jeffrey L. Meikle, *Twentieth Century Limited: Industrial Design in America, 1925–1939* (Philadelphia: Temple University Press, 2001), 53.

page 109   *Teague (Figure 5.3) was by temperament*: Ibid., 47.

page 109   *Loewy (Figure 5.4) characterized*: Raymond Loewy, *Never Leave Well Enough Alone* (New York: Simon & Schuster, 1951), 77.

page 110   *Dreyfuss was educated*: Russell Flinchum, *Henry Dreyfuss, Industrial Designer: The Man in the Brown Suit* (New York: Rizzoli Publications, 1997), 24.

page 111   *discipline of ergonomics*: Henry Dreyfuss, *Measure of Man: Human Factors in Design* (New York: Watson-Guptil, 1950).

page 112 *those who did not*: Quoted in Jeffrey L. Meikle, *Twentieth Century Limited. Industrial Design in America, 1925–1939*, (Philadelphia: Temple University Press, 1979), 84.

page 112 *Bell returned to Dreyfuss*: Henry Dreyfuss, *Designing for People* (New York: Allworth Press, 2003), 102–103.

page 114 *agricultural revolution*: Carl Ortwin Sauer, *Land and Life: A Selection from the Writings of Carl Ortwin Sauer*, ed. John Leighly (Berkeley: University of California Press, 1963), 164.

page 115 *Crystal Palace*: Edward Macdermott, *Routledge's Guide to the Crystal Palace and Park at Sydenham* (London: George Routledge & Co., 1854), 7. *Tallis's History and Description of The Crystal Palace and the Exhibition of the World's Industry in 1851*, ed. Beard Mayall, et al. (London and New York: John Tallis and Co., 1852).

page 116 *Original Crystal Palace*: Tallis, ibid.

page 117 *A Work Table Displayed*: Tallis, Ibid.

page 117 *Charles Eames*: John Neuhart, Marilyn Neuhart, and Ray Eames, *Eames Design: The Work of the Office of Charles and Ray Eames* (New York: Harry N. Abrams Publishers, 1989), 8, 14–15, 355, 358.

page 119 *"stay/no stay."*: Courtney G. Brooks, James M. Grimwood, and Loyd S. Swenson, Jr., *Chariots for Apollo: A History of Manned Lunar Spacecraft*. NASA Special Publication-4205 in the NASA History Series (1979), 317.

page 122 *controller of its Wii*: Gregory Trefry, *Casual Game Design: Designing Play for the Gamer in All of Us* (Burlington, MA: Morgan Kaufmann, 2010), 7–12; see also William Lidwell and Gerry Manacsa, *Deconstructing Product Design: Exploring the Form, Function, Usability, Sustainability, and Commercial Success of 100 Amazing Products* (Beverly, MA: Rockport Publishers, 2009), 208– 209.

page 130 *two opposed ideas*: F. Scott Fitzgerald, "The Crack-Up" *Esquire*, February 1936 (first in a series of essays published in *Esquire* in February, March, and April, 1936).

page 130 *Opposable Mind*: Roger L. Martin, *The Opposable Mind: How Successful Leaders Win Through Integrative Thinking* (Boston: Harvard Business School Press, 2007).

page 131 *future is already here*: Gibson made this statement on several occasions. One example is an interview called "Finding Science in Science Fiction," Talk of the Nation, National Public Radio, November 30, 1999.

page 132 *nearly five times as many*: *Modern Living Up From the Egg. Time* LIV, no. 18 (October 31, 1949).

Interlude Yesterday, Today, Tomorrow: Data Storage

page 135 *SABRE airline reservation system*: S. K. Singh, *Database Systems: Concepts, Design and Applications* (New Delhi: Pearson Education, 2006), 35–38; see also Duncan G. Copeland and James L. McKenney, "Airline Reservations Systems: Lessons from History," *MIS Quarterly* 12, no. 3 (September 1988): 352–370.

page 137 *public information space*: This is a vision that was first articulated 20 years ago in David Gelernter's *Mirror Worlds, or: The Day Software Puts the Universe in a Shoebox . . . How It Will Happen and What It Will Mean* (Oxford, UK: Oxford University Press, 1992).

Chapter 6 Design Science on Trillions Mountain

page 139 *We are as gods*: Stewart Brand, Ed., *Whole Earth Catalog*, (Menlo Park, CA: Portola Institute, 1968), 2.

page 140 *Design thinking*: Peter G. Rowe, *Design Thinking* (Cambridge, MA: MIT Press, 1987).

page 140 *Comprehensive Anticipatory Design Science*: R. Buckminster Fuller, "A Comprehensive Anticipatory Design Science," *Journal-Royal Architectural Institute of Canada* 34 (1957): 357.

page 140 *Fuller teaches us*: Richard Buckminster Fuller and E. J. Applewhite, *Synergetics: Explorations in the Geometry of Thinking* (New York: Macmillan, 1975): 4–9.

page 141   "*[devising] courses of action*: Herbert Simon, *The Sciences of the Artificial* (Cambridge, MA: MIT Press, 1969), 111.

page 142   *Workscape*: J. M. Ballay, "Designing Workscape: An Interdisciplinary Experience," in *Proceedings CHI 94 Human Factors in Computer Systems* (Boston: ACM, 1994), 10–15.

page 143   *11 patents*: U.S. Patent Numbers 5499330, 5528739, 5544051, 5600833, 5613134, 5621874, 6012072, 6012074, 6151610, D395297, 5528739.

page 143   *three-dimensional document management system*: S. K. Card, G. G. Robertson, and W. York, "The WebBook and the Web Forager: An Information Workspace for the World-Wide Web," ACM Conference on Human Factors in Software (1996). Data Mountain: George Robertson, Mary Czerwinski, et al., "Using Spatial Memory for Document Management Microsoft Research (January 1998), in *Proceedings, UIST '98*, p. 154. Cindy Pickering, John David Miller, Eleanor Wynn, and Chuck House, "3D Global Virtual Teaming Environment," Fourth International Conference on Creating, Connecting and Collaborating Through Computing (C5 '06) (2006), 126–135.

page 147   *ISO-9000*: ISO 9000 Quality Management, 12th ed. (Geneva: International Organization for Standardization, 2009).

page 147   *stage-gate model*: Lawrence P. Chao and Kosuke Ishii, "Design Process Error-Proofing: Benchmarking Gate and Phased Review Life-Cycle Models," Proceedings of IDETC/CIE 2005, ASME 2005 International Design Engineering Technical Conferences & Computers and Information in Engineering Conference, Long Beach, California, September 24–28, 2005.

page 150   *design methods.*: John Christopher Jones, *Design Methods: Seeds of Human Futures* (London: John Wiley & Sons, 1970); 2nd ed. (New York: John Wiley & Sons, 1992).

page 154   *superstitious behavior even in pigeons*: B. F. Skinner, "Superstition in the Pigeon," *Journal of Experimental Psychology* 38 (April 1948): 168–172.

page 156   *information-centric manipulation*: P. Lucas, S. F. Roth, and C. Gomberg, "Visage: Dynamic Information Exploration," paper presented at the Association of Computing Machinery, CHI '96 Conference, Vancouver, Canada (1996); P. Lucas and S. F. Roth, "Exploring Information with Visage," in Video Proceedings of the Association of Computing Machinery CHI '96 Conference, Vancouver, Canada (1996); S. F. Roth, P. Lucas, J. A. Senn, C. C. Gomberg, M. B. Burks, P. J. Stroffolino, J. A. Kolojejchick, and C. Dunmire, "Visage: A User Interface Environment for Exploring Information," *Proceedings of Information Visualization, IEEE* (San Francisco: IEEE Computer Society Press, 1996): 3–12; Fact File, A Compendium of DARPA Programs, August 2003, Command Post of the Future, 40.

page 157   *Computation in Context*: Portions of this section appeared previously in P. Lucas, "Mobile Devices and Mobile Data: Issues of Identity and Reference," *Human Computer Interaction* 16 (2001): 323–336.

page 160   *Geographic Names*: The U.S. board of geographic names is responsible for domestic place names, but non-U.S. names are the responsibility of the National Geospatial Intelligence Agency, an agency of the U.S. Department of Defense. See http://geonames.usgs.gov /foreign/index.html. The proprietary *Getty Thesaurus of Geographic Names* may be found at http://www.getty.edu/research/tools/vocabularies/tgn/index.html.

page 161   *service discovery problem*: Golden G. Richard III, *Service and Device Discovery: Protocols and Programming* (New York: McGraw-Hill Professional, 2002), 2.

Chapter 7 Architecture with a Capital "A"

page 167   *Technologies get obsolete*: Ishii has made variants of this statement many times. The particular quote came from his Twitter feed (@ishii_mit) dated February 20, 2010.

page 168   "*architectonic*": Architectonic = of architecture or architects; constructive; pertaining to systematization of knowledge (*The Concise Oxford Dictionary*, 6th ed.).

page 169   "*organic architecture*,": Frank Lloyd Wright, *Modern Architecture: Being the Kahn Lectures for 1930*, intro. Neil Levine (Princeton, NJ: Princeton University Press, 2008), xl, xli, 59, 62.

page 169   *more natural than nature*: Kimberly Elman, "Frank Lloyd Wright and the Principles of Organic Architecture," Legacy Essay, http://www.pbs.org/flw/legacy/essay1.html. Accessed January 23, 2012.

page 171   *one irritant is absent*: Walter Dorwin Teague, *Design This Day: The Technique of Order in the Machine Age*, rev. ed. (New York: Harcourt, Brace and Co, 1949), 207.

page 175   *tests*: J. Nichols, B. A. Myers, M. Higgins, J. Hughes, T. K. Harris, R. Rosenfeld, and M. Pignol, "Generating Remote Control Interfaces for Complex Appliances," in *UIST 2002*: 161–170; see also Jeffrey Nichols, Duen Horng Chau, and Brad A. Myers "Demonstrating the Viability of Automatically Generated User Interfaces," http://www.jeffreynichols.com/papers/viability-chi2007-final.pdf.

page 176   *PUC Testing Results* Brad Myers and Peter Lucas, "Personal Universal Controller (PUC)," February 2002, 7. (A joint project conducted by MAYA and Carnegie Mellon University funded by the Pittsburgh Digital Greenhouse.) Accessed March 2, 2012. http://www.cs.cmu.edu/~pebbles/papers/PUC_PDG_02-13-02.ppt. Accessed March 1, 2012.

Chapter 8 Life in an Information Ecology

page 181   *apple pie from scratch*: Carl Sagan, *Cosmos* (New York: Random House, 1980), 179.

page 186   *Gödel, Escher, Bach*: Douglas R. Hofstadter, *Gödel, Escher, Bach: An Eternal Golden Braid* (New York: Random House, Vintage Books ed., 1980).

page 186   *Shepard Tones*: Roger N. Shepard, "Circularity in Judgements of Relative Pitch," *Journal of the Acoustical Society of America* 36, no. 12 (December 1964): 2346–2353.

page 186   *Earwig, Man, Elephant*: Iona Archibald Opie and Peter Opie, *Children's Games in Street and Playground: Chasing, Catching, Seeking, Hunting, Racing, Duelling, Exerting, Daring, Guessing, Acting, Pretending* (Oxford: Clarendon Press, 1969), 27.

page 186   *bacteria within the digestive system*: B. Kerr, M. A. Riley, M. W. Feldman, and B. J. Bohannan, "Local Dispersal Promotes Biodiversity in a Real-Life Game of Rock-Paper-Scissors," *Nature* 418, no. 6894 (2002): 171–174; see also B. C. Kirkup and M. A. Riley, "Antibiotic-Mediated Antagonism Leads to a Bacterial Game of Rock-Paper-Scissors in Vivo," *Nature* 428, no. 6981 (2004): 412–414.

page 187   *winning strategy*: Douglas Walker and Graham Walker, *The Official Rock Paper Scissors Strategy Guide* (New York: Fireside, 2004).

page 189   *water cuts the alluvial banks*: Mark Twain, *Life on the Mississippi* (New York and London: Harper & Brothers, 1901), 134–135.

page 190   *Phineas Gage*: Malcolm Macmillan, *An Odd Kind of Fame: Stories of Phineas Gage* (Cambridge, MA: MIT Press, 2000).

page 191   *watch that basket*: Andrew Carnegie, *The Empire of Business* (Garden City, NY: Doubleday, Page & Company, 1913), 18.

page 192   *"transactional consistency."*: Philip A. Bernstein and Eric Newcomer, *Principles of Transaction Processing*, 2nd ed. (Burlington, MA: Morgan Kaufmann, 2009).

page 195   *quantum entanglement*: For an accessible introduction to these topics, see Louisa Gilder, *The Age of Entanglement: When Quantum Physics Was Reborn* (New York: Alfred A. Knopf, 2008).

page 197   *(actually recycled) chips*: Joel Brenner, *America the Vulnerable: Inside the New Threat Matrix of Digital Espionage, Crime, and Warfare* (New York: Penguin Press, 2011). See also United States International Trade Commission, and Katherine Linton et al., "China: Intellectual Property Infringement, Indigenous Innovation Policies, and Frameworks for Measuring the Effects on the U.S. Economy," *Investigation*, no. 332-514 (Washington, DC: U.S. International Trade Commission, 2010), 3-1 to 3-25.

page 197   *electronic shipping tags*: Hosang Jung, F. Frank Chen, Bongju Jeong, eds., *Trends in Supply Chain Design and Management: Technologies and Methodologies* (Springer Series in Advanced Manufacturing, 2007).

page 199   *You have zero privacy anyway*: Scott McNealy. Quoted in Hal Abelson, Ken Ledeen, and Harry Lewis, *Blown to Bits: Your Life, Liberty, and Happiness After the Digital Explosion* (Boston: Pearson Education, 2008), 296.

page 199   *the jig is up*: For a discussion of privacy versus freedom, see David Brin, *The Transparent Society: Will Technology Force Us to Choose Between Privacy and Freedom?* (New York: Basic Books; First Trade Paper Edition, June 1, 1999).

page 200   *O.J. Simpson murder trial*: Abelson, *Blown to Bits*, op. cit., 11.

page 200   *automatic OCR*: National Research Council (U.S.), Transportation Research Board, Airport
            Cooperative Research Program (U.S.), Federal Aviation Administration, and Jacobs Consul-
            tancy, *Guidebook for Evaluating Airport Parking Strategies and Supporting Technologies*
            (Washington, DC: Transportation Research Board, 2009), 97, 126. See also Kemal Koche,
            Vijay Patil, and Kiran Chaudhari, "Study of Probabilistic Neural Network and Feed For-
            ward Back Propogation Neural Network for Identification of Characters in License Plate,"
            7–12, in *Advances in Power Electronics and Instrumentation Engineering*, ed. Vinu V. Das et
            al., *Proceedings of the Second International Conference, PEIE 2011*, Nagpur, Maharashtra,
            India, April 21–22, vol. 148 (New York: Springer-Verlag 2011).

page 200   *VisiCalc*: Daniel Bricklin, *Bricklin on Technology* (Indianapolis: John Wiley & Sons, 2009),
            423–465.

Chapter 9 Aspects of Tomorrow

page 205   *The only simplicity*: Oliver Wendell Holmes and Sir Frederick Pollock. Holmes-Pollock
            Letters: *The Correspondence of Mr. Justice Holmes and Sir Frederick Pollock, 1874–1932*,
            2 vols. in 1, 2nd ed., ed. Mark DeWolfe Howe (Cambridge, MA: Harvard University Press,
            1961), 109. The Holmes quote is often given as "I wouldn't give a fig for the simplicity on
            this side of complexity; I would give my right arm for the simplicity on the far side of com-
            plexity," and is variously attributed to Holmes Senior or Junior.

page 206   *Net's traffic is aggregated*: Jonathan E. Nuechterlein and Philip J. Weiser, *Digital Crossroads:
            American Telecommunications Policy in the Internet Age* (Cambridge, MA: MIT Press,
            2005), 131–132.

page 209   *new manufacturing techniques*: C. D. Dimitrakopoulos, S. Purushothaman, J. Kymissis, A.
            Callegari, and J. M. Shaw, "Low-Voltage Organic Transistors on Plastic Comprising High-
            Dielectric Constant Gate Insulators," *Science* 283, no. 5403 (February 1999): 822–824.

page 212   *Information Commons*: See, for example "Designing the Future of Information: The Internet
            Beyond the Web." Harbor Research Whitepaper, September 2005, http://www.scribd.com/
            macurak/d/15481864-Designing-the-Future-of-Information-The-Internet-Beyond-the-Web.
            Peter Lucas, "CIVIUM: A Geographic Information System for Everyone, the Information
            Commons, and the Universal Database," MAYA Design Group, Inc., presented at the Inter-
            national Institute for Information Design (IIID), Vision Plus 10 Conference, Lech/Arlberg,
            Austria, 2003.

page 214   *against pending legislation*: *Stop Online Piracy Act*. H.R. 3261. 112th Cong. (2011–2012);
            and *Protect IP Act*. S968. 112th Cong. (2011–2012).

page 217   *"The Erlenmeyer Flask"*: *X-Files*, season 1, episode 24, production code 1×23. Original air
            date May 13, 1994.

page 220   *we put the thought*: J. R. R. Tolkien, *The Fellowship of the Ring* (London: HarperCollins,
            1994), Ch. 8, Book 2, 486.

Epilogue Thriving in the Spacious Foothills

page 221   *three kinds of companies*: Gary Hamel and C. K. Prahalad, *Competing for the Future*
            (Boston: Harvard Business School Press, 1994), 100.

page 223   *Library at Alexandria*: Stuart Kelly, *The Book of Lost Books: An Incomplete History of All
            the Great Books You Will Never Read* (New York: Random House, 2005).

page 225   *custom ring tones*: John Fletcher, "Shrinking Ringtone Sales Lead to Decline in U.S. Mobile
            Music Market," SNL Kagan's Wireless Investor (2009).

page 225   *Zynga*: Dean Takahashi, "Zynga Reports a Profit for Third Quarter on Eve of IPO,"
            November 4, 2011. http://venturebeat.com/2011/11/04/zynga-reports-a-profit-for-third
            -quarter-on-eve-of-ipo/.

page 225   *15 billion apps*: Ben Camm-Jones, "App Store Downloads Hit 15bn Mark," *Macworld
            Australia Magazine*, July 8, 2011, 6; Phillip Michaels, "Apple Reports Record Sales, Profits
            for Third Quarter," *Macworld Australia Magazine*, July 20, 2011.

Page 226   *Underwriters Laboratories*: Ernest C. Magison, *Electrical Instruments in Hazardous Locations*, 4th ed. (Research Triangle Park, NC: Instrument Society of America, 1998), 3–5; see also James Gerhart, *Home Automation and Wiring* (New York: McGraw-Hill, 1999), pp. 96; Quentin Wells, *Htl+ Home Technology Integration in Depth* (Boston: Thomson Learning, Inc., 2004), 246–247.

page 227   *numerous government awards*: http://archive.darpa.mil/DARPATech2004/awards.html; http://www.army.mil/article/16774/.

page 227   *decision making and mission planning effectiveness*: William Wright et al., "Command Post of the Future: Limited Objective Experiment – One (LOE-1), Some Results," NATO Workshop on Visualization of Massive Military Multimedia Datasets. Quebec, Canada. June 7, 2000, http://www.vistg.net/VM3D/.

About the Authors

PETER LUCAS is founding principal at MAYA Design, which he cofounded in 1989. He is also adjunct associate professor of Human Computer Interaction at Carnegie Mellon University. He holds a PhD from Cornell University, where he studied educational and cognitive psychology and psycholinguistics. He has authored numerous scholarly papers and co-authored a book on language perception. He served on the Committee on Networked Systems of Embedded Computers of the National Research Council.

JOE BALLAY is a nationally known industrial designer, former head of the School of Design at Carnegie Mellon University, and founding principal of MAYA Design. He holds an MFA in design from Carnegie Mellon University. He also holds a BS in industrial management from Carnegie Institute of Technology and a BFA in industrial design from the University of Illinois. He has taught design at institutions throughout the world including the University of Cincinnati, Georgia Tech, Virginia Tech, the Samsung Design Institute in Korea, and the University of Lund in Sweden.

MICKEY McMANUS is president and CEO of MAYA Design. He holds a BFA in industrial design from the University of Illinois, with extended studies in communication design and mathematics. His work has been published in *Bloomberg Businessweek*, *Fortune*, *Fast Company*, the *Wall Street Journal*, and *Harvard Business Review*. He is a frequent speaker on the topic of design, pervasive computing, and business innovation.

Index